Not Remotely Controlled

Not
Remotely
Controlled

Notes on Television

LEE SIEGEL

BASIC BOOKS

A Member of the Perseus Books Group
New York

The essays in this book, including the introduction, originally appeared, sometimes is substantially different form, in *The New Republic* and The New Republic Online.

Copyright 2007 by Lee Siegel

Published by Basic Books,
A Member of the Perseus Books Group

Books published by Basic Books are available at special discounts for bulk purchases in the United States by corporations, institutions, and other organizations. For more information, please contact the Special Markets Department at the Perseus Books Group, 2300 Chestnut Street, Philadelphia, PA 19103 or e-mail special.markets@perseusbooks.com.

Designed by Brent Wilcox

Library of Congress Cataloging-in-Publication Data
Siegel, Lee, 1957–
    Not remotely controlled : notes on television / Lee Siegel.
        p.   cm.
    ISBN-13: 978-0-465-07810-3 (hardcover : alk. paper)
    ISBN-10: 0-465-07810-9 (hardcover : alk. paper)
    1. Television programs—United States.   2. Television broadcasting—
United States.   I. Title.
PN1992.3.U5S55 2007
791.45'750973—dc22

                                                                2007004702

10 9 8 7 6 5 4 3 2 1

For Janet Malcolm

Contents

Introduction

The reviews and essays in this book originally appeared in the *New Republic*, where I served as the magazine's television critic from 2003 to 2006, writing essays for the print magazine and shorter, weekly pieces for the *New Republic* online. One of the people who thought profoundly about television was the *New Republic's* first television critic, Paul Goodman. In an essay on TV that appeared in the magazine in January 1963, Goodman wrote:

> This is too beautiful a medium to be thrown away. . . . It offers opportunities for the frequent spontaneous emerging of plastic and poetic invention, the rapid dissemination of radical ideas, many kinds of training and instruction, . . . [The networks cannot get in] touch with the real, for they are not set up for that. It is evident that the present top-down decision-makers have no notion of whatever a free medium is. The best is simply to get rid of them, break up the networks by a complete new deal in the franchises, and decentralize control as much as possible. . . .

Goodman's prescience was extraordinary since this "complete new deal" is nearly exactly what the cable revolution created. What we have on television now is an overlap of eras. The advertising-hungry networks exist like amphibians alongside subscription-hungry cable channels that are beginning to walk upright, on two legs. This peculiar time-warp is one complication facing the television critic.

Another is that whether you are tuned into CBS or HBO, you are still watching the unique entity known as TV. No form or medium—in the realm of either art or diversion—has television's consequential intimacy, and its alarming immediacy, and its *seeming* seamlessness with reality. If television is a miracle of pleasure and information it is also an ongoing emergency in consciousness. Being a television critic, therefore, is not like being any other kind of critic.

The marketing people are going to kill me when they read the following, but if you've picked up this book looking for straightforward television reviews, you're going to be disappointed. Television inspires me to talk about a lot of things outside television. That is the nature of the glowing, flickering beast. Television as an object of critical discrimination is very different from the "thick" expressions of a poem, a novel, a painting, a serious biography. They are so rich with dense layers of meaning and structure that you have a great deal of work to do before you can start talking about the world outside them. But a television show, no matter what form it takes, is deliciously thin. Its nature has been so stretched in different artistic, cultural, social, economic and commercial directions that you can dive right through the small screen into the world outside it. If, that is, the world doesn't come striding through the glass to you first.

In other words, television's unreality can be very real indeed. You have only to pay it the attention it deserves.

Cops

1 Why Cop Shows Are Eternal

He is there, David Caruso, week after week, with his red hair and narrow eyes and bitter irony, aided by the other *CSI: Crime Scene Investigation* officers, picking up the pieces of incredible violence and following them back, like Hansel in the asphalt jungle—though he follows computerized simulations of entry wounds, not pieces of bread—to the deformative trauma that shattered a life; and there is Jerry Orbach, a nice Jewish actor playing a nice half-Jewish cop, as Lenny in *Law & Order*, who hates the scumbags with matter-of-fact irony and feels for the helpless unlucky guys driven beyond the law to defend themselves; and there is Vic in *The Shield*, brutal, good-hearted, and corrupt, way behind *CSI* in technology, and way beyond *Law & Order* in psychology. And there are a lot of other guys, and also a few women, running around the tube with a badge and a gun. The proverbial complaint that there's never a cop around when you need one may or may not be true, but there's always a cop show around, whether you want it or not.

Here is a sample of the police dramas currently on television, both new shows and old: *CSI, Without a Trace, Law & Order, 24, The Shield,* a new *Dragnet, The Division, Fastlane, Cops, The Sentinel, Streets of San Francisco, True Crime, Boomtown, The Wire,*

NYPD Blue, Hawaii Five-O, Columbo, Miami Vice, U.S. Marshals, Hill Street Blues, Forever Knight. At any moment on American television, someone is either committing a crime or getting arrested, shooting or getting shot, chasing or being chased. There is even a show called *Animal Cops*, which—alas—is not about animals empowered by the state to pursue and apprehend bad animals ("Up against the wall! Spread your legs! Now spread your other legs!"). This particular brainstorm depicts real cops pursuing and apprehending miscreant schnauzers and so forth.

And in the unlikely event that you tire of any of the countless television series about the police, you can flip between cop movies and cop shows—between *Training Day*, in which a good cop battles a corrupt cop, and *The Shield*, in which good cops become bad cops while battling to remain good; or between the wildly successful black-cop and white-cop teams in *Lethal Weapon* and *Die Hard with a Vengeance* (where Samuel L. Jackson isn't a cop but acts like one) and the current incarnation of *Law & Order*, whose writers have given Lenny a new black partner. The configurations are the same; only the names have been changed to protect against the hypercritical. On the big screen and the small, cops enthrall us the way gods and demigods captured the imaginations of the ancient Greeks and Romans.

Like the demigods of mythological yore, like Achilles with his divinely wrought shield, cops on television—they also have shields—occupy a hybrid, liminal realm. They are half ordinary citizens constrained by laws, customs, and convention, and half divinities, free to exert their will, to thwart someone else's, to punish and to kill, to set matters straight: that is, they are glamorously unconstrained by laws, customs, and conventions. When you sit for an hour in a traffic jam and fantasize about taking the motorcycle away from the guy ahead of you and tearing straight up between the lanes, you are fantasizing about being a cop.

Of course, all the subliminal energy packed into the figure of the cop has a strong symbolic dimension. The dramatic, untrammeled doings of television cops appeal to the American self, with its daydream of a dramatic, untrammeled existence: television cops represent the fantastic consummation of the American promise of radical individualism. They seem simultaneously to have their way and to possess the power to keep other people from achieving theirs. The power offered by a plastic card with a big line of credit is half like the power represented by a badge.

The cop who goes too far in battling his conventional or dumb or corrupt superiors, who themselves have gone too far; or who passes beyond legal boundaries while fighting a conventional or dumb or corrupt system that has exceeded all legal boundaries; or who slugs it out with bad guys just as unconstrained by law, custom, or convention as he is; or who wrestles with his own demons; or who finds himself lost and ineffectual in that realm where unthinking exercise of the will can alienate the object of desire (the realm of romantic love)—it is not too grandiose to say that the image of the American cop embodies the perpetual American dilemma: how far can individual freedom go before one person's freedom becomes another person's crisis?

That conundrum has a long history. In American pop culture, there was always the good outsider sheriff squaring off against the bad insider sheriff—Wyatt Earp; Gary Cooper in *High Noon*—or the good stranger vanquishing the established authorities that had become villainous, as in *Shane* (which means "beautiful" in Yiddish—did its Jewish writer do that on purpose?). But though the good outsiders and strangers often had complex natures—like Shane himself, whose noble motives were entangled with his desire for the wife of another good man—they usually remained incontestably good. Film noir, with its morally ambiguous heroes, only occasionally influenced the cinematic image of the Western lawman.

Matters were even more clear-cut on television, where after World War II the Western kept bad guys and good guys as distinct from one another as the city was from the suburbs. During the postwar exodus from urban centers, morally reassuring Westerns such as *Gunsmoke* and *Bonanza*, meant to be watched by the whole family, catered to the suburban imagination just as all those morally unsettling postwar film noirs, meant to be watched alone in a dark theater, appealed to the urban imagination. The cop shows of the time were even more black and white, as if these police series were as comforting as the sight of their black-and-white patrol cars. Shows such as the old *Dragnet* and *Adam-12* portrayed law-enforcement figures unobstructed by complex natures or dubious superiors. A comedy police show would be inconceivable now, but back then you had series like *Car 54, Where Are You?*—on cable you can still catch the reruns, which seem like prehistoric cave paintings—and *Mayberry RFD*, humorous cop shows featuring bumbling policemen akin to *West Side Story*'s Officer Krupke. Even the serious police dramas of the time, viewed now, seem to have a comic spirit animating their simple divisions between good and bad.

We have all heard about how the Vietnam War, and the 1960s, and the race riots, and Watergate, changed popular culture; how they made the movies, and the television, and the songs, and the musicals, more cynical, more ambiguous, more "real" about buried motives and hidden conduct. Indeed, the chief cause of reality television is that in our commercial society people have cynically come to associate artistic pretense with entrepreneurial misrepresentation; and as popular art has absorbed this skepticism of pretense and become more ironic about itself, people have come to suspect any strain of sincerity in actual life. Cop shows belatedly reflected the social and cultural movement toward "the real." In the early 1990s, *NYPD Blue* revolutionized television cops by dramatizing their inner lives and depicting cops torn by anger, and alcoholism, and lust, and infidelity. Though these figures remained for the most part on the right side of the law, they enacted private transgressions that were at the heart of the public crimes they were dedicated to investigating.

It might seem that with this riveting and beautifully done series, television cops had become more like real cops, more like actual life. Yet since most people's perception of the police is the simple one of men and women who really are there to serve and to protect, the cardboard cops of *Adam-12* and the old *Dragnet* are closer to real life than *NYPD Blue*'s dramatic, exciting, conflicted cops. For the black or Hispanic kid being brutalized by a cop, the hackneyed simplicity of the good cop gone bad is obviously more real than the romantic image of authority figures tormented by the burden of their jobs. Justin Volpe, the cop now serving time for torturing Abner Louima, is Joe Friday turned on his head.

Rather than bringing the viewer closer to actual cops, with their (to the ordinary citizen) obscure and unknowable inner lives, *NYPD Blue* ended up making these half-divine figures of authority—the authority to interrupt a life, or the authority to take a life—transparent and comprehensible. The show simultaneously demystified them and made them unreal. It glamorized sordidness rather than exposing it. And it made the revelation of psychological forces into just another type of information. With its portrayal of cops who are just as screwed up as the rest of us, but who, like the rest of us, still get up in the morning and do their jobs, *NYPD Blue* made mysterious quasi-divinities rationally apprehendable.

Three different types of police shows grew out of *NYPD Blue*. The first is the simple good guy/bad guy police show like the new *Dragnet*, which is really the old *Dragnet* with more vicious crimes; and *Law & Order*, where the inner lives of Lenny (who, we learn, lost his daughter to drugs) and his partner obtrude tastefully on the plots, which are almost always complex and intelligent and wholly absorbing.

The second type is the gritty police series, which goes even further than *NYPD Blue* in portraying cops as torn, conflicted, gone rotten, and in extremis. There aren't many of these: *24* has some raw, ambiguous moments, and so does *The Wire,* and so did *The Beat,* the last now defunct. The raw police show par excellence is *The Shield*, a series that has remarkably shorn itself of glamour and romanticism. Interestingly, the "reality" police show, *Cops,* which seems to be on cable twenty-four hours a day, is closer to the old simplistic police dramas than to something like *The Shield,* since its policemen always get their culprit and we never see corrupt, tormented, or brutal cops. What the gritty police shows share with *Cops* is the shaky, hand-held camerawork, one of the few romantic elements of *The Shield* and the most down-to-earth feature of *Cops*.

The other, and far more plentiful, species of cop show took from *NYPD Blue* its style of making the cop, suspended between mortal and immortal realms, rationally knowable. For in the end, the latter's Andy Sipowicz's drinking, and his violence, and his unhappiness amplified the perception of him as a figure who could enforce his will despite the obstructions to his will. His weaknesses empowered him; the disclosure of his weaknesses empowered the viewer. The more explicit the revelation of what motivated him, the more familiar and predictable he became as a person. And this psychological omniscience of *NYPD Blue*'s scriptwriters seems to have passed into the minds of *CSI*'s and *Without a Trace*'s investigators, who couple their psychological mastery with technological fluency.

When you watch *CSI* or *Without a Trace,* you are enjoying the fruits of *NYPD Blue*'s fantasy of omniscience. There is very little violence on these shows, which already distinguishes them from a television universe where a series like *Oz,* set in a prison, has pushed the boundaries of graphic violence about as far as they can go on television. *CSI*'s cops, though they carry highly visible, oversize guns on their hips—as if to compensate for the show's lack of violence—catch their criminals by means of forensics and various kinds of technology. Such violence as there is the show enacts through the *CSI* investigators' graphic computer simulations of knives penetrating skin, tissue, muscle, and bone. It's where Sherlock Holmes meets Popeye Doyle. Not the least of the show's enthrallments is the illusion it offers that by imagining and then rationalizing the worst, the worst will never happen.

Without a Trace, in which detectives piece together the puzzle of a life to find missing persons, is more cerebral and more subdued, yet the series also has a consoling faith in the ability of its cops to uncover the truth, always accurately, in this case by deciphering the meaning of a pause in conversation or a shift in someone's glance. *Law & Order* takes a different tack. By dividing the program into police show (first half) and courtroom drama that includes the categorization of information about the crime (second half), it offers a complete spectacle of the rationalization of the irrational.

While *The Shield* and the other gritty police shows enact the old drama of the American will enmeshed in its paradoxical freedoms, *CSI*, and *Without a Trace*, have submerged that drama in the world of the video game and the Internet, where the technology-created culture of engaged isolation meets the old-time crime drama. *NYPD Blue*'s moral ambiguities have become the hard new scientific certainties. A gritty, morally shadowy drama such as *The Shield* is really a throwback to a soft bygone humanistic complexity.

The most significant thing about these shows, particularly *CSI*, is that they fuse the crime drama with the medical drama. The body is the most intimate, and potentially the most threatening, dimension of a person's existence. In *CSI*'s forensic obsession with bodies—you can also flip to the fact-based series *Forensic Files*—viewers can be held rapt and also reassured that no wound, no invasion of the body is, in the end, fatal.

For though *CSI* is an innovative (as they say) police show, it has also pushed the medical drama into a new phase. The doctors on *ER* race to save a person's life. The cops on *CSI*, fiber by fiber, semen stain by semen stain, wound by wound, work to capture the perpetrator of the fatal blow, and thus, by finding the agent of the formative wound, they do not save a person's life—they resurrect a person from the dead. In a similar way, the detectives on *Without a Trace* redeem a person from the ranks of the missing.

As American society goes, so goes the American crime drama. If ever there were shows that expressed our solitary, computer-riveted sense of being there but not being there, of being mysteriously injured or depressed yet feeling healthy and optimistic, of being helpless to influence events but feeling strangely that we are powerful enough to do so, they are these raw, entertaining, gripping, utterly delusive fantasies of transparency and control.

MARCH 31, 2003

2   The New *Kojak*

In the late 1970s, when the bald, blatantly ethnic Telly Savalas played tough, compassionate Kojak in the television police show of that name, New York was in the doldrums. Since 1958, when *Naked City* aired—the first television cop series to be set in New York—much had changed. The city was economically depressed. Crime rates were soaring. Racial tension ran to skin-crawling highs, reaching a crescendo—a paradigm shift, as it were—in 1987 in the case of Tawana Brawley, a young black girl who falsely accused six white men, one of them a law-enforcement officer, of raping her. The recession induced by the vast expenditures of the Vietnam War had caused an enormous crisis. The liberal "idealism" in foreign policy that had created the catastrophe in Southeast Asia had receded along with the economy and left the liberal idealism that still guided the country's social policies to take the fall. And no city in the country was as liberal in its social attitudes as New York.

So a new mayor named Ed Koch swept into office on the Democratic ticket and started talking tough, which laid the groundwork for Rudy Giuliani, who did tough. The Jewish, unmarried, and seemingly romantically unattached Koch accentuated rather than played down what some people might have construed as his otherness. Back then, the media was less prosecutorial. Koch was a *tummler*, a clown, a kind of Allen Ginsberg in political clothing. He had come out of the progressive wing of the city's Democratic Party, and his headquarters early in his political career were in Greenwich Village, on the corner of West Fourth and Seventh Avenue—in the heart, that is, of New York's artistic/bohemian precincts. There was some element of camp in Koch's public persona, and behind it a hardness and impatience, and behind that even a kind of wry sadness.

All these layers were encased in a seemingly impregnable egotism. As the city grew more and more depressed, Koch inflated his ego to larger and larger proportions. Inflation, in fact, became public and economic policy. He and his banker-prince, Felix Rohatyn, borrowed more and more money, slowly raising the city out of its slough—in much the same way as Ginsberg and others had tried to levitate the Pentagon a decade before. That whole epoch in New York had a bloated surreality: the mayor puffing himself out; he and his banker floating bonds on the thin air of trust and taking out loan after loan; the city's bankers venturing, junk-bonding, and leveraging; and behind it all, a massive media campaign to sell New York—"I ♥ New York"—as the best investment, the capital of the world, the "Big Apple," a bite of which would give you worldliness, secret thrills, and a permanent buoyancy instead of the fabled Fall. Everyone was wafting about on the collective construction of a spotless, shining self-conception fabricated out of their depressed sense of a faltering environment.

Telly Savalas' Greek American New York City police detective was, like Koch, bald (though Savalas liked to leak to the press through his publicists that he shaved his head and could thrust upward a virile tract of hair anytime he wanted to). He was, like Koch, brash, brassy, wisecracking, buoyant, irrepressible. Like Koch, he was unabashedly ethnic. Both men cultivated personas that were an ad-man's dream of "New York." Koch liked to theatrically ask his constituents during his public appearances: "How'm I doin'?" Kojak liked to cockily ask, "Who loves ya baby?" (We love New York!) Both men—rather, both fabricated characters—gave the impression that they could handle any situation, that fighting social malaise and crime was really a matter of style more than anything else, and that there was a secret source of their invincible confidence that no one would ever know. For Koch, its traces lay perhaps in the fact that he always appeared in shirtsleeves; for Savalas' Kojak, the fedora seemed to hold the key to his bravado. Not to mention the lollipops that he liked to suck on and hand out to people, colorful pacifiers that he said he needed to quit smoking but that hinted at a dark rage in their absence, and also looked like harmless candy caricatures of bludgeons.

What's most significant about the current revival of *Kojak*— a show so boring that it makes you angry at yourself for nodding through murders and beatings—is its revelation of cultural distance. Today, the Democratic Party headquarters in Greenwich Village that Koch worked out of at the beginning of his career is a nail salon. And, indeed, this new *Kojak* is more polished than its predecessor ever was. Its claws are sharper, too. Savalas' Kojak was tough, but for the most part he stuck to the straight and narrow. Ving Rhames' Kojak, like so many other detectives on TV nowadays—as well as the counterterrorist types on *24*—tortures suspects in custody and generally pushes people around, and members of his team routinely remove evidence from people's apartments without warrants.

But the really interesting thing is that if this Kojak is brutal where the original was merely tough, he is also maudlin, soft, and teary where the other was merely sympathetic and warm. What was an organic intensity to Savalas' character—the tough guy with a tender side—is an almost psychotic set of extremes in Rhames' version. One minute he's using a baseball bat to psychologically torture a suspect, and the next minute he has tears running down his face when he remembers the trauma of his father's murder when he was ten. Violence begets violence, you see—they hit us and we have to hit them back, again and again. But the greater our violence, the keener the need to think of ourselves as compassionate. (Giuliani is the master of breaking heads and, in a later incarnation, shedding tears.) In this context, the lapse of having Rhames' Kojak suck on lollipops without making his attempt to quit smoking the motive behind it is appropriate. Rather than a rational mental strategy, the lollipop habit seems like a mentally unbalanced compulsion.

As for the "innovation" of making the Greek American detective an African American detective, Joe Papp was casting black characters in white roles in his productions of Shakespeare's plays a generation ago. As usual, TV is far behind the times it's often accused of, or credited with, creating. When they do a black *Little House on the Prairie*, I'll be impressed.

MAY 3, 2005

3 CSI: New York

HBO may well be a revolution in television, as the cable network's near sweep of the Emmys last night made clear, but not everything on the networks is cotton candy. I was never that big a fan of the *CSI* franchise: There is some cultural perversity at work in the presentation of graphic X-ray images showing brains hemorrhaging and neck bones breaking, disclosing with such fake gravitas—and exciting MTV dramatics—the material secrets of human suffering. On one level, it's a kind of medical porn. But the show's premise is also an ingenious evolution of the sleuthing genre, and like *Law & Order*, its closest competitor, *CSI* itself is an X-ray of the society that the hugely popular show entertains.

Both series offer the illusion of control after great painful upheaval. In *Law & Order*, a crime shatters social forms and personal lives, and then cops, district attorneys, and others try to piece society back together again. Even when the rationalizing system doesn't work, you see precisely how it doesn't work. Dark, unfathomable-seeming forces have been illuminated. Knowledge is created out of horrible deeds committed in obscurity. Irrationality, if not always vanquished, is for the moment understood. And the culprit is always the frail human ego, prey to appetite and emotion.

17

CSI explores the same depths but from a different angle. Its culprit isn't ego but body. Mortality itself is the perp. Week after forensically illuminating week, the fact of biological vulnerability is what does in the series' various victims. If it were not for flesh that yields to sharp cold hardness, for bones that break, and organs that burst, and membrane that tears, no amount of malevolence could upset a life. What reassures you at the end of every *CSI* episode is not the satisfying tableau of a bad guy or guys being brought to justice. It's the almost mythological insinuation that Death itself has been flushed out, apprehended, and, at least this once, defeated. *Law & Order*'s illusion of control is tentative and social; *CSI*'s is absolute and scientific.

And if it's science that has flushed death out from behind all the material instruments of death, it's particularly American science—specifically, American technological know-how. The cops and investigators on *Law & Order* have to use all their faculties to get their man: their minds, five senses, intuition, and feelings. On *CSI*, all you need is a lot of incredibly expensive equipment and a good pair of eyes. In other words, *CSI* represents the triumph of the money culture: On the one hand, with the right amount of money, you can buy the right technology, and then no mean secret is safe from your probing, luminous eye. On the other hand, the only things the *CSI* cops need are those faculties and activities that the money culture privileges—seeing, collecting, counting, calculating. That's why the *CSI* franchise began in Las Vegas, the money culture's subconsciousness and id.

The show now comes to New York via *CSI: New York*. Sooner or later, *CSI* had to come to Gotham, and not just to compete with *Law & Order* on its own turf but because New York is where all the tendencies of a money culture reach their perfection: it is the consummate modern city. The great German sociologist

Georg Simmel wrote a famous essay in the early part of the last century called "The Metropolis and Mental Life" in which he might have been describing two essential qualities of New York, and of *CSI*: impersonality and emotional withdrawal. Simmel wrote:

> Instead of reacting emotionally, the metropolitan type reacts primarily in a rational manner, thus creating a mental predominance through the intensification of consciousness. . . . The reaction of the metropolitan person . . . is moved to a sphere of mental activity which is least sensitive and which is furthest removed from the depths of the personality. . . . Money economy and the domination of the intellect stand in the closest relationship to one another. They have in common a purely matter-of-fact attitude in the treatment of persons and things in which a formal justice is often combined with an unrelenting hardness.

A formal justice combined with an unrelenting hardness— that's a pretty good description of David Caruso's Horatio Caine on *CSI: Miami*, a man who won't let anything stand in the way of his pursuit of the bad guys. This quality is crystallized in Gary Sinise, the star of *CSI: New York*. Sinise is a more reflective Gene Hackman, if reflective is the word. In the face of this exceptionally gifted actor, thought seems to be slowly simmering over an emotional fire, but it never comes to a boil. He is about to come to clarity about something yet he never does. If he suddenly decides to take action, the matter has been resolved deep inside him; he doesn't clue you in. Whatever his rational purposes, they are hidden in rich emotional folds; whatever his feelings, they are shrouded in thoughts that hover near the surface but never break through. Sinise is the perfect actor for a series in which ratiocination has replaced individuation, in which "the reaction of the metropolitan person . . . is furthest removed from the depths of personality."

You would have to "process"—*CSI* jargon for getting clues off a damaged body—Sinise to get to what he's thinking. He's a living enigma just as the victims who comprise his métier are dead enigmas. The pilot episode, airing this Wednesday, is a tour-de-force in the way that, like Sinise, it perfectly expresses the spirit of the show. It begins with Sinise looking out over Manhattan from Brooklyn—just as *CSI: Miami* begins with Caruso gazing out over that city—only Sinise is looking at Lower Manhattan, where the Twin Towers used to stand; he is gazing at an absence. Soon you learn that his first case is a woman killed by, we learn later, a serial murderer. "Someone out there," Sinise says, looking once more at the empty space above Lower Manhattan, "is missing a wife."

From that point, the episode gives us a victim who can move only one eye—the eyes being the organs that see, collect information, calculate—and a medically trained killer, who induces in his prey something called "locked-in syndrome," in which they live only in their minds and cannot move any part of their bodies. The killer's motives are, as Sinise puts it, "all about control." And this recalls the forensically, somewhat medically trained *CSI* investigators themselves, who are also, like the entire series, locked-up emotionally, super-controlled, as they seek to control their environment. So in seeking a medically trained killer, adept at all kinds of medical technologies, who himself or herself seeks absolute control, the show's first episode is hunting the perversion of its own spirit of benign technological domination. And it is also searching for a way out of its own radically "locked-in" condition—its "intensification of consciousness"—by liberating people from the same condition. Since the ultimately incomprehensible events on September 11, the show seems to be saying, we have all moved further into our own psyches. Though this first episode is itself too controlled, too slick, and moves too fast for its own good, its mental life is about right for this particular moment in its new metropolis.

SEPTEMBER 20, 2004

4 ▢ *Numb3rs*

Television and movies have a strange relationship with the idea of "the genius." On the one hand, both mediums traffic in the exceptional person or event, so the exceptional gifts—the event, even—of a genius are right up their alley. In fact, the figure of the detective is a type of genius, and the detective is the ur-figure of American popular culture. Just about every protagonist on television, for example, is some kind of detective, whether it is the surgeon, the psychiatrist, the spy, the gangster—the detectee, you might say, manipulating clues to elude capture—or the desperate housewife trying to fathom the mystery of her neighbor's death, or the secrets behind her living neighbors' lives. Detectives are problem-solvers, and everybody on TV is trying to solve a problem, from Judge Judy to Dr. Phil to Charlie Rose, who cheerfully tries to untangle the riddle of a personality.

On the other hand, there is nothing more inimical to the spirit of mass entertainment than the idea of the genius. After all, there is nothing more hostile to democratic taste—popular culture is one great inflation-deflation machine, building up and tearing down, celebrating the mediocre, exposing the exceptional as flawed, mirthless, "removed" from common life. Thus the shaming reality shows, and the daily celebrity scandals, and our current pre-deflated, and therefore deflation-proof, talentless inhabitant of the White House, a building whose modest, graceful excellence is like a faith in the average person's inherent nobility that society refuses to bear out.

One of the paradoxes of becoming a leader in any sphere of life is that the people who do so almost always ascend on their capacity for obeisance to other people. They are, as the sociologists used to say, conformists. It is like Tolstoy's theory of history: "great" men are humanly diminished in proportion to their ascent; they are the puppets, rather than the orchestrators, of history. Elevating, differentiating nobility is the last thing they exude. "Genius," however, is true to itself, follows its own nature, marches to the beat of a different drummer, and so on. So the portrayal of genius is a problem for television channels and networks that want to be "leaders" in their industry, that want to win the greater share of the market.

Popular entertainment is stuck in a dilemma. Genius is attractive as yet another special, interesting human case; genius repels because of its superior qualities, its authenticity. But television and movies have found several ways around that dilemma. The favorite one is to portray genius as malady, a festering wound that lays its possessor low even as it raises him or her above other people. There is psychological truth to the notion of wound-nourished gifts. You get a very sensitive, and gently funny, portrayal of that in *Monk,* one of television's best police shows, which depicts an uncannily intuitive detective—uncannily played by Tony Shalhoub—who is also debilitated by obsessive-compulsive neurosis. His gifts are palatable to anyone who might covet them because no one would covet the torment that enlivens them. It's like an equation. For the addition of superlative gifts, you suffer a precise subtraction of mental comfort. This is the way popular culture quantifies and makes tolerable the figure of the genius.

Numb3rs doesn't base its protagonist-genius on this type of quantifiable trade-off between psychic qualities; it makes its genius a professional quantifier. Charlie Eppes is a brilliant and famous physicist and the younger brother of Don, an FBI agent. The show's premise is that, as its website says, "In the world of crime, people lie. Numbers don't." Or as a voice speaking over the credits tells us at the beginning of every episode, we use numbers every day to figure out the world around us. Numbers solve life's mysteries.

This genius is not made acceptable to the audience on account of crippling neurosis, paranoid schizophrenia—à la *A Beautiful Mind*—or alcoholic self-destruction in the manner of Ed Harris in *Pollock*, a sensitive, understated film that nevertheless ended up reducing its hero to his disease. Charlie is handsome, renowned, affluent, and capable. He is not even romantically or sexually inept so much as entirely folded into his thoughts. His cerebrations leave him no time for romance or sex. Charlie's superior talents are domesticated for mass consumption not through illness, but by means of his occupation. He deals with numbers, and numbers are the stuff of money and the marketplace, and the marketplace dangles before us the promise that, if we are rational enough and hard-headed enough about trade-offs between costs and benefits—if we are diligent enough about numbers—we will thrive and prevail. Charlie Eppes is like a priest of modern economics, his feelings, his desires, his thoughts tonsured in devotion to the pursuit of happy, harmonious quantities.

He is not, in other words, the genius, not in the quaint romantic notion of the word—already a debasement of superior gifts—handed down to us from the nineteenth century. Charlie works for his brother, for the powers that be, and the drumbeat that he marches to inside his head is the very same drumbeat the feds, and the local cops, and all the forces of law and order are playing outside him. When he thinks, his thoughts are portrayed in action-like sequences, with dramatic music and slick visual effects. Even the very lineaments of his brain have been cast into an entertaining idiom—an idiom of obeisance, if you will.

You feel gratified by this genius who is not a mess, yet you feel let down by this genius who might as well be a corporate accountant. He solves crimes, whereas in the bad old days, genius itself was a crime, or at least a malfeasance—Sherlock Holmes was addicted to cocaine. The old conception of the genius does survive in *Numb3rs,* though. The bad guys are all Byrons-gone-bad: the evil physicist out to hack into the Federal Reserve; the egomaniacal architect (not quite a bad guy; rather a bad-guy facilitator); the disaffected train engineer who is also a criminal mastermind. For all those geniuses out there who aspire not to be leaders, the future is bleak indeed.

MARCH 7, 2005

⑤ *RENO 911!*

"Car 54, where are you?" Those were the days—1961, to be exact—weren't they, though I have no memory of them. How much different cultural expectations must have been at a time when JFK airport was called Idlewild, the name itself connoting a patience, maybe even a liking, for implicitness, and a low level of self-consciousness, and a tolerance for possibly playful ambiguity. I mean, who would call any public structure now, especially an airport, Idlewild, without fearing a thousand op-eds? And Idlewild was originally the name of a golf course that had been on that very site: Imagine. Then Kennedy was shot, and just over four weeks later Idlewild Airport became John Fitzgerald Kennedy Airport, as if American sunniness, destructive and sustaining both, had to convert the horrific image of the dead young president into the disembodied name for a place of worldwide flight, of almost infinite possibilities for a better life. Today the big, international airport symbolizes almost infinite possibilities of apocalypse. In other words, a comedy like *Car 54, Where Are You?* about two bumbling New York City cops, which ran from September 1961 to September 1963, would be pretty much unthinkable now. As a friend of mine quipped, you would have to call it *Car 54, We Need Back Up*. And it wouldn't be funny.

No, now the hunger to have a police presence with us in our living rooms, and as often as possible, has given us, most recently, *NYPD 24/7,* a reality show about the New York City Police Department that understandably, and justifiably, calls itself a "documentary" to distinguish itself from the debased and debasing genre of reality television. The concept of *24/7* is the phonetically symmetrical antidote to 9/11, which we are now cheerily told was simply the result of a lack of vigilance. The show is also the opposite of *NYPD Blue* and similar series, because it is not about the surprisingly tortured lives of men and women whom we depend on to be strong and uncomplicated in their protection of us. For all its real-life intimacy and disclosures, *24/7* returns us to the old-fashioned image of the cop as someone whose work is separate from, and uncomplicated by, his private life.

In this atmosphere, where the figure of the cop has acquired an urgency on top of the symbolic quality it always possessed, Comedy Central's *RENO 911!* seems, at first glance, a mildly astonishing phenomenon. Because of the richly symbolic nature of the cop, film comedies about the police have been far fewer than serious crime dramas—the very first, the *Keystone Cops,* was as wildly irreverent toward law enforcement as the tiny genre ever got. Then there was Abbott and Costello's *Mike the Cop* and, taking a leap from the prehistoric age into our own time, there is *Police Academy* and its sequels, and *Beverly Hills Cop* and its sequels, and *Lethal Weapon* and its sequels, and so on. Television comedies about the police have been almost nonexistent: *Car 54* and, maybe, *The Andy Griffith Show* and its later offshoot, *Mayberry RFD,* are the only shows that come to mind. But Comedy Central's often funny series could only have been set in Reno, Nevada. Big cities are too dangerous for comedies about police incompetence; putting bumbling cops in a small town is disrespectful; and setting them down in a suburb would be just plain boring. Reno is just right: the stuff of small legend; sort of artificial in a vaguely Vegas kind of way. Reno is one of those places you think you know without ever having been there or wanting to go. So the show's creators found a real town with a semi-fabled environment, a setting for a satire on murder and various kinds of violence and crime that wasn't going to stimulate comedy-obstructing thoughts or feelings. In one episode, you see the chalk silhouettes of murder victims drawn in the most improbable positions—sitting against a building, lying on the sidewalk with one arm neatly drawn down the side of the curb and then perpendicularly sticking out onto the street—and you think, this could only happen in this place, and you laugh.

You also laugh because *RENO 911!*'s satire has a very specific target (there is no more intimate relationship in art than between a satire and its target). The series isn't sending up cop shows, it's sending up reality cop shows—in particular, *Cops*, one episode or another of which seems to be on the air, well, 24/7. *RENO 911!* is at its funniest when it is true, as it were, to its relationship with its subject, when what is being inverted, exploded, travestied is a familiar, or familiar-seeming, scene being blown to comical smithereens. You don't have to be familiar with *Cops'* frenetic hand-held camera, and the blurred faces of the perpetrators, and its actual cops making commentary before and after arrests. The slightest familiarity with the faux-sincere reality-TV genre is enough, not just to laugh with this show, but to be relieved by it.

FOX network bought, held onto, and never aired *RENO 911!*, finally selling the series to Comedy Central. In this, FOX was true to its nature as one of the most prodigious generators of reality-schlock on television; perhaps it understood what a dissonant presence *RENO 911!* would have been in its lineup. Comedy Central is exactly the right forum for this show, the appearance of which amounts to a public service. The show is least funny when it meanders into sub-storylines about the personal lives and relationships of its characters: Lieutenant Dangle's estranged wife; his strained relations with the other members of the department; various sexual shenanigans between the Reno cops. But when it connects solidly to the reality-TV genre, *RENO 911!* is often very funny, almost liberating.

The premise of the show is that the camera follows the cops on their rounds, raising the expectation that viewers will be privy to the exciting arrest of dangerous or peculiar menaces to society, but that things will, of course, go horribly, hilariously wrong. On the night before Halloween, a pair of officers stop the car and get out to ask two masked kids to leave a cemetery where they've been horsing around. Suddenly a dozen more masked trespassers pop out from behind headstones and begin pelting the cops with eggs and tomatoes, and the cops retreat, shouting into their radios those familiar TV phrases, "Officers under fire, we need back-up," etc. etc., but the ridiculous situation upends the tiresome stock phrases like lifting a weight off your shoulders, or like picking you up and setting you down in a new place with a new landscape that replaces the one you see every day of your life. I'm sorry, this kind of thing cracks me up. It's like a vacation for the faculties.

In another episode, two cops respond to a call from a man who tearfully tells them, when they arrive, that his dog is terminally sick and suffering and should be put out of its misery, but that he doesn't have the heart to do it himself. He asks the two officers if they have the compassion to end the animal's life. One of the cops takes pity on the man, draws his gun out of the holster and shoots the poor creature. As the patrolmen leave, the one who did the deed wiping tears from his eyes, a woman comes running out of the house next door and screams, "What did you do to my dog?!! What did you do to my little Freddie?!" (or something like that) and the man who called the cops runs back into his house laughing wickedly. The dog's barking had been annoying him. This kind of useless, non-rational, purposeless impiety is profoundly liberating (it is not the kind of impiety that outrages decency just to show that it can, just to make a rational, purposeful point about its own power).

But the show is most comically freeing when it gets the reality genre in its sights and bears down without letting up. A near-virtuoso episode sent up reality cop shows and reality romance shows in one stroke. It involved lonely, slightly humpbacked Detective T. Wiegel, played to the peak of comic perfection by Kerri Kenney, who finally falls in love, which is nice, except that the other members of the department are pretty sure that her beau is a wanted serial killer. When Kenney extols her new boyfriend's qualities, she doesn't do it with a predictably clueless air which implies that everyone except her knows who this guy really is. She performs this with such an attitude of weary, impatient desperation that she gives the impression of knowing, but not caring, about who her boyfriend really is—after all, she's in her late thirties or early forties, and he's not married, and he's not gay. This self-aware acknowledgment of her situation keeps down the level of absurdity by giving the absurdity a practical origin, thus giving the comedy its edge. "I feel that I'm really falling for this guy," she tells another cop as the latter is helping her look for new clothes. "I mean, for the very first time in my life, with the combination of the anti-depressants, which are working very, very well, that and him, I feel like I might make it another year." That "I might make it another year" does the trick. It averts the potentially merely silly situation of an unwitting cop having a romance with a serial killer by making this cop very witting, and self-knowing, and comically, desperately open to the most fatal situations. It reincarnates the absurdity as a reality.

And this is unlike the reality shows, which edit reality until it becomes totally absurd. *RENO 911!* makes you nostalgic for a time when the imagination was flattered, not manipulated and shoved around. A time when Idlewild was an airport, and when no one knew where Car 54 was because no one really cared.

JULY 6, 2004

6 *Monk*

One evening last October, Mark Fisher, a nineteen-year-old student at Fairfield University in Connecticut, who had gone into Manhattan with friends, met a girl in a bar on First Avenue on the Upper East Side, got separated from his group, and was found dead the next morning on a Brooklyn sidewalk, his body wrapped in a yellow blanket, five gunshot wounds in his chest. According to a long article in the *New York Times*, Fisher's case remains unsolved mostly because no one who was with him that night seemed to want to tell the police everything they knew. This uncertainty was a further affliction on the young victim's parents, Michael and Nancy Fisher, who explained that their son's trip into Manhattan was the first time he had gone there without them. You felt so enraged by their suffering that you searched the article looking for clues on their behalf, or simply to reassure yourself that the world was not such a senseless place that a young person could not venture into it alone, without protection. You put down the paper thinking that you knew who the murderer was; and so you couldn't help wondering what might have happened that night if Mark Fisher had picked up all the clues that you did, not as clues but as warnings of an imminent doom. The ego being the avid entity that it is, you even ended up putting yourself in the poor young man's place, grasping the clues as hints about the future and thereby avoiding his terrible fate, in this way experiencing a catharsis for the pity and the terror that his story had aroused in you in the first place.

Surely, that illusion of control is what lies behind the popularity of police shows such as *CSI,* in which cases are solved by the kind of fancy technology that we have come to depend on—alarm systems, drugs, Blackberries, TiVo—to organize the senseless world more and more in our favor. (We call this rearrangement of the real "customization.") But what kind of mental condition would result if a person could apply his or her powers of detection not to looking into the past but to looking into the future, so that every uncertain portent of trouble became a divination of certain disaster? This would be paranoia; and it would place the detective's pellucid intuition a hairbreadth away from mental illness.

Adrian Monk, the protagonist of what is now television's most original cop show, is both a detective and a seer—excuse me, a victim of obsessive-compulsive disorder (OCD), as well as of myriad phobias. He is, in other words, a type of paranoid. Monk worked as a detective for the San Francisco Police Department until his wife was found murdered in an underground garage. Her murder went unsolved, and Monk grew unhinged. As viewers discovered during this, the show's third season, Monk has had a tendency ever since he was a boy to throw up neurotic defenses against a threatening world. (He never used the swing set his father bought for him when he was eight because the young Monk considered it a "death trap.") With the killing of his wife, Monk's clinical complexity, especially his fantastical vigilance toward germs, intensified to the point where it interfered with his work, and his superiors had to let him go. But he is such a genius at detection that his former boss, Captain Stottlemeyer, keeps him on as a consultant for the most difficult cases, which he investigates with the help of Sharona Fleming, his shrewd, earthy nurse and personal assistant. Naturally, he always solves these cases: there never has been a detective show in which the sleuth does not get his man—or woman. Viewers have to be able to sleep. *Monk*'s complication of the cop show's happy ending, its own innovation in its genre, is that an unsolved crime, the murder of Monk's wife, is what animates everything from its pathos-laden atmosphere to its characters' motivations.

In a sense, *Monk* is one more example of a larger development that has been growing stronger and stronger in recent years: the culture's subtle uprising against its own images of perfection. Reality shows, which celebrate the imperfect, the defeated, the humiliated, are one phase of this phenomenon. Television shows and movies in which the hero is a neurotic, or even a semi-paralyzed obsessive-compulsive, express another instance of rebellion. (The revolt of the messes.)

These heroes come in two main varieties. There are OCD heroes such as Jack Nicholson in *As Good As It Gets* and Nicolas Cage in *Matchstick Men,* their forerunners probably ranging from Dustin Hoffman in *Rain Man* to Cliff Robertson as the retarded man in *Charly.* (Larry David, though hardly hampered by his neuroses, certainly portrays a neurotic of the first order.) And there is the increasing frequency of movie and television heroes, often criminals of one kind or another, who are in therapy: Robert DeNiro in *Analyze This,* William H. Macy in *Panic,* Pierce Brosnan in *The Thomas Crown Affair,* Tony Soprano. The very effective—and entertaining—purpose of these scenes with a shrink is to bring out the interior nature of a character, but these outlaw analysands also conventionalize and even glamorize certain antisocial traits that seem to be growing more socially accepted: selfishness, greed, a total rejection of responsibility toward other people except as instruments of gratification.

But the former group, the autistics and the obsessive-compulsives and the chronic phobics, are different: they offer comfort for our strangeness. These funnily and not-so-funnily tortured characters are alone even when they are in public; and they make us grateful that we, unlike them, have not revealed our private, unassimilable peculiarities so openly. We see Hoffman's public display of utter individual strangeness, we watch Nicholson's or Cage's neurotic performance of our deepest anxieties and fears, and we leave the theater buoyant with the thought that our secret selves remain secret and hidden, that we are in better shape than these people. It is like waking from a repression dream in which we find ourselves, to our horror, sitting at the office, or back in a college or high-school classroom, naked or wearing pajamas. We come out of the dream—or we leave the silver screen—relieved: our private rituals of self-protection, our petty and not-so-petty traumas, are still safe inside us, silent and unseen.

Yet Adrian Monk, who is every bit as wounded as his OCD predecessors, and who also sees a therapist, is in his own category. He does not exhibit pathological behavior. On the contrary: his psyche is still reeling from his wife's murder, and he has no tolerance for the dark, violent side of human behavior. Indeed, unlike the outlaw analysands, he does not really tell his therapist, who sometimes seems as vulnerable and defenseless as Monk, anything significant about his inner life. In one lovely moment, an almost perfect comitragic mixture, Monk's therapist asks him what his sex life with his late wife was like, and Monk, rather than answer, sits in his chair and sings an old torch song. (The show's charm is that it moves from one wildly inventive whimsy to another; if the series has a flaw, it is

that it sometimes does not know what to do with itself between whimsies.)

But Monk is also nothing like his OCD precursors, whose
maladies are pure negatives that make us feel grateful for our
positives, or for the lesser magnitude of our negatives. Monk is
sui generis because his curse is his blessing. The condition that
is obstructing his wish to be back in the department is also what
makes him indispensable to the department. He is a modern-
day Philoctetes, the legendary archer of ancient Greek mythol-
ogy whose prowess with the bow was the reverse side of a
festering wound, which emitted such a noxious odor that his
fellow soldiers isolated him even as they depended on his gift to
save them. The uncannily gifted Monk is the wounded detective; his wound comprises his gift.

This is what makes the show something new. For once, popular culture does not drag the fact of creative genius down—as it
did in *A Beautiful Mind* and *Hilary and Jackie*—by making it
seem as if some kind of unique suffering is the price that must be
paid for great creativity, as if one could be thankful for not being
brilliant, or feel that in not "choosing" genius one could avoid suffering. Instead, *Monk* elevates intuitive genius by demonstrating
how it elevates and transforms suffering, and by presenting suffering as a condition that everyone shares, no matter what their
gifts may or may not be. Nearly everyone on the show has some
inflection of Monk-like torment, whether it is Stottlemeyer, who
becomes briefly deranged when his own wife is nearly killed in a
car accident; or Monk's agoraphobic brother, portrayed in a small
tour de force by John Turturro in a guest appearance; or the helpless, naïve upstairs neighbor who is deceived and nearly murdered by a vampish grifter; or Sharona, whose solitary devotion
to Monk is something like a renunciation of earthly pleasure. At

the core of *Monk* is the unsolved murder of Monk's wife, which colors the show like a metaphor for universal precariousness, for the bruise of mortality on the heart of the world.

"It's a jungle out there," Randy Newman sings in the show's theme song, and into this jungle comes Monk, traversing the thin line between comedy and tragedy, sanity and madness, his gift fueling his illness and his illness stimulating his gift. In the same way, his obsessive-compulsive straightening of crooked objects, his repetition of gestures, and his avoidance of germ-laden surfaces alternates with his alertness to clues: a sundial moved when the perpetrator ran out of a house; a single shoe in a garbage pail that makes him suspect that the other shoe disappeared when its owner was murdered; a case-cracking clue that comes from scouring the newspaper, of all things, for if the world is a jungle, the newspaper is its daily drumbeat. Monk's weakness is his strength: he is preternaturally aware of the external world.

The gentle, almost rueful humor of the show derives from this double motion: just about every incident and scene undulates between absurdity and poignancy. The doubleness is reflected in the extraordinary performance of Tony Shalhoub, who does not play Monk as helpless or nebbishy in the slightest way, but as a shaken yet undefeated worldly man both harassed and reassured by an enigmatic thought or image somewhere in the recesses of his psyche. Shalhoub's Monk goes around half-buried within himself, not so much distracted from the world around him as intensely focused on both the grief and the gift inside him, so that when he is startled out of his mysterious inwardness, which happens constantly, the foolishness of his preoccupied air is immediately absorbed by the intensity of his eccentric attention to the matter at hand. (Turturro, by contrast, instead of playing the agoraphobic brother shifting between his inner world and the world around him, as Monk does, portrays the brother as being lost within himself while interacting with other people at the very same time. Seeing these two masterful character actors work together was a special treat.)

So the symbiotic relationship of Monk's illness to his gift is embedded in the show's structure and style. A very old resonance hangs about this character. He is "always sickly or morbidly sensitive"; his chosen vocation "allows him to expend [his] nervous force freely"; he exists on "a vital plane that shows him the fundamental data of human existence, that is, solitude, danger, hostility of the surrounding world." I take those descriptions from Mircea Eliade's great book, *Shamanism*. Adrian Monk is the ancient shaman as modern shamus. His strange interlude in his therapist's office recalls "the famous Yakut shaman Tusput (that is, 'fallen from the sky') [who] had been ill at the age of twenty; he began to sing, and felt better."

But, Eliade goes on, "the shaman is not only a sick man; he is, above all, a sick man who has been cured, who has succeeded in curing himself. . . . The shamans, for all their apparent likeness to epileptics and hysterics, show proof of a more than normal nervous constitution; they achieve a degree of concentration beyond the capacity of the profane; they sustain exhausting efforts." Monk succeeds in curing himself every time he solves a crime by means of his superhuman powers of concentration. If his wife's murder remains unsolved, and he has to try to solve another crime to fend off madness, that is as it should be. Like that aboriginal detective Oedipus, Monk, when he finally solves the riddle of his wife's senseless death, will also solve the riddle of mortality. That will be his final season.

MARCH 22, 2004

Sitcoms

7 Friends

Sophisticated taste doesn't like the phenomenally popular *Friends*, whose final episode this Thursday will end the series' ten-year run, but when was the last time sophisticated taste did anything for you? Dante, Shakespeare, and Mozart liked fart jokes—and you're afraid to be silly? Or does invoking Dante, Shakespeare, and Mozart before writing favorably about *Friends* make a critic seem afraid to appear unsophisticated in his defense of silliness?

Oh, the self-consciousness of the critic. So let's start another way. Twenty-five years ago the federal government commissioned the sculptor Richard Serra to build a work of art for New York City's Federal Plaza. Serra came up with *Tilted Arc*, a curving wall of naked steel 120 feet long and 12 feet high that he placed in the middle of the vast urban space. The people who worked in the offices around the plaza, and who used to relax there during lunch and coffee breaks, protested that Serra's work broke up the little vista that soothed their burdened minds and nerves, and they called for the government to remove it. Serra himself agreed that *Tilted Arc* did not have a calming effect: "The viewer becomes aware of himself and of his movement through the plaza. . . . Step by step the perception not only of the sculpture but of the entire environment changes." In other words, art unsettles, disorients, and reorients: Serra arrogantly refused to budge. Eight years and a sprawling controversy later, a panel convened by the United States General Services Administration, which had commissioned the sculpture, ruled that it should be taken down. An angry Serra declared in high modernist fashion, "I don't think it is the function of art to be pleasing. Art is not democratic. It is not for the people."

Well, yes and no. The *Tilted Arc* controversy touched a sore spot in American culture that rarely gets exposed except in the context of protests against cultural "dumbing down," an argument that takes place between marketers, editors, producers, artists, and critics but that never includes the phantom audience on whose behalf and for whose dollars the dumbing down is being instigated. (Shut up, you'll love it versus Shut up, we hate it.) But the hornet's nest that Serra stirred up is about taste, and the reason it's so hard to talk about taste in America is that it's almost impossible to avoid dragging the issue into the realm of morality, where you end up associating good taste with good education, with good income, with being good. And no one who wants to appear good would ever dream of publicly associating moral goodness with material things. Certainly no one who learned the value of appearance at a good school.

It's a good bet that the people who worked at Federal Plaza were more likely than Serra and his admirers to go home in the evening and watch a show like *Friends*—or *MASH*, *The Mary Tyler Moore Show*, *Kate and Allie*, *Cheers*, *Seinfeld*. It's a good bet, too, that few of the tens of millions of viewers who will be dabbing their eyes at the close of Thursday's two-hour finale were as absorbed in what happened between Carrie and Big in *Sex and the City* as they have been in the outcome of the relationship between Ross and Rachel. That's because Ross and

Rachel are Carrie and Big in a parallel universe. Through all the former couple's permutations—marriage, divorce, having a child together out of wedlock—they are emotionally connected. For Rachel, Ross is not unattainable; he's just not tolerable. Big remains unattainable, emotionally distant, unfulfilling in every way except for his thrilling elusiveness, which responds not to Carrie's emotional center and needs but to her de-centered lack of self-esteem. The function of *Friends* is to be comforting, or "pleasing" as Serra would say. The function of *Sex and the City* was to entertain, yes, but also to unsettle and to provoke in its candor. You could enjoy both shows, but you couldn't be devoted to both shows.

Debuting in 1994, when Rachel left her fiancé standing at the altar and rushed, wedding gown and all, from her suburban demesne into the coffee lounge in Manhattan where her closest friend from high school liked to hang out, *Friends* followed the lives of people in their twenties trying to make their professional and romantic way in the big city. The show was absurd; its people were caricatures; its humor was often silly, even sophomoric; it could have been set in Akron so un-hip were its situations and environment (yet its indifference to Manhattan chic was a relief); its popularity made it more and more stilted, self-conscious, and empty as the seasons wore on—and when it was good, it was consoling and hilarious. It did the work that sitcoms have always done. *Friends* ennobled the setback, lent dignity to ordinary experience, proclaimed mere survival a triumph greater than wealth, or success, or fame. Adorno would have plotzed. Surely the harmony is illusory harmony and the catharsis is shallow, so that the critical intellect is defeated (by advanced studio capitalism!) with fake expectations and ersatz pleasures.

But since the Frankfurt Schoolers didn't know from Winona Ryder, or Bruce Willis, or Brad Pitt, or Reese Witherspoon, they would not have noticed that the series wasn't merely sucking up to the celebrity culture by having stars appear from time to time. It was also using such appearances to emphasize the function and allure of *Friends*, and of nearly all situation comedies, which is to restore to comedy's long view the daily obstructions and little calamities that loom so large when they occur. One such calamity is disappointment, which looms especially large in our celebrity-littered landscape of glittering images of splendor and opulence. In *Friends*, the celebrities are afflicted by disappointments that are served up by the ordinary inhabitants of the series: Rachel dumps Bruce Willis, who has been playing a weepy character against type; Monica dumps Tom Selleck, who is undercut by her ordinary demand for children; Phoebe (played by the sublimely funny Lisa Kudrow) upstages Alec Baldwin, who plays a glamorous, sunny, and clueless character. In fact, in traditional sitcom fashion, nearly every show turned on some disappointment, whereas *Sex and the City*'s four girls seemed less disappointed than unsatisfied and ungratified. Phoebe, looking forward to two weeks with her naval officer, gets chicken pox; Ross can't get on his new leather pants; Joey, the struggling actor, loses a shot at a movie role when he gets too dramatic with his butt (it's a stand-in for Pacino's). But they all survive. They have each other.

In reality (I assume there is still a consensus on what that word means), relationships with other people are often the cause of disappointment. The people in *Friends* are disappointed by circumstances—by situations—more than by people. People—that is, the friends—are the refuge they come back to after being disappointed. Sitcoms are family shows that portray, week after week, strangers who have come to relate to each other as family—shows like *MASH, The Mary Tyler Moore Show, Cheers,* and so on. In the early sitcoms, *I Love Lucy* and *The Honeymooners,* the Mertzes and Norton and Trixie represent the outside world that loses its teeth and claws and comes to sit at the Arnaz' and the Cramdens' table, makes trouble, and always returns for a hug. A sitcom's dialogue often seems like a string of non sequiturs because this is a world where all the sharp and rough edges of ego cut and slash yet have no negative effect on a relationship. That is what's so funny, and that is what's so consoling.

It could be that those of us who enjoy silly sitcoms are people who need the shallow escapism of illusory warmth and family feeling more than those who can come home after a weary day, throw their feet up, and watch someone being sodomized on *Oz.* It could be that the former audience lacks the emotional and material security necessary to watch images of violence and degradation without feeling threatened. And since emotional and material security are often associated with wealth and success, there might be some correlation between "advanced" taste and economic status and education. Then again, the automatic attraction of "advanced" taste to violence and degradation, to anything "edgy," might also say something about the hollowness of the highly educated classes. Will I be watching the finale of *Friends* this Thursday? Probably.

MAY 4, 2004

8 *Joey*

Never mind all the worrying about whether Americans still know how to read serious, difficult books. It's time to start worrying about whether Americans still know how to watch and enjoy television. Or at least that class of people whose job it is to make sense of television for everybody else.

Joey, NBC's new sitcom, stars Matt LeBlanc in the role of Joey Tribbiani, the clueless, charming character he made famous in *Friends*. Joey has moved to Los Angeles, where his sister Gina—played by *The Sopranos*' Drea de Matteo—lives with her twenty-year-old son, Michael, and where Joey intends to make a career for himself as an actor. The show is quick, and crazy, and funny and, among other things, a refreshing antidote to *Entourage*, another comedy set in Hollywood which glamorizes the mores of that strange town behind the shallow pretense of—as the critics like to say—"skewering" them. But you wouldn't know what a pleasure this new show is from the reception it's gotten. That's because nobody seems able to write about it as a simple pleasure.

Instead of approaching *Joey* as entertainment, critics treat it as part of an overarching corporate strategy. The response to the show is almost as funny as the show itself. It is, we are told, NBC's attempt to compensate for the loss of *Friends* and *Frasier*;

NBC is replacing *Friends* with a spin-off from *Friends* because the network is playing it safe; the show's "concept" also resembles that of *Frasier*, another show with a main character who moves to the other side of the country to be with family; *Joey* is NBC's attempt to revive the sitcom genre, which is now dead (the same critics declared it dead in the spring. So it is dead); NBC is trying to fill the vital primetime Thursday night slot so as to compete with Fox, which is moving its hit show, *The O.C.*, to the powerfully profitable 8 P.M. Thursday night slot. And on, and on.

Television is so transparently commercial that people who appraise it often have to demonstrate that they are hip to the commercial imperatives driving a particular show in the same way that they have to demonstrate that they are hip to the theatrical conventions animating a political convention. Ironically, when they write about fiction on television, they see only the hidden hand of economic interest; when they scrutinize politics, they see only the blatant fictions driven by political purposes. But there has never been a politics, democratic or tyrannical, that presented itself raw and unmediated to its citizens or subjects, and there has never been a work of art or entertainment that was not, in one degree or another, influenced by commercial considerations. What is to be done?

Relax and enjoy! Blake threw off the anxiety of Milton's influence, and, yes, *Joey* has sloughed off the onerous precedent of *Friends*. The running joke in the first episode is Gina's surgically enlarged breasts, which she invites Joey to touch when she goes to pick him up at the airport. Critics—the same people who explicate with such patient sensitivity HBO's graphic violence and sex—were scandalized. The entire episode, declared the *Washington Post*, had "weird sexual overtones." "The premiere leans too heavily on boob jokes," reflected the *Boston Globe*. Commenting on Joey's reference to his sister's "fake boobs," *Time* paternalistically snapped that such language was not "for our Joey." (Talk about weird.) But the show is so cleverly written that this running joke, far from being gratuitously vulgar or sexually depraved, unifies the entire episode.

For Joey has arrived in a fake place. When the show opens, he's riding in a cab and going excitedly on about L.A. to the cab-driver, who informs him that he's actually in Dallas—Joey mistook the connecting city for his destination. What better introduction to the fluid half-place and headquarters for the Department of National Illusions that is Los Angeles? The pilot episode weaves such displacements throughout its humor. From his soulless apartment complex, Joey can only see part of the fabled Hollywood sign: it spells "OLLYWOO." The movers fail to bring his furniture. He shows his nephew, Michael, a pair of pilot's wings he bought at the airport, and Michael immediately puts them in his pocket, wrongly assuming that they're a gift. Gina tells Joey that if he hadn't liked the apartment she found for him, she was going to lie and tell him that Tom Cruise used to live there. (He believes her anyway.) The pretty blonde who lives next door and who seems like a romantic possibility turns out to be married. Standing on the set of a television police show he's appearing in, and wearing a gun and a T-shirt splattered with the blood of a man he's just pummeled, Joey tells Michael that when he was young, Gina used to "hit me all the time, she used to hold me down and force me to say, 'I am gay for David Cassidy.'" In fact, Gina herself has lied to her son about how old she was when she had him (she was sixteen). Nothing in this fake place is how it appears; and if even mothers aren't what they seem to be to their children, why should their breasts be any less illusory?

So this show has its own momentum and its own identity. One of its delights is Drea de Matteo, late—very late: she was whacked—of *The Sopranos,* whose acting on *Joey* is so easy, and funny, and resourceful that it will add another dimension to *The Sopranos'* original blend of comedy and tragedy for anyone who returns to watch the HBO drama. And the contrast between Matteo's HBO style—a mixture of naturalistic and theatrical— and Matt LeBlanc's pure sitcom manner, an assortment of histrionic facial expressions, outsized gestures, and dramatic acoustics, is surprisingly harmonious.

Matteo and LeBlanc work beautifully together, and you chuckle at the show's mischief when Joey tells Gina that the series he's appearing on is "for cable, so there's a combination of nudity and swearing that I find intriguing." There used to be a distinction between television acting and movie acting; *Joey* offers the revelation of distinct cable-acting and network-acting styles. Jennifer Coolidge, who plays Joey's agent, and who delivers to him the most depressing news through a frozen smile, is in a comical class by herself. And on network television yet, where the sitcom is supposedly dead. Sometimes the thing that everyone expects to be fake is real after all. In the media business, that is known as a "non-story."

SEPTEMBER 13, 2004

9 *My Name Is Earl*

Critics have pronounced *My Name Is Earl* a masterpiece. A weird comedy, they say, that signals a rebirth of the sitcom. Innovative. Original. Heralds NBC's return as a contender. Hysterical. Dark. Several steps above most network sitcoms. A paradigmatic shift away from reality television. Good-natured. Yet wicked. Provocative programming! But good-natured.

Is there any form of popular or serious art that has it as critically easy as a television series? The critics who emitted the effusions cited (and paraphrased) above had likely only seen one episode of the series. Since using the first episode to pass judgment on an entire series is the conventional way of doing television criticism (and I'm as guilty as anyone else), the judgments of television critics have precisely zero effect. A rave or a pan is going to leave the reader equally indifferent because a pilot episode is a pilot episode, and everyone knows that the season has a dozen more installments with which to rise or fall. But being tied so tightly to the news cycle as it is, reviewing television is never going to change.

The problem is that most television, and most movies too, are part cultural products, part news events, and part sheer commercial ventures. In other words, they are inherently incapable of holding our absolute attention because they are inherently unable to pay undivided attention to themselves without being distracted by themselves. (That's why such creations are perfect for network television's commercials.) A Vermeer, say, or a story by Chekhov, arose out of an absolute attention and draws our absolute attention. But not our media. That's why they're called media. The entire value of television and movies does not lie in themselves. Rather, they mediate between us and other things. They are not works. They are reference points.

You can therefore review a whole series on the basis of only the first episode because the television critic's job is not really to pass judgment at all. It's merely to announce a new reference point. After all, the greatest success a TV show can have is to become established in speech as the shortcut to an experience—Trump's "You're fired," for example, mercifully short-lived as that phrase's common usage was.

Consisting of multiple parts, the best TV shows provide the occasion for pundit-commentary, water-cooler conversations, and sometimes moral panics or controversies. *Earl*—about a petty criminal and ne'er-do-well who wants to repair his fate by making up for the various wrongs he's done to people—has already been trotted out by trend-proclaiming journalists as evidence of rising interest in Eastern religions and the concept of karma.

But, most of all, TV shows as reference points offer you a way to certify your relevance, that is, your independence from the ravages of time and your continuing viability on the market. It's odd how the upper echelons of hipness and with-it-ness run along the same lines as elementary-school popularity. Do you remember what happened if you showed up at your fifth-grade class without having seen the latest episode of the latest, hottest TV show? The same goes for culture references in the so-called adult world of media.

Heaven help you if you refer to a Nautilus instead of a Cybex machine. Can you imagine referring to a Walkman rather than an iPod in public? Nightmare. (Ten years ago I would have written, "What a nightmare.") Of course, staying abreast of reality is essential for every thinking, acting person. And being able to listen to thousands of songs on your device is as significant an addition to reality as it is a nice new pleasure. But like TV shows, these new technologies are part happy-making little things, and part commerce-driven entities. Go ahead, enjoy listening to the new Blow-Job Puffin while you're on the treadmill. (Don't tell me you don't know this Paramus, New Jersey, band. Are you serious?) You're still dancing to someone else's tune.

Why the degree to which your speech and style and behavior have been shaped by the products of someone else's self-interest—Apple, for example—is generally considered a mark of your relevance, rather than a sign of your passive inauthenticity, is beyond me. The sole original virtue of *My Name Is Earl* is that the series offers a sly comment on that curious perception.

Earl is the latest entertainment in a long-lived genre of "stupid." From Stan Laurel through Dobie Gillis and Beavis and Butthead, it's been a relief to be tickled by the self-imploding—and usually ultimately triumphant—antics of the mentally ungifted. It doesn't get dumber than white-trash Earl and his brother and Earl's deliciously nasty ex-wife. (The comically appealing Bitch is a growing staple on television now: intellectually superior, radically autonomous, and morally deficient, she is feminism and its backlash clenched into one person.) The show's conceit of Earl running around with a list of people he's wronged, trying to make amends to each one and then checking off his successes, is like the stupid conceptual correlative to the show's stupid characters. And for the most part, the situation of each episode is so absurd that its outlandishness outpaces its comedy. Absurdity and farce have to concretely present everyday reality and then wash it away in a torrent of nonsense, or else the entertainment is all just nonsense—that is, it's all like what passes for everyday reality.

But there's one thing that *Earl* does that perks me up. It anchors its characters' stupidity in false consciousness. How does Earl get the dumb idea of improving his karma by pursuing the people on his list? By watching an episode of *Last Call with Carson Daly*, also on NBC, in which Daly one night admiringly describes and prescribes the practice of karmic accumulation of good earthly deeds. This is rich because it's *Earl's* way of using itself to promote the network while satirizing the inbred nature of network self-promotion. But the hermetic culture references don't stop there.

In another episode, and in separate scenes, Earl and his brother Randy both say something and then you see, in a flashback—and also in separate scenes—each of them standing or sitting inattentively in front of a television on which someone is saying the exact thing Earl and Randy will repeat later. In still another episode, a purported meal that Bruce Willis had with Demi Moore and Ashton Kutcher becomes the reference point for a farcical misunderstanding between Earl, his ex-wife, and her fiancé. What adds to the fun is that Willis, Moore, and Kutcher had actually caused a stir—yes, this caused a stir—by appearing on *That '70s Show*, a sitcom on FOX, itself often the stupidest television network in the history of the medium.

How clever. Like all television shows, *Earl* hopes to work itself into the way people speak through a line of dialogue that gets repeated until it becomes a general expression, or through a physical gesture, or even an exclamation. But if the show does achieve that supreme success, the viewers it will be holding in its thrall will have become as victimized by false consciousness as Earl and Randy. The show's success will be everyone else's personal failure—if you ever find yourself talking or acting like any of the show's regular characters, you'll have disappeared into the same prefabricated mental numbness in which they are enveloped. So if you really do like this idiotic new series, and you really do think it's "weird" and "original" and several steps above most network sitcoms, the best compliment you could pay it is never to watch it again.

NOVEMBER 22, 2005

10 *Everybody Hates Chris*

Everybody Hates Chris is being praised as a wise, tender, funny portrait of a black working-class family, and it is exactly that. Narrated by Chris Rock and starring a really marvelous cast of actors, the series tells the story—or the way the comedian wishes to tell his story—of Rock's experiences growing up poor in Brooklyn's Bedford-Stuyvesant neighborhood with his younger brother, younger sister, mother, and father—"My father never said 'I love you.' He was one of only four married fathers on our street, so just coming back home to us at night after work was the way he said 'I love you.'"

That's one of the wise, tender parts. The funny parts happen by the second: Chris gets bused to a school in Brooklyn Beach (i.e., Howard Beach) where he's the only black kid there. The place is called Corleone Junior High. After multiple beatings, little Chris ends up with a star position on the basketball team without even trying out for it simply because he's black, the only problem being that he can't for the life of him play basketball—besides being hysterically funny, the absurd turn of events offers a triple swipe at racial stereotypes, affirmative action, and white ethnic prejudice. So if you're smart and politically engaged but have no sense of humor, don't worry, you'll still like the show.

And if you'll pardon another example (my quotes are paraphrases), Rock tells us that whenever his parents went out, his father put Chris in charge and left him with specific instructions in case of emergency—this is depicted in rapid sequences meant to portray different nights: "If there's a fire, call the fire department and get your brother and sister out of the house." "If your brother catches fire, call the fire department and get your sister out of the house." "If your brother and sister catch fire, call the fire department and get out of there as fast as you can," and so on. All through the comedy, however, the father's character—as well as all the other characters—develops and deepens in different dimensions. Pathos is always present just below the show's surface, as if, along with fancifully portraying his childhood and youth, Rock wants you to see beside his comic gift the painful source of his gift.

The formative event in this boy's life isn't that everybody "hates" him. His parents are remarkably loving people. It's that his need for love is so intense that little Chris exaggerates every instance of a shortfall in the world's affection into the type of comical calamity the performance of which will, finally, win him the world's affection. The show might have been called *Portrait of the Comedian as a Young Man*.

But *Everybody Hates Chris* is something more than the wise, tender, funny portrayal of the evolution of a gifted mind. It's actually something very rare on television, even rarer in the movies, and almost nonexistent in contemporary fiction. It's the wise, tender, funny portrait of a poor kid.

You can't argue with the beneficial effects of having bucks. In artistic terms, though, the adventure of either seeing through or rising through society is a lot more interesting than portraying very wealthy people as having their own problems, dilemmas, and so on, and going about telling such a story without exposing the pathologies of privilege. After all, the greatest American novel, *The Great Gatsby*, was written, as it were, by Fitzgerald, not Gatsby: Nick Carraway narrates Gatsby's story rather than the other way around. But, then, the novel itself as a form of art was a middle-class invention, fostered by the prosperous conditions created by the new titans of the Industrial Revolution. The novel was the way middle-class authors and readers used the accumulation of experience to compete with the accumulation of wealth, the downside and the upside of capitalism being the crazy multiplication of experiences.

But in the last decade or so, serious and popular art has more and more often been overtaken by uncritical images of wealth and privilege. Ours must be the only civilization that has ever existed whose art yokes together material riches and spiritual success. Think of the film *Indecent Proposal*, in which the shallow, crass millionaire who offers a husband and wife a million dollars if the latter will sleep with him is presented, in the end, as a person of more character and integrity than the couple who says yes. And a recent "hot" novel has as its hero a trust-funder whose unsatirized problem in life is . . . not being able to make up his mind! Reviewers rushed to proclaim this dilemma a Representative Conflict, as if the main problem facing our terrified, confused, post-Katrina, Iraq-quagmired country were what to do about its spoiled rich kids. At least the author of this emotionally sterile tale had the politic, if not the artistic sense, to abruptly transform his adorable young plutocrat into a socialist at the end of the book.

In other words, now it's Gatsby's empty crowd that's writing fiction. It would doubtlessly hate little Chris and definitely spur him ever upward.

OCTOBER 10, 2005

Comedy

⑪ Jon Stewart

Just when American politics is becoming no laughing matter, the job of commenting on American politics has fallen to the comedians, to "political satirists" such as Al Franken and Bill Maher, who have aligned themselves with the Democrats, or Dennis Miller, who has aligned himself with the Republicans. For the first time in the history of comedy, you have to register to laugh. And now, Jon Stewart and his *Daily Show* are following the same trend. With the comedians' solemnity about their politics, with their *grave concern* about the direction the country is headed in, comedy is fast becoming no laughing matter, either. The marriage of comedy and politics is even more unhealthy than the marriage of church and state.

Laughter is the essence of individuality. Sobs sound alike, so do moans of pleasure and pain, so do terrified screams; but each person has his or her own laugh. A horror of individuation was why Stalin asked a group of Polish communists how Comrade Z was and when they stared at the ground in silence, he burst into laughter, because he and they knew that he had had Comrade Z killed a few days before; it is why the Uruguayan junta called the prison where it tortured and killed suspected leftists *Libertad*. Those were instances of politics pursuing and catching laughter and then having the Last—the eschatologically last—Laugh.

Politics hates the naked, unbridled ego that laughter sets free; it hates it with the intensity with which laughter heaps its furies on the naked unbridled ego that hides behind the high-flown sentiments of politics. When American presidential candidates make the by-now obligatory pilgrimage to the late-night comedy shows and grovel, and pander, and even humiliate themselves, it's not just because they want to reassure some anxious voters that, in this particular case, they shouldn't worry about feeling diminished by a leader who is dignified, intelligent, and true to his or her individual self. It's also because they've sensed that the comedians have put laughter in the service of high-flown sentiments and gotten it under control.

Lenny Bruce had a field day with Eisenhower, but no one would ever have identified him as a mainstream liberal. Nixon put comedy on steroids, but none of the comics who took him as their target, from George Carlin to Robert Klein, actually got indignant about his policies the way a smug Bill Maher gets indignant about Bush's policies. Indignation is to comedy what turning the lights on is to a party. Indignation implies earnest thoughts about a better world; but those comics of yore were wholly, unrelievedly negative—that's what made them so refreshing. In a country where everyone believes today can be repaired like a car so that tomorrow will run more smoothly, they harbored no recommendations for the future in the havoc they wreaked on the present. That got you thinking about how rife with unprescribed possibility was the present. Like the id, comedy exists only in the here-and-now. But by aligning themselves with an ideology, with a politics, Franken, Maher, and Miller weigh their comic negativity down with a positive premise. They actually believe in the power of the ballot box to shape the country's future. That's not funny.

So it's not just bizarre but disappointing to see Jon Stewart blazing the same trail. To be honest, I was never a huge fan of Stewart's humor, which he custom-crafts for a mostly college-age audience. *The Daily Show*'s intention of showing clips from the news in order to mock the conventional coverage of the news and get to the bottom of what's really going on in the world always seemed to me too dependent on the thing it derided—the comic equivalent of covering an old song. Stewart's deflate-the-talking-heads shtick consists too much of sarcastic jibes at the Pompous or Deceitful Public Figure, at the Underlying Reality of Self-Interest: it's more like throwing fruit than making jokes. Sometimes it's just plain stupid, as when he made a running commentary on the, like, totally hilarious Taiwanese elections, with their throngs of people pushing to get to the polls ("and that's just the line for the bathroom"). This led into a whole Asian thing, at one point with Stewart providing captions for illustrations from Sun-Tzu: "rah-rah ruts, kick 'em in the nuts!" And then it was on to Indonesia's impending first-time democratic elections, for which the Indonesian government televised instructions so that its citizens could practice voting. Here Stewart got confused, quipping that the Indonesians "simulate democracy," whereas we "simulate terrorist attacks." Even Stewart's brainwashed audience couldn't be prompted to laugh at that one, for the simple reason that no one could figure out what he was saying.

Stewart can be funny when he's not playing his new role as *comique engagé*, though it's strange that he can't mimic or do accents—he's the only American comic I've ever heard who can't do a British accent. My Korean grocer can do a British accent. Most peculiar is that he keeps using the identical outrageous-silly voice Johnny Carson patented decades ago. Maybe someone should give him a nudge. But the really discouraging thing is that nowadays, Stewart seems to consider it more important to be a good citizen than a funny fellow. According to the newspapers, a substantial number of younger viewers get their news from *The Daily Show*. So for some time now, Stewart doesn't just want to skewer the conventional news and the mendacious politicians. He wants to clarify the news, and to educate his audience.

The result is that Stewart weighs down his jokes with a kind of Government 101 knowingness. He's not just funny about politics, you see, he's savvy about the way the system works, and he's going to help us through the maze. In Washington, "you have to cut through the partisan gridlock just to get to the bureaucratic logjam." Stop, you're killing me. But when it came to Richard Clarke and his controversial book, Stewart gave up even the pretense of being funny.

For days preceding Clarke's appearance on his show, Stewart transformed himself from a "political satirist" to a Clarke spokesman. Clarke's book was "mindblowing"; it was "insane"; his book and his testimony at the 9/11 hearings "provided a window into how our government functions." Now, as a Serious Citizen, I think Clarke's charges against the Bush administration are wholly credible, I think the administration's response to him is wholly scurrilous, and I hope a thousand Clarkes bloom and drive the insolent near-sociopaths who currently run the country out to sea and over to Iraq, where they should open a department store and stay forever. As an *animal ridens,* however, I think Clarke is a genuine political satirist's bull's-eye. Here was a slick, malleable, professional political advisor/operator, who had the choice of resigning in protest against an invasion of Iraq months before it took place, when such a protest might have had consequences, but who chose instead to wait until his slighted ego burst at the seams. This Clarke, a true embodiment of human foible and folly, deserved to be manhandled by the spirit of laughter every bit as much as his accusations deserved to be defended by the spirit of truth. But like everybody else in public life, from politicians and pundits to performers and poets, Stewart wants to seem edifying and instructive. He wants to seem good. Exerting a positive, educative influence has become the self-conscious premise of his show.

So after showing a clip of 9/11 Commission member (and Republican) James Thompson questioning Clarke and exposing Thompson as the no-good, ideologically driven, politically motivated hack he most surely now seems to be (audience hoots and laughs), and after exalting Clarke as the Saint of the Beltway he most surely now seems to be (audience cheers and laughs), Stewart got the prize of Clarke's actual physical appearance on his show. And what followed was so unfunny that it seemed like a glimpse of what late-night comedy might look like after a revolution has killed all the comics.

Rather than chide, tease, or otherwise discombobulate this smooth veteran courtier, Stewart worried with Clarke over the state of the nation, which prompted Clarke to make a nod to the show's target audience and express concern about how today's politics might breed cynicism, a bad thing "because we need young people to go into government . . . and try to change things on the inside." Stewart then thanked Clarke for providing, in his book and in his testimony at the hearings, "an eye-opening examination of the true workings of government." Such earnestness on the part of a "political satirist" who had just bravely lampooned the Taiwanese and Indonesian political establishments, on the part of a comedian who had beckoned to comic immortality by calling Robert Novak a "douchebag for liberty" only days before (the audience roared), was anti-comical enough. But right after Clarke's visit, Stewart had Karen Hughes on the show. Hughes, whom Stewart treated with sly irony, dutifully made a nod to the audience in a way that made her sound just like Clarke: "I hope to inspire young people about the political process." And Stewart then thanked Hughes as though he was actually still thanking Clarke, saying that "it's very interesting to see the inner workings" of government.

So beyond Stewart's positive and increasingly unfunny political agenda is his commercial and absolutely unfunny pandering to the show's demographic. Apparently, comedy has become too important to be left to the comedians, who are rushing to refashion themselves as politicians in the fullest sense of the word.

APRIL 12, 2004

(12) *Extras* I

This column has commented on the remarkable number of television series (not to mention feature films) that portray the real life of actors, or of famous actors playing themselves, or of television shows that explore acting as some sort of representative activity. *Extras,* HBO's British import, continues this trend. It is a black comedy that is currently the most original and brilliant show on television. The series plays with the pretense of acting, sees through it, and makes sense of it in a new light; it deconstructs celebrity and stages a collision between reality and cinematic art. *Extras* deserves more than a review.

And so, this column will take up the subject of this extraordinary show, in two parts. The first part, which follows, is a sort of theoretical overture. Next week's essay will be about the series itself.

The recent preoccupation with dispelling acting's enchantments is an inevitable development in our restless, ceaselessly enterprising nation. But it reflects some widespread social impulses, too. People are more and more fed up with the celebrity culture—celebrities are almost always actors, or at least performers—which is a good thing. But people are also in revolt against any type of authoritative presence, which is not always a good thing.

Anyone the media builds up, regardless of his or her accomplishments or lack thereof, has to immediately get torn down. Yet, since most media constructions of instantaneous fame are driven by commercial purposes, the rapid backlash—which seems to come more and more quickly—is a healthy corrective to an empty phenomenon. In commercial terms, the almost immediate deflation is also a necessary corrective. Room has to be made for the next Sensational Person, whose coverage earns money for various people and entities: the media organ in question, which makes its own coverage essential once it proclaims the thing that must be covered; the journalists who then feast on the New Personality; any product or service associated with said personality. But the dynamic surrounding the making and unmaking of celebrity is not simply a quality of the marketplace.

The fascination with celebrity perhaps represents, on another level, a response to the remoteness and inadequacies of politics. Let some pretty face with an action-movie resonance intervene in a global crisis where politics has yet to make a difference! Some social scientist would probably be able to draw a definite connection between Bush's fraudulence and incompetence and an intensification in the national obsession with celebrities. And for those of us who regard, in the current case, four years in the White House as the equivalent of a geological epoch, the quick inflation and deflation of instant fame is a satisfying symbolic deconstruction.

Never mind that glittering celebrity-interventions are usually merely fantastical catharses, or vehicles for vicariously inserting ourselves into a world tragedy the way teenagers engage in video-battles set in foreign places. The more ineffectual politics becomes—and the more commercial society makes one's own fantasies the center of reality—the more urgent the national desire to travel with the pretty cinematic faces from crisis-zone to crisis-zone.

This radical alienation from politics is partly justified, given our current leadership. But it's also a general alienation from boring, unexciting politics, which is the nature of a liberal, "democratic" politics. There is a reason why fascism had such a strong cinematic component. It replaced the democratic tedium with suspense. One of totalitarianism's paradoxes was that it depressed the mind and the spirit yet kept the adrenalin running at the same time. What is "suspense" in film, anyway, but a normalized paranoia?

The strange development is, though, that the increasing general enthusiasm for global celebrity-intervention runs parallel to another, antithetical trend. There is also a growing intolerance of the very movie-illusions that the roaming celebrities specialize in. Reality-television and the proliferation of shows that penetrate and expose acting's enchantments—*Entourage, Unscripted, The Comeback, Fat Actress, Joey,* and so on—reflect a rising suspicion of art. (Not to mention all the novels based on real events or on previous novels, or the memoirs disguised as novels.) Movies from *Being John Malkovich* to *My Date with Drew* are further dismantlements and exposures of celebrity's thin numina. It is as if the conventional gimmick of the cameo appearance were being stretched into entire movies and television series. At the same time, the enchantments of religion, whose stories are as potent as art's illusions, have a stronger and stronger hold over people's imaginations.

Charismatic politics—that is, authoritarian politics—also exhibits an ardor for exposure and an impatience with pretense. Fascism built its credibility on its claims of seeing through the petty corruptions and compromises of a democratic system. *Letter to*

D'Alembert, maybe the greatest intellectual assault on the theater, was written by Rousseau, one of the proto-architects of an authoritarian politics. *Extras'* pilot is about a movie set in Nazi Germany. Its second episode has Ben Stiller metamorphosing from the insensitive, narcissistic director of a film that seems to be about the Serbian massacre of Bosnian civilians to a cruel, monstrous director whose professional purposes seem to allow, even foster, the impulses that lead to genocide. And this is all done lightly, and lethally. You don't merely laugh; laughter as a response to the show becomes a disturbing new reality. If you promise to stay awake, I'll tell you why next week.

OCTOBER 17, 2005

⟨13⟩ *Extras* II

Nietzsche said that jokes were epigrams on the death of feelings, by which he meant that comedy comes at the expense of sympathy. It's an uncomfortable truth. Think of any joke you want, and I guarantee you that the humor in it depends on a diminishment of feeling, on a hardness toward something or someone where there should be a softness. Laughter briefly snaps the human bond; it makes the solitary ego soar with power. To cause people to laugh is like standing on a platform in space and watching the planets plunge.

But the phrase "the death of feelings" is not exactly right. The funniest people are usually nursing the deepest wounds. And to be hurt as keenly as that, they had to possess feelings deep and unguarded enough to yield great pain. Their feelings are bruised and buried, not necessarily dead. Some subterranean part of funny people is more alive than life can bear.

A lot of critics are fond of comparing Ricky Gervais' socially maladroit, calamitously blunt, sad-sack character in *Extras* to Larry David in *Curb Your Enthusiasm*. You read a lot now about a special department of comedy called "cringe-humor," which is "politically incorrect" in the way that it insults protected groups like blacks, gays, Jews, and handicapped people, and "cringe-inducing" in the way that it ultimately causes the humiliation of the hapless naïf who unwittingly is doing the insulting. But in the death-of-feeling sense, all comedy, and probably every type of laughter, is politically incorrect "cringe."

And Larry David is not naïve; rather, he has suppressed his superego. He's still a very canny comedian; it's just that he's a comedian in plainclothes, a stand-up comic at a sit-down dinner. The expression of feeling, of sympathy, is often a reflexive response to the superego's socializing dictates, but the comic exists in asocial solitude: he's pure id. Which is to say, he's pure appetite. So it's no surprise that David's show is such a sensational success. In a society constantly cajoling everybody to gratify every appetite and impulse, David has burst the socially elemental inhibition that keeps people from surrendering to the impulse to say what they are thinking. If I can, for example, get on the Internet—or fly to Thailand—to satisfy unspeakable desires, why can't I say whatever I want to say, regardless of whose feelings I might be hurting, or what generally decent sentiments I might be trampling to death?

Like Larry David, Ricky Gervais says what he thinks in *Extras,* but unlike Larry David, he's playing an unsuccessful actor named Andy Millman instead of himself. Millman is not rich and famous, and this new series—created by Gervais and his writing partner Stephen Merchant, who plays Millman's agent to a comic T—is up to a lot more than *Curb Your Enthusiasm.*

On the one hand, *Extras* is a highly original deconstruction of celebrity, and also of the movie industry that is largely responsible for the culture of celebrity. On the other hand, this extraordinary show is asking what instincts celebrities and movies keep in check: it's inviting you to imagine what kind of life we would have if the movie-illusions of courage, and decency, and universal sympathy gave way to a general conviction that cowardice, the relentless pursuit of self-interest, and indifference to other people were the most fundamental facts of human nature, and therefore as necessary to practice yourself as essential to avoid in other people.

Every episode of the show follows the same pattern. Each one opens with the filming of a scene from a movie on which Andy Millman and his best friend, the clueless Maggie, are working as extras but trying to get speaking parts—though Maggie is more interested in finding a boyfriend and a happy relationship, which is something like looking for a larger part in life. The movie scene is presented so expertly that you think at first you're watching a feature film and not *Extras* itself. The scenes are so riveting that you wish the movie would continue.

They are also either outright disturbing or subtly discordant. The pilot episode began with a film set somewhere in Nazi-occupied Europe; the second showed a group of probably Bosnian civilians being massacred by Serbs. The third episode, which presented a seventeenth-century romance with all the portents of being ill-starred, was unsettling in a smaller dimension, while the most recent installment hinted at present-day political tensions between the United States and England, though in a satirical key. After the movie scene is shot and finished, you meet another of the series' conventions: the famous guest-celebrity.

There have been four so far: Kate Winslet, Ben Stiller, Ross Kemp (known mostly in England), and Samuel L. Jackson. And here is where *Extras* puts some friction into its fiction. With the exception of Jackson, the stars play themselves as assholes. Winslet marvelously plays a nun who, while wearing her habit, tells Andy and Maggie during a break that she took the role because it's a Holocaust movie, and actors who play in films about the Holocaust "have Oscars coming out of their arse." As for herself, she thinks the Holocaust is overrated: "Okay, we get the picture. It was grim. Move on." Andy and Maggie listen to her with their mouths open in astonishment.

The truly superb Stiller, in a tour de force, plays the director of the film set in the Balkans and based on the real experiences of a Bosnian man who is there on the set. Stiller first gives a speech to the film crew about how important this film is to humanitarian purposes, a speech that is an almost inexpressibly delightful mixture of narcissism, self-delusion, and saccharine Hollywood rhetoric. The episode ends with Stiller trying to get a child-actor, who is playing a Bosnian boy, to cry by holding a gun up to his real mother's head and threatening to shoot her. Maggie protests and Stiller insults her, at which point Andy defends Maggie and gets himself first humiliated and then fired by Stiller.

The first two episodes certainly fulfill the show's brilliant conception most completely. Throughout every episode, in their search for a speaking part—and a boyfriend—Andy and Maggie inadvertently embarrass themselves and other people. They are, in a mostly innocuous, run-of-the-mill way, cowardly, relentlessly self-interested, and indifferent to other people. Indifferent to the Bosnian survivor's horrific experiences, Andy pesters him for a part. Maggie wrangles a date with a cute guy who works in the film company's office, only to deal a blow to his ego when she finds out—thanks to Andy's gross indelicacy—that one of his legs is several inches longer than the other and publicly rejects him. These two are not people so much as walking mindless and heartless nightmares. Or so you think at first.

But the stars are much worse. Winslet's cynicism isn't merely thoughtless or maladroit. It's coldly calculating. Stiller is downright homicidal, and his trespasses against decency are lined with ego and cunning, two qualities that Andy and Maggie wholly lack. In fact, the two extras are really just extreme versions of anyone who goes through life without the benefit of a script. That is to say, all of us. We never say exactly what we should say; we never say what is exactly right in any given situation. Actors playing a part, though, speak scripted lines that are just what is called for by the character, the particular situation, and the larger story. Andy's and Maggie's search for a speaking part is really a kind of comic metaphysical quest.

Andy and Maggie are not content to live, as audiences do, vicariously through the actors on the silver screen. They want—as more and more people seem to want, by means of all the instruments of control society makes available to us—to inhabit a prefabricated life, with a coherent beginning, middle, and end. In this sense, *Extras* has a dark twist that is a sort of test. To the degree that we think Andy and Maggie are "losers," our minds have been shaped by the unreal standards set up by the movies' images of splendor and perfection. To the degree that we think Andy and Maggie are far preferable to the hypocritical Stillers and Winslets—these two real actors whose portrayal of hypocrites in *Extras* has the effect of redeeming their professional inauthenticity—we are still tolerant and humane, capable of forgiving other people's intolerance and petty lapses of humanity.

Yet the show also offers a very different perspective. Do we want a world of Andys and Maggies who inadvertently break through the pretenses of virtuous-seeming directors and nun-playing actresses? A world of blunt speakers and ruthless realists who will stop losing in every situation as their numbers grow and their values proliferate? Do we want, in other words, the current trend of television shows, and movies, and books, like *Extras,* that shatter popular art's sentimental, but mundanely sustaining illusions? Or do we want to hold on to popular art's mostly, but not completely, false-but-necessary images of humanity and heroism?

Extras is the only comedy I know that uses laughter to try to define the contemporary sound of laughter. Rather than signaling the death of feelings, the show's hilarities are perhaps pointing the way to new feelings altogether—whatever they might be.

OCTOBER 24, 2005

(14) *Curb Your Enthusiasm*

It is a cultural platitude that American society, over the past twenty-five years or so, has absorbed and normalized various types of behavior that would once have been considered deviant, in the precincts of sex, sexuality, dress, speech, and manners. This development has put the comedian, who likes to outrage convention with the frank display of underlying instincts and motives, in a tough spot. A challenge looms for comic artists working in an unshockable era. Now it is the frank display of unsocialized behavior—rap, talk shows, radio rants, celebrity narcissism, the "outrageous" rhetoric of some pundits and politicians—that has to be exposed for the virulent new respectability that it is. And since the comedian's tools have always been various inversions and outlandish inflations of sex, sexuality, dress, speech, and manners, he or she has to get on with the business of letting go without seeming complicitous with the weird sort of go-go pretentiousness and street boorishness that is all around us. He must be loose, but tightly so.

Larry David started out in the 1970s doing stand-up in comedy clubs such as Catch a Rising Star, where if he came out on stage and did not like the audience he would stare at them deadpan, say "fuck you," and walk off. This was a form of integrity in comedy. Back in the 1970s, when David was appearing with corrosive performers like Richard Pryor and Richard Lewis, his shtick grew organically from his edge, and his anger satisfied some people, even if he did not make them laugh.

I never saw those early routines, but I would think that David's appeal, such as it was, lay in the fact that the abrasive dis from the stage came from a struggling young performer, and the more intense his hostility, the more flagrant his helplessness. His outburst might have lacked vindicating humor, but it had the vindictive disposition out of which humor paradoxically creates its sympathetic bonds. The dis was really a cry of complicity with the audience's undiscovered feelings—it was as if David was coming out and trying to tune the room's conscious to its subconscious by hitting the low note of his own nether impulses. He was speaking down to them, but from below.

Or so it must have seemed. But it is now many years later, and David's anger has had a career. Having made it big as the co-creator of *Seinfeld,* he walked out on that sensationally successful show and moved to Los Angeles and created *Curb Your Enthusiasm,* a partly improvised series about Larry David in which the super-wealthy comedy writer plays himself, living in a luxurious house, eating at expensive restaurants, hanging with the rich and the famous, rambling around Santa Monica and Malibu and Beverly Hills, complaining, quarreling, picking fights, and sometimes actually slugging it out with people who irritate him—that is, just about everyone he meets—pausing every few minutes to nail his antagonist with a deadpan stare that says "fuck you," and occasionally actually uttering the imprecation, maybe for old time's sake.

Rather than coming full circle, David has stepped from one parallel line to another. These days his edge is growing out of his shtick. The deadpan dis now comes from a wealthy and to some extent powerful man, which means that the more intense his hostility, the more flagrantly helpless his target, when the latter happens not to be also wealthy or powerful. David is speaking down to people, but from above. "There but for the grace of God go . . . you," David says to Jeff Green, his portly Sancho-esque manager and foil, after being startled to find a comedy writer he once knew down on his luck and working as a sandwich man in a deli. "Not you?" challenges Jeff. David smiles and looks down, saying quietly and confidently, "No, not me." From the Little Tramp to the Cashed-Out Champ.

There has been a lot of hand-wringing during the past thirty years over the way mainstream culture has appropriated the adversarial energies of the avant-garde. But comedy was a last bastion of lucid insanity: long after Rothko sold paintings to the Four Seasons, Lenny Bruce was still manically holding forth on stage. With *Curb Your Enthusiasm*, however, comedy's citadel of genuine opposition has finally been overrun, and the hilarious barbarians have been driven out by the uptight hordes. The respectable deviance created by consumerism's ever-expanding arena of appetite has devoured the comedic impulse itself. Rather than taking as his targets the Stuffed Shirt, the Self-Absorbed Sucker, and the Bully—as Chaplin once did, and the Marx Brothers, and Laurel and Hardy, and W. C. Fields, and Sid Caesar, and Woody Allen, and Bob Newhart, and Mel Brooks— David sets his sights on the little guy, the perennial target of the Stuffed Shirt, the Self-Absorbed Sucker, and the Bully. David's wit is a huge exercise in defection, a way of making the death of sympathy seem like a price worth paying for a chuckle.

David's afflictions assume many forms. *Curb Your Enthusiasm* portrays him getting exasperated by long waits at the doctor's office, and at the pharmacy, and at restaurants; by salespeople, and garage attendants, and caterers; and by things, like houses that make mysterious sounds at night, and sunglasses that he buys as a gift that are not prescription and thus are rejected by the intended recipient, and phones that won't ring when you want them to ring, and unsightly telephone wires suspended over your backyard. Hath heaven no more thunderbolts? But what really drives David into fits of animadversion are people who impede his desire for instant gratification. This would be funny if the figures in question had the power truly to do David harm; and it would be effectively humorous if the objects of David's wit were all the anti-human forces ranged against his heart and soul. But David's nemesis is usually just the service industry and all the people who work in it. *Curb Your Enthusiasm* resembles more than a little those Roman comedies in which some ineffectual slave keeps the trouble boiling. David almost never picks on someone his own size.

One episode has the programmatically poker-faced David stalked by an angry Asian American parking attendant who claims that he didn't give her money that he owed her; in another segment, the rich comedy writer—who, we are told, is worth $475 million, which of course is nothing to laugh at—is pursued by an enraged salesman at Barney's, who explodes against David when the two meet in the street because the latter has decided not to buy a pair of shoes that the salesman has put aside for him. Caterers steal David's food after a party at his house. Snooty maitre-d's make him homicidal by asking him to wait for a table. Airline ticket agents drive him into such despair that you would think they were Spanish border guards driving away refugees in flight from Nazi Germany. Sometimes, though, a ray of sunlight pokes through the plague of bad service: a waitress makes him laugh at her obsequious manner.

Comedy used to be about the *iron,* the ancient Greek word for the original little guy, who appeared in classical comedy puncturing the sometimes just maddening, sometimes harmful pretensions of the big guy. It set the spiritual order right by turning the social order upside down. But Larry David has returned the social order to its upright position by standing comedy on its head. For perhaps the first time in the history of the genre, he has put comedy on the side of the big guy.

It makes you wonder exactly what that young comic was angry about. The insult-humor of Pryor and to a lesser extent Lewis derived from the fact that they, especially Pryor, felt like Invisible Men, and they wanted to startle the audience out of their blindness and make them see the human being storming and ranting in front of them. From watching *Curb Your Enthusiasm,* as well as *Seinfeld* where David expressed his rage through the sociopathic (in the bad sense) character of George Costanza, you get the impression that for David it is everybody else who is invisible. Nothing vexes him so much as the sudden visibility of another person; nothing drives him into snits of irritation so much as the slightest pressure of another ego on his own.

The thing about Invisible Men is that they internalize other people's misperceptions of them, and Pryor and Lewis ultimately were angry at Pryor and Lewis. The lacerations that they flung into the faces of the people who came to hear them were attempts at shattering those misperceptions by exploding their objects, that is, themselves. They rode their anger as far as it could go, to extinction in the case of the former, to an alcoholic breakdown and years wandering in the professional wilderness in the case of the latter. (Even poor, shrieking Sam Kinison could move his audience.) Lewis's appearances on *Curb Your*

Enthusiasm, in fact, make up most of this occasionally droll show's funniest and most genuine moments, and David should get credit for placing Lewis's fine despairing anger against his own pettiness and pique. Lewis to David: "You told him I was high maintenance?! Why did you do that? It took me seven years to get my life together. . . ."

David's anger, by contrast, is merely the anger of frustrated entitlement. Consider his deadpan stare. It is not the deadpan of Jack Benny, for instance, which reacted to the absurdity of a situation, itself often created by a flaw—almost always the flaw of stinginess—in Jack Benny; or the inviting, conspiratorial stare of Johnny Carson, which reacted to the absurdity of a universe of headlines, of current events, or to the warm-hearted naïveté of Ed McMahon, whose genial antagonism with Carson was based on the transparently sympathetic bond between them. Larry David's deadpan is in the same line as David Letterman's (who has softened it in recent years) and Conan O'Brien's: they all react to an unresponsive audience by looking at them as if they weren't laughing not because they did not have a sense of humor, but because they did not have the knowledge to laugh. The absence of laughter denotes, for these dancing bears of knowingness, not a failure of humor in the comedian but a failure of intelligence or hipness in the audience.

But the biggest influence on David's deadpan is Jerry Seinfeld's deadpan, an impermeable expression of suburban complacency that says: "This is just too crazy to be real!" This represents an absolute inversion of the comedy of Lenny Bruce, or George Carlin, or even the tamer but still subtly subversive Robert Klein, the guiding sentiment of all of whom was: "This is too alarmingly real to be replenishingly crazy!" Seinfeld's look was the smugly defensive posture of teenagers from some affluent Long

Island town—Massapequa, to be exact—in Manhattan for the first time, putting down as abnormal or stupid everything that went beyond what they knew at home. The ideology of Manhattan that you encounter in shows such as *Sex and the City* was indeed concocted by people more anxious about the city than at home in it.

David has perfected Seinfeld's superior, uninviting stare into a cold, cruel sneer. The reason so many people like it is that they want it to like them. David's gleaming bald head, his hard, sloping Joe Camel nose, his long face that curves in and away from you: all these features are less like the elements of a mortal physiognomy than like a blunt weapon. He is the anti-nebbish whose worst pratfalls will end with him going home to his multimillion-dollar house or to his next power lunch. Even his glasses—whose wire frames are barely visible, thus making his eyes look not vulnerable and lensed but plated with some hard substance—are the antithesis of Woody Allen's large black pathetic frames, often askew on his face, just waiting to be snatched away by some cold, cruel hand.

On one level, *Curb Your Enthusiasm* provides catharsis for a middle-class society that lives as though it were an affluent society, which is drowning in things and whose perpetually stimulated appetite is constantly outraged by phenomena that delay satisfaction for anywhere from twenty minutes to indefinitely. Not to mention the therapeutic justification that the show offers to selves whose prosperous, self-sufficient isolation has less and less need of other people as its sense of prosperity and self-sufficiency grows larger and larger. And I suppose that the show's allegedly anhedonic protagonist, who seems so miserable with all his money, offers some kind of banal commentary on the powerlessness of money to make us happy.

But Larry David is not miserable; he is annoyed. He is not anhedonic; he takes infinite pleasure in himself. The star of this universe of tony things is himself a tony thing. And he is a thing whose every situation consists of his entanglement with other things. The episodes all have to do with the way inconvenience keeps spoiling a life of placid privilege and possession. The worst event that befalls David is the loss of something: his eyeglasses, his plane tickets, his notebook, his bowling shoes, his take-out Chinese dinner, his wife's prescription. It is not commercialism that gets in the way of his humanity. It is other people's humanity that gets in the way of his acquisitive appetite. This is a very small predicament. The "wisdom" of *Curb Your Enthusiasm* is said to consist in the understanding that life is made up of little things, and that little things are big things; but little things are usually just little things, and a life that is made up only of little things is just a little life. Maybe being trapped in a little life is why Larry David reflexively despises the little guy. As for this big guy, his biggest accomplishment is that he has banished largeness from laughter.

JANUARY 13, 2003

15 *Weeds*

When all else fails, when American life gets too complicated and wacky to get a good satirical hold on it, writers repair to the suburbs. The unlovely secrets harbored by the ranch houses and bi-levels, by the lawns and empty sidewalks of the towns lying just beyond the fervid cities, have been to American novelists, screenwriters, and television writers what plutocrats were to Daumier. Behind every traveling sprinkler there is a penis longing to wander.

Artists and intellectuals have always hated the suburbs, probably because it's the cities that produce works of art and intellect. People leave the cities and move to the suburbs because they've attained enough financial security and professional status to exchange the struggle to keep building a life for the determination to live happily ever after. But artists and intellectuals know that no one is contented and happy for long. The struggle to create and build a life exists alongside, among other obstacles, conflicted desires that sometimes make a person defeat his own happiness in his very attempts to achieve it. If Gatsby's mansion couldn't win him bliss, your renovated garage certainly won't. You can leave the city with all its mire and complexities, but the city won't leave you. At least, that's the caricature of suburban life that you often get in movies and in fiction.

Movies and fiction have gone about portraying the suburbs in very different ways, however. For screenwriters, the caricature is sufficient. They're content to expose the seething libido beneath the manicured surface. From *Peyton Place* to *American Beauty,* Hollywood has depicted the suburbs as a place animated—or paralyzed—by a simple contrast between public respectability and hidden sordidness. Deep within every marriage straining to appear stable and satisfying lurks a sex-starved wife and a husband in hock to dangerous gamblers. Nothing is as it appears, but you know how things really are because all you have to do is turn appearances on their heads and, voilà! Truth.

But for the best suburban novelists, *echt*-suburban chroniclers like Updike and Cheever, no easy irony exists between surface and depth. Later novelists like Richard Ford and Don Delillo mined the vein first exposed by Richard Yates in *Revolutionary Road,* a glib, movie-like indictment of suburban self-delusion and hypocrisy. For Updike and Cheever, though, the suburbs were as complex as the cities, suburbanites plagued not by self-delusion and hypocrisy but driven by age-old ambitions ruled by the tragic ironies that twisted the fates of ancient Greek heroes.

You would think that after Todd Haynes' weird, chilling *Safe,* a movie about the suburbs that has its heroine—the incomparable, the divine Julianne Moore—slowly dying of some undiagnosable disease that is really the spiritual mange of the suburbs themselves, writers for the silver screen would have been hard-pressed to keep plowing the field of suburban malaise. Perhaps the genre is slowly waning in Hollywood, but now television has gotten its hands on this deathless subject. *Weeds,* Showtime's answer to the phenomenally successful *Desperate Housewives*—ABC's answer to cable's candor—cannot, to my mind, touch the bottom of *Housewives'* azaleas. The ABC sitcom strikes just the right note of campy, soap-opera-like theatrics and self-parody. It is not a satire of the suburbs; it is the *reductio ad absurdum* of suburban satire.

Weeds, though it tries hard to be funny, wants to break out into new, undiscovered territory. Its only means of doing so, though, is to stretch candor to the breaking point, as if portraying the once-unportrayable might astound and silence hypocrisy for good. Yet what follows from all this scandalous exposure is mere contempt for the environment being exposed. How appropriate that the show's theme song is "Little Boxes," composed in 1962 by Malvina Reynolds, who performs it here. In its subtly annihilating, smug condescension about everyone not in Reynolds' campus-coffeehouse audience, it's perhaps the most repellent folk song ever written.

The song's assumption that life's variegated plenitude, even in the dreaded suburbs' "little boxes," can cease to exist and that great numbers of people are as shallow and knowable and similar to each other as a row of driveways doesn't bode well for *Weeds'* satirical purposes. Nor does the song's gross socioeconomic error of equating houses that are "ticky tacky"—the dwelling places of the working class—with lives that are highly mobile and upper class.

"Little Boxes'" inauthenticity is reflected in *Weeds,* which has Mary-Louise Parker playing Nancy Botwin, a recently widowed mother of two who has to turn to dealing pot to make ends meet. The first problem is Parker herself, who is to acting what "Little Boxes" is to song. Her approach seems to be to perform her characters the way she thinks they would act in real life, and the result is to import such self-conscious "naturalness" into her parts that she ends up being utterly artificial. When I saw her on stage in *Proof,* her self-consciousness made me wince. Somehow, in her roles, she retains the narcissism actors have when they are not acting. On film, she's unbearable. She crafts her facial expressions—the film and television actor's essential instrument—only for the camera, not for the scene she's playing with other characters, so that the impression of narcissism you get from her on the stage is multiplied tenfold on the screen. I can't understand how she has gotten any kind of career for herself at all, unless some audiences, more and more suspicious of art, feel relieved to see an actor incapable of disappearing into her roles and acting just as self-absorbed as ordinary people who don't appear on stage or screen.

Weeds itself unfolds in this phony spirit. For example, Nancy's suppliers are black. The show wants to portray them as being real, as being antidotes to all the synthetic suburban postures, but they are, after all, the only black characters on the show, and the only black characters on the show happen to be drug dealers. Why couldn't *Weeds* have some "real" black doctors, or lawyers, or business executives? Because they're all living in those ticky-tacky houses, I guess, and they all look just the same. Better to have the "realness" of these black caricatures that seem to have sprung out of the very parochialism and narrowmindedness the show wants to hold up to derision.

As for the rest, the show can't seem to find a consistent take on anything—except for some primal, haunting moments during one episode in which Nancy's son plays on his camcorder, again and again, images of his dead father. We have no idea what Nancy thinks about having to sell pot to make a living—is she guilty, resentful, ironic about it, sort of having a good time? She never says a word. And *Weeds* doesn't know whether it wants to use Nancy to make caustic commentary on conventional morality, or on materialistic values, or on the venality and unhappiness of her clients, or on the hypocrisy of these affluent forty-something potheads who want to appear straight (and respectable) when they are usually stoned. And the idea that a marijuana haze is a metaphor for the self-deluding pursuit of the suburban-American dream is as unfocused in the show as it is a banal premise for the show's satire.

Predictably, to fill in its blanks, *Weeds* throws in cable's usual shock-and-awe ingredients: adultery, homosexuality, teenage sex, and *beaucoup de* sex talk—"He went down on me for days," chirps a philandering husband's young Thai girlfriend about her furtive lover's sexual skills to his middle-aged spouse, when the two women have a showdown over drinks, an encounter that leads to an intense bonding session between girlfriend and wife. If the suburbs are as cool as all that, I'm heading out there with my sprinkler right now.

AUGUST 11, 2005

16 The Life and Death of Peter Sellers

About ten years ago, a movie called *Funny Bones* was released, a delightful and original flick. It's about a fledgling American comedian, played to perfection by Oliver Platt, who is trying to follow in the footsteps of his father, a legendary American comedian. In Platt's debut performance at a big Las Vegas hotel, he's upstaged by his father and nearly booed off the stage. So he takes a little hiatus and makes a pilgrimage to Blackpool, England, a seaside resort town renowned for its comedy acts in the era before television, in order to look for original material that he might use to buck up his act. Blackpool also happened to be the place where his father started out, and the movie's climax involves the father's return to his old stomping ground and a not-at-all-funny confrontation with his son at the edge of the sea.

Watching *The Life and Death of Peter Sellers* reminded me of that movie about American comedians in England, because Platt's legendary father is played by Jerry Lewis, who like Sellers is Jewish, and whose Jewishness strikes a richly speculative chord in the British context. Jerry Lewis could well have been a British comedian. Forgive the extreme example, but Jackie

Mason—to stick with the Jewish theme—could not have been anything of the sort. Nor could Bill Cosby, or Richard Pryor, or the Irish-Catholic George Carlin have started out in England with the acts that made them famous; and nor could any number of American comedians whose comedy lies in the furious inflation of their ethnic, racial, or religious identities.

Consider Jackie Mason's one-man show in a London theater that's sometimes aired on cable. The audience is engulfed in hilarity. But it's not humor that's getting them going. It's a kind of astonished embarrassment at the almost brutally asocial return-serve of their own secret prejudices. Their laughter is actually anti-comical. It's a desperately polite attempt to socialize Mason's unspeakable revelations. You get the feeling that behind the loud gales of laughter is an effort to drown this cunning comic out.

Impersonation is the British comic's forte. In *Monty Python,* the funny voices and accents, the costumes, the outrageous physical postures are even more essential than the routines themselves. That's why the routines almost always dissolve into absurdity. It's the other way around in the United States. The classic *Saturday Night Live* skits, for all the role-playing, were really about the way the comic situation unfolded. No matter how outrageous, the situations stayed coherent, and the dialogue always mattered more than the funny accents or ridiculous get-ups. The magnificently demonic Robin Williams is the only American comedian of note I can think of whose shtick consists of (brilliant) impersonations. As for Jerry Lewis, his British side, as it were, expressed itself through his total submergence of ego and identity into the persona of the Nutty Professor. For the most part, whether it's Lenny Bruce, or Mort Sahl, or Johnny Carson, or Jay Leno, or David Letterman, the

stuff of the American comedian's stock-in-trade is the monologue or some version thereof—like Jon Stewart's running com-
mentaries on the news.

The ego run amok during the course of an ego-destroying,
ego-recreating monologue is a perfect comic catharsis for
American social life, in which the ego seems at times to know no
boundaries. In England, however, the social forms and rules of
decorum still require, certainly compared to American society,
the utmost suppression of ego. And so rather than the monologue, the reigning form of British comedy is the impersonation
of another identity entirely, which is the perfect comic catharsis
for the constant social suppression of the ego. The Australian
Barry Humphries' very funny Dame Edna, a sensation on stage
in New York and London, is the perfect fusion, in fact, of the
egotistical comic monologue and the self-surrendering comic
impersonation. As Jewish comedians in America, Peter Sellers
and Ali G, a.k.a. Sacha Baron Cohen, might very well have
played with their Jewishness in wildly inventive ways. As English
Jews, they are wildly inventive impersonators—though Ali G
has all the abrasive, corrosive undertow of the most aggressive
assertion of self.

The Life and Death of Peter Sellers is no more successful than
any other biopic at conveying a performer's inner life. It has a
wonderful performance of Sellers by the very fine Geoffrey
Rush, himself an Australian impersonating a great imperson-
ator. It has a surprisingly unhackneyed sort of Brechtian inventiveness, maybe because Sellers was so self-estranged—a
character will suddenly be revealed sitting, for example, on a
movie-set; Sellers will be confronted by his first wife, who tells
him that she's leaving him, and then he'll play his first wife, in
the same scene, telling him that she is going to stay with him

and tolerate his infidelity and physical abuse forever. It has wonderful music—I could listen to its title song, Tom Jones singing "What's New Pussycat," on treadmills from here to Kathmandu.

But it never even gets close to what made Sellers tick, or what made him funny, or what made him often not as funny as he was supposed to be and should have been. The best this very handsome production can do is tell us that Sellers inhabited so many different people because he had no sense of self. This, for some reason, the movie sees as a tragic flaw rather than an artistic prerequisite. The movie should have been called *Negative Disability*. For some reason, whenever the movies take up the life of a great comic, the result is the old Vesti La Giubba treatment—laugh through your tears, you poor pathetic clown, laugh. Recall Dustin Hoffman in *Lenny*.

In the case of Sellers, he apparently had a smothering, driven mother, an uncontrollable libido, a liking for fancy cars, and a terrible, childish temper. And despite it all, he became a famous movie star, who turned all of his dark psychic shit into risible gold. That transmutation is the oldest joke in the world.

NOVEMBER 29, 2004

Cartoons

17 *The Boondocks*

Racial stereotyping—like any kind of stereotyping—turns the objects of its derision into cartoons. And so a kind of poetic justice lies in the fact that *The Boondocks,* the most corrosive racial satire on television, is a cartoon. It's striking how deep an affinity prejudice and satire have with each other. In both cases, the Procrustean idea of a person shapes and disfigures him into a caricature doomed to that idea. In prejudice, bias precedes the caricature; while in satire, hateful or ridiculous behavior verging on caricature provokes the satirist's mordant bias. Satire is prejudice meted out on a case-by-case basis.

Of course, for satire's rigid intellectual constructions to work, the satirist and his audience have to share a common social and psychological framework even more than a common set of values. Maybe that's why great satire is so rare now.

You have no idea what a relief it is for this critic to watch *The Boondocks*' psychologically accurate lampooning after trying to read dozens of contemporary novels a year. The art of reproducing, through words, plausible people with credible psychologies seems about as lost to history as the technique used to raise the giant slabs at Stonehenge. All the technologies of mass entertainment have, paradoxically, cut us off from the masses of other people. Television, iPods, DVDs, the Internet, e-mail—you can order a date, dinner, or a movie online, and if you happen to work at home, you never have to leave the convenience and security of your four walls. Romantic movies used to be about the difficulty of meeting the right person, or the calamity of meeting the wrong one. Now they're about the hardship and inconvenience of just being with another person, period.

As a result of our pleasurable, isolating technologies, people act in public as if they were all alone in private. Shouting into cell phones. Wearing baseball caps in fancy restaurants. Holding a symposium in a darkened movie theater. The other day I saw a guy at the gym wearing . . . flip-flops. But I did not see flip-flops. I saw the broken wall, the burning roof and tower, and Agamemnon dead.

It's not that these people are rude. It's that, in the evolutionary sense, their adaptability to a social setting has atrophied from disuse the way eons ago our flippers and fins dried up and disappeared when we started living on dry land. Our fiction writers are prey to the same conditions. The music of their own consciousness drowns out the meaning of other people. So when they reach for characters, they come up with cartoons.

Encountering in the pages of a novel a cartoon when you expect to find a character numbs the faculties, all the more so when the novelist really has no inkling of what he's created, or failed to create. But to encounter a cartoon nourished by insight and imagination, a cartoon working itself into a character—that's a different story. Such intelligent animation acknowledges the primacy of visual over literary culture nowadays; it capitalizes on the new reality of the eye being sharper than the intellect. We're used to movies telegraphing meaning to us through the shrewd manipulation and sometimes even the poetic orchestration of potent, pregnant images. It's becoming harder and harder to do the heavy lifting of verbal explication. What a liberation when images come in to do the heavy lifting for words.

The Boondocks is about a poor, elderly black man named Robert Freeman ("Granddad") who moves from the South Side of Chicago to a wealthy suburb when he comes into an inheritance. He brings with him his two teenage grandchildren, Huey and Riley, the former an angry nihilist with a sharp intellect and a fantasy of revolution, the latter a gangsta-wannabe and general mischief-maker.

I can't think of another recent work of art, popular or serious, that's as caustic about race as this wild little cartoon. And not only race. In one episode, the R&B superstar R. Kelly is accused of having sex with a fourteen-year-old (specifically, urinating on her), and the ensuing antics portray the general social craziness of present-day American life more vividly—and more entertainingly—than any work of contemporary fiction I've read. (You would think that fiction, being the older, more distinguished genre, would be bolder and less constrained; on the contrary, its august status has made fiction formal, self-conscious, and uptight.)

Complications multiply (the episode is based on a real incident involving Kelly, for which he's still facing charges): Kelly is depicted as an abusive creep living in celebrity-narcissist Cloud-Cuckoo Land; his supporters are just as divorced from reality, yet right to point out the hypocrisy of society condemning Kelly while fostering the conditions that create Kelly as a star; the singer's William Kunstler–like lawyer is noble on his client's behalf, and offensively patronizing in his blindness to this black pop-star's capacity to do harm; and—most outrageous of all—the very precocious fourteen-year-old consented to and enjoyed the experience ("I've even let guys who weren't stars piss on me," she lackadaisically explains to the court).

In the end, everybody is (figuratively) pissing on everyone else for his own hedonistic or acquisitive purposes, and Granddad's ironically innocent conflation of Kelly's sex act with the American Dream ("A golden shower everyday—that's what I want") is the uplifting *coup de grâce*. Don't even get me started on the portrayal, in another episode, of a black-gangsta-speaking rich white suburbanite teen who's just come back from Iraq and asks Riley to fire a shotgun into his bullet-proof vest so that he can prove his street mettle. We've had Danny Hoch's black-rapper impersonations in *Whiteboyz,* and Michael Rapaport's tender assimilation of blackness in *Zebrahead,* and the ill-fated junior white gangsta in that masterful film *Fresh,* and Eminem and his appropriation/homage/usurpation—but no one, with the exception of *The Boondocks,* has *satirized* the white appropriation of the partly white-induced black pose of extreme violence and, at the same time, the congruence of violent black-gangsta culture with, as Huey might say, the "white power structure's" senseless military violence overseas. With animation like this, who needs the stasis of the contemporary novel?

NOVEMBER 28, 2005

⟦18⟧ *SpongeBob SquarePants*

The funny thing about television is that it distracts you as you watch it. It doesn't hold your attention, it eases it. The phrase "glued to the tube" is profoundly inaccurate, unless you envision it meaning, somewhat macabrely, that your body is stuck to the screen while you move your head and look around the room. Television stills your mind and lets it roam, as if the mind were a crying infant that the television took in its glowing arms and soothed so that it could sleep and dream.

That quality of holding without engaging is why we have gotten used to doing other things while enjoying television; that's why, as a recent Kaiser Family Foundation study reported, kids are now doing several "new media" things at once while watching the tube: instant-messaging, talking on the phone, listening to music, and so forth. The dismaying news is not only that kids' minds are now almost entirely absorbed by various kinds of screens and disembodied experiences. What's really discouraging is the extent to which television cultivates distraction into a new kind of discipline.

So I have to demur to the conclusions that my colleague, Michelle Cottle, arrived at in her column about the Kaiser report. Cottle admonished the Kaiser study and everyone alarmed by it for exhibiting "hysteria." The fact, Cottle argued, that kids watch TV four hours a day is mitigated by the fact that adults watch between four and five hours of TV a day. This means, Cottle writes, that kids engaging in other activities while sitting in front of the television is a hopeful sign, "a recognition by the younger generation that most TV is too mindless to deserve one's full attention." But this is a pretty illogical conclusion to reach, since kids are still sitting in front of the mindless television for four hours a day, and the interests they absent-mindedly pursue while watching the tube aren't interests at all, but different phases of inattention. The really significant thing is that these kids seem to be having a hard time not just paying attention, but staying distracted.

The fact is, as Bruno Bettelheim once said, "television captures the imagination but doesn't liberate it." A book pulls your active imagination into it. Television's powerful combination of fast-moving images and music shuts the imagination out. Rates of violence in society have soared since television really took hold fifty years ago, and this might have something to do with the fact—pardon the Freudian formulation—that violence is a shortcut for libidos that have no outlet in the imagination. Then, too, spending so much time alone, with television's caricatures of life and people—rather than in the companionable solitude of a good book with its deep apprehension of life and people—isn't so great for learning how to be social. Fifty or so years ago, the imagination had a different fate in America. You had the abstract expressionists, cool and bebop jazz, Bellow, Ellison, Mailer et al., Lenny Bruce, *Death of a Salesman*, to mention a few artistic names and trends.

This sort of worrying isn't cool, I know. It's never cool to get too excited about anything. But fifty years ago it was cool, and even twenty-eight years ago it was cool when Marie Winn published her classic attack on television, *The Plug-In Drug*, in which she traced the changes wrought by television on consciousness and society. (The Bettelheim quote is from her book.) New phenomena about to become permanent conditions provide a small window of time through which to regard them critically before we take them for granted. We hardly think about television as formative in any way now. Cool, unflappable people don't. But once upon a time, the coolest and most unflappable people had utter disdain for television's greedy appropriation of the viewer's imagination. Winn's concern and even her idiom might strike some readers as quaint now, but her book is as urgent and current as it ever was.

Television has changed over the years, and I enjoy and even admire good TV. But kids often don't watch the best kind of television. Which brings me to the great exception that is *SpongeBob*. Of course it's not subtle propaganda for a gay lifestyle—although a typical show had this adorable and intrepid little character impersonating a psychotic athletic coach, a hilarious comic liberation that recalled Nathan Lane hysterically impersonating a rabid football fan in *The Birdcage*. Another episode had him redefining the word "cool" (sitting in a library reading, for example, was cool; partying all night wasn't). He's just a smart, sensitive, sweet kid trying to go his own way amid all the pressures to join the herd, a cross between Holden and Huck with some weird short pants. Sure, he likes to sing a lot. So did Sinatra.

It seems to me that the right's panic over this cartoon was the misplaced expression of a good and authentic fear, which is that anything goes in popular culture if it makes money. Especially in the realm of television. But these negatively obsessed fans of *SpongeBob* don't want to acknowledge that the free market they support is responsible for the popular culture they deplore. So they retreat into the safe, if crude, certainties of the moral higher ground, away from the realm of the market. Moral panic is perhaps their way of defeating the market's amoral influence and winning back a non-economic space. But they could use a little less time in front of the television themselves and a little more of SpongeBob's defiance and pluck. No wonder he stirs them up.

MARCH 14, 2005

Race

⑲ *Unforgivable Blackness*

Even as American Indians were being exterminated or put in reservations, representations of them in the culture became sentimental. As the issue of race and its connection to poverty in America continues to vanish from political discourse, cultural representations of blacks have become reverential, sentimental, and condescending: Richard Powers' novel, *The Time of Our Singing,* and the play *Caroline, or Change* are two recent examples. And now comes Ken Burns' four-hour-long documentary about the life of the great black heavyweight boxer, Jack Johnson, a film that brings Caucasian condescension to a new low. This film is not, however, the product of a guilt-ridden white mind. Burns seems absolutely free of guilt. He seems, on the contrary, and with wide-eyed cynicism, adept at ransacking the painful historical experience—now long past—of another group of people for his own gain.

Jack Johnson was—outside the ring—a violent and arrogant bully, a misogynist, a wife-beater, a predator of prostitutes and helpless women, all of whom were white and could thus serve as targets for his justified rage against white people. He spent the huge sums of money he earned on expensive cars, booze, and lavish orgies, and not a penny on any cause other than himself.

You'd think that the lily-white Ken Burns' decision to cele-brate Johnson as, in the words of one of the show's "experts," "one of the three great black leaders of the early part of the [twentieth century]" would have inspired withering, ironic re-sponses, especially from black intellectuals, who could have ex-posed this almost-textbook case of deeply rooted racial bias and passive aggression on the part of Burns and his colleagues. But no, the film has been hailed all across the land as the long-awaited corrective to Johnson's conviction—and eventual im-prisonment—on trumped-up, racially motivated charges of white slavery. Burns has even bravely been lobbying President Bush to posthumously pardon Johnson, who died in a car acci-dent in 1946. Just think how inspiring such a pardon would be for poor black kids everywhere in the year 2005!

Unforgivable Blackness—the nice phrase is W.E.B. Du Bois' explanation for why he believed whites despised Johnson—is yet one more entry in a tried-and-true American genre: the Ap-pearance of Goodness. All you have to do is show that you're on the side of good, not evil. You might want to make it clear that you think evil is, as it were, a bad thing. Or you can simply prove your goodness. You can write a novel about someone mentally impaired, compose a play about someone who is terminally ill, make a movie about a victim of genocide—or create a docu-mentary that seeks to expose and indict universally acknowl-edged social injustice. You are going to, in fine enterprising fashion, reap the concrete dividend of—to use Benjamin Franklin's words—"Reliable Appearance" from all this safely re-moved and certifiably monstrous historical and imaginary suf-fering. The moral rebate for appearing moral is unsurpassingly sweet and large. And don't worry about anyone seeing right through your pretense. People are supposed to see right through it. If anyone thought you were really excellent and good, they'd either ignore you or run you out of town.

Johnson had courage, Olympian persistence, and extraordinary gifts. He was one of the greatest boxers who ever lived, but he also had dramatic skills, and musical skills, and such a keen intelligence that he even took out a patent for a new kind of wrench. He defied the crushing racial prejudice of his time by pushing and pushing until first Tommy Burns and then Jim Jeffries, reigning heavyweight champions, agreed to fight him, dropping American boxing's prohibition against black fighters contending for the heavyweight title. He beat them both; after his defeat of Jeffries, riots erupted across the country because, as the film would have it, white people couldn't bear the idea of black physical superiority. Racism it was, savage and frenzied. But racism wasn't the only feeling behind the fury against Johnson.

Throughout the 1930s, as Joe Louis—the "Brown Bomber"— pounded his way to the heavyweight title in 1937, he didn't meet anything like the racist invective and death threats that followed Johnson wherever he went. Blacks were still being lynched in the 1930s. *Unforgivable Blackness* wants to tell us that part of the reason white people despised Johnson was that he was so open about his many relationships with white women. But Louis had many liaisons with white women. In his case, though, they were women like Sonja Henie and Lana Turner. Johnson preyed on prostitutes, usually three or four at a time, and in full public view, as he led his louche entourage from hotel, to café, to expensive home, to hotel.

It's doubtful that any boxer, black or white, would have escaped public outrage if he had, like Johnson, done everything he could to outrage the public. Johnson drove as fast as he was able to, defying the police to give him a ticket; one time, when they did, he threw down a thousand-dollar bill and explained that he was going to come back at the same speed and wanted to pay the fine in advance. He beat up a smaller man in a bar, and when the police gave him a summons, he tossed it away. All this attention on the part of the police the film considers violent bias against an uppity black. It implies that not acting so heedlessly and selfishly would have made Johnson an Uncle Tom. Burns does not offer a wide range of being to his black subjects.

Johnson was a brutal misogynist, a violent black performer who, though rich, debased himself by appearing in vaudeville shows that caricatured his own image. He made a lot of people rich—white people. The film never takes up the many charges, made throughout his career, that Johnson threw his fights for his own profit and that of his white handlers. Those charges were widely cast about, but the film doesn't consider the possibility that Johnson's dishonesty, rather than his skin color, was part of what fueled the rancor against him. Stanley Crouch—himself a vapid bully—at one point bizarrely says about Johnson, "He made people upset because they had a more circumscribed idea about what individual freedom should have been for [Johnson]." This from a critic who ostentatiously heaps scorn on the white business culture's manipulation of the image of the violent black rapper.

And the film ridiculously wants to make Johnson's compulsive seduction of white prostitutes into a brave statement about racial resistance. It wants to turn a voracious particular appetite into "Letter from Birmingham Jail." Too bad the movie doesn't include the testimony of the black singer Ethel Waters, who said that when Johnson came on to her, she declined, explaining, "You have the white fever."

Worst of all, Burns bends over backward to cover up Johnson's violence against women, in particular his first wife, the white Etta Duryea, an upper-class woman who turned her back on her class. Johnson seemed particularly to need, and to hate, her.

Here, as elsewhere, Burns treats Johnson like a sacred relic. Of Johnson's countless infidelities in his marriage to Etta, Randy Roberts, one of Johnson's (white, of course) biographers, informs us that he was "heroically unfaithful." (Burns never interviews Geoffrey Ward, Johnson's best and most definitive biographer, only the crude and obsequious Roberts. Was there a problem between them? Ward's book is far more skeptical.)

Burns' own misogyny hits bottom when he takes up the story of Etta's suicide. Johnson had cheated on her, ignored her, beat her, made her accompany him on week-long bouts of group sex with him and several other white girlfriends. All this naturally drove Etta, who seemed attached to Johnson in the desperate, helpless way of battered women, into deep depression. She tried to kill herself twice before finally succeeding in September 1912. For Burns, Johnson's mistreatment of Etta had nothing to do with her self-destruction. No, "Etta's horrible dread had finally overwhelmed her." We're treated to extended commentary meant to prove Johnson's devotion to her. He "collapsed in grief" when he learned of her death. Four weeks later he was on the road with a nineteen-year-old prostitute, whose mother set the cops on him, leading to his legally indefensible, but morally well-deserved, indictment under the Mann Act.

The irony is that, in the end, *Unforgivable Blackness* is a new kind of minstrelsy. The show is obsessed with Johnson's sexual relationships with white women, juxtaposing over and over again his naked powerful black body with pictures of scantily dressed white prostitutes—at the same time, of course, stressing how the whites in Johnson's time were threatened by that very same sexuality. Certainly, some of these white people viciously hated Johnson's blackness and his human gifts. Others, however, were probably not threatened by his power but disgusted by his lack of decency and self-control. Burns never considers this—he's in thrall to the commercial value of Johnson's physical beauty and sexual encounters. He's brought racial projections to a whole new level. Like Johnson's white promoters, like a lot of white cultural promoters nowadays, he's enslaved a piece of black history and made it dance sensationally to his audience's appetites.

JANUARY 24, 2005

⃞20 *Lackawanna Blues*

There is a striking disjunction in *Lackawanna Blues,* the story of a poor black community in the late 1950s in Lackawanna, New York, where a woman named Rachel "Nanny" Crosby owns a rooming house in which she welcomes and cares for various drifters, misfits, and marginal black people. All the honesty, the rawness, the creative weirdness, and originality belong either to the actors or to the film's music—fabulous blues songs and R&B classics from the 1950s.

You'll find nothing new or startling in the story, by Ruben Santiago-Hudson, or in the film's direction, by George C. Wolfe, the former head of New York's Public Theater, where this film first appeared in the form of Santiago-Hudson's autobiographical one-man play. Wolfe's style is so tightly structured, so ultra-calculated and tidy—every shot is wrapped in nice paper and tied with a pretty bow—that it is less like film directing and more like a study in conscientiousness and caution. Santiago-Hudson's script is something else again. It's a special kind of mush, the kind of mush you mostly find in movies that recall Jewish domestic life in past American epochs: films by Neil Simon, Woody Allen, and others.

As a tale of arrival, struggle for identity, and ultimate triumph, the Jewish experience in America has come to a close as a special story. The majority of the prison population isn't Jewish; Jewish children aren't consigned to inferior, underfunded schools with overwhelmed or indifferent teachers; affirmative-action quotas for Jews aren't a political issue. Just about every other immigrant group has success stories. Yet even those that don't are closer in their collective experience to a happy ending than American blacks are. The odyssey of black Americans—as a group—is nowhere close to fulfillment.

So where are the stories reflecting the black experience in today's America? They should be pouring from the minds of black writers. But they aren't. Instead you get, say, Ken Burns on jazz in America, or Ken Burns on the racist persecution of the great black heavyweight, Jack Johnson—even Burns' best documentary, on the Civil War, was to a great extent taken up with the issue of slavery. Spike Lee is the only black filmmaker I can think of who tries to make sense of the contemporary black experience. Younger black directors—often Lee's protégés, like John Singleton, Matty Rich, and the Hughes brothers—end up making action movies with trite or caricatured nods to themes about race. Maybe what is needed, as Lee recently said, is simply more blacks flourishing in corporate America and then investing their money in films and producing plays. But the experiences of blacks in corporate and professional America, and in middle- and upper-middle-class America, are precisely the stories that should be reimagined; they are the stories that should be fascinating us.

Irving Howe once rightly enraged Ralph Ellison and other black writers and intellectuals by decreeing that Ellison should concern himself, in his fiction and nonfiction, exclusively with the racial issues of his day. Of course they were enraged. Why should anyone reduce an imaginative artist to the color of his or her skin? Wasn't the whole point of Howe's airy exhortation to push black writers to protest society's reduction of their humanity to the color of their skin? Yet here was Howe, a Jewish intellectual who perhaps was urging black writers to be "more black" in order to feel himself all the more successfully integrated into American society, all the more comfortable with his status as a Jewish writer who didn't always have to write about the Jewish experience.

And to think, Howe was writing around the time of bebop and cool jazz and not long before an explosion of black countercultural works—just recall the raw, original plays of Ed Bullins and Leroi Jones, for example. Even Lorraine Hansberry's play *Raisin in the Sun,* performed around the time Howe was wagging his finger, hit a nerve with its themes of black passivity versus black ambition, integration versus segregation, economic security versus heroic risk-taking, though black writers at the time condemned it as being too tame. But in 1959, the year of the play's debut, Hansberry's issues were alive and festering and unresolved. In other words, *Raisin in the Sun* was about 1959. *Lackawanna Blues*, airing in 2005, is about 1956. Howe, to my mind, was pompous and inflated in his remarks about Ellison. Today he would make sense.

Black themes today would have something to do with the psychic story behind the dramatic social and political saga of integration; something to do with the psychic story behind the social and political drama of blacks who have been socially "integrated" but not economically assimilated. Black literary art would get inside the minds of its characters the way the great Russian novels got inside their characters' minds. Instead you get, in *Lackawanna Blues,* a period piece, the film version of a Reginald Marsh painting (if Marsh had made his caricatures of black life in the 1950s rather than the 1930s). The film's disappointing note is struck in its opening scenes, when Wolfe cuts back and forth between a woman giving birth to the movie's protagonist, a man and a woman having sexual intercourse in the backseat of a car, and a jealous woman cutting her rival with a knife. You know, at that very moment, that *Lackawanna Blues* is going to reduce its characters to stereotypes the way it blurs all these highly particular events into one blurry and bleary panorama of the Human Comedy.

Except, as I said, for the actors. (And that music. Robert Bradley's blues-singing will cut through your bones. And Mos Def will melt your new plasma TV.) As Nanny, S. Epatha Merkerson tears the guts out of this hokey character, this Hattie McDaniel with an edge. Nanny gives and gives and gives. She's a Plymouth rock of strength and hope. As Ruben, who narrates the movie, says, "Nanny gave every drop of herself to people. My biggest fear was that Nanny would give all of herself away and that there wouldn't be anything left for her." We learn that the death of her only child created this need to sublimate her suffering into the care of other people. The strange shape of the self-sacrificing, near-obliteration of her personality never gets revealed by the script. But Merkerson doesn't give us some impossible creation of goodness. Her Nanny is not some stock black character, the self-sacrificing mother who wears herself out for her special child and then, minutes after college graduation, drops bathetically dead. Merkerson's eyes are heavy with the price her goodness exacts from her self-interest; her kind face is animated by pain and loss. Sometimes her eyes are so clouded by mysterious desire—for the satisfaction of love or hate, you don't know—that you feel her greatest scenes and lines are offscreen. She has created an echo of the character Nanny should have been, and really is, somewhere out there.

But far and away the shocking, powerful heart of this movie is Jeffrey Wright, who portrays a double-murderer named Small Paul living as a roomer in Nanny's house. Wright is one of the greatest American actors alive today. I cannot think of another actor who so completely inhabits his characters, from Basquiat to the drag queen in *Angels in America*. As Small Paul telling his story to the young Ruben, Wright is woeful, contrite, quietly enraged, subtle, cunning, resolved, doomed—ruefully, almost unwillingly, indestructible. He has inside him all the qualities and experiences you just wait for black writers to come along and re-create on stage, screen, and page.

Maybe that's why *Lackawanna Blues* serves a purpose where it fails to delight. It proves that the finest actors in America today are black (and often straitened by timid, myopic Hollywood into the same old stock roles). Perhaps the most artistic black men and women today, lacking art that reimagines their experience, have nowhere to go but deeper and deeper into the multitudinous meanings inside themselves, and then out again, into someone else. They are still, to some extent, invisible people. What a film that would be.

FEBRUARY 14, 2005

Religion

21 *Joan of Arcadia*

Television is about to surpass film as the dominant entertainment medium, and if you're not convinced of that, take a look at the number of movies coming out that seem defensively to depend on music, close-ups, and special hi-tech effects, features that don't translate easily to television. Not yet, anyway. But that will all change this fall, when Sony and Zitellii Contractors introduce their new telehouses, in which the living space, thanks to the miracle of computerized sheetrock and cutting-edge fiber optics from New Zealand, will allow you to merge into your favorite television shows and interact with your favorite television characters when you are at home. OK, I'm joking. But it is, as they used to say, a dialectical certainty that sometime in the near future television will become more and more participatory, more and more emotionally immediate.

Film actors know this, and the film actors who know it best are the ones who do not possess the glamorous, physically beautiful dimensions of movie stars. A lot of television now is a rebellion against the perfect images purveyed by advertising and the movies, in much the same way as the fan magazines have always kept movie stars from becoming oppressive presences by reminding readers that celebrities have drinking and drug problems, get plastic surgery, experience mental breakdowns, and so on. Television now offers an alternative universe of flourishing psychological, physical, and moral imperfection: the confrontational, confessional talk shows; the reality shows; the wounded-detective shows; the shows about sex as an addiction; the shows about violence as a universal condition. Perhaps the reason the upper echelons of our national politics are filled with so many sorry figures is that people associate the appearance of dignity, character, and success in a politician with the wearying slick and shallow images they have come to angrily resent. A public figure who wears his peccadilloes, even his moral deformities, winkingly on his sleeve is, alas, a kind of relief from all that cold, distant beauty and perfection.

There is a bright side to this in the creative realm, which is that unlike most movies, television now abounds with actors who don't spend six hours a day in the gym, with actors who can more plausibly inhabit ordinary people and bring to life scripts that have substance and conceptual verve. CBS's critically acclaimed and commercially successful *Joan of Arcadia* is one such show, and average-looking Joe Mantegna—a cross between Pacino and Matthau—who plays one of the series' principal characters, is one such actor. There aren't many successful film actors who have made the transition from movies to television so smoothly. So artful, in fact, is Mantegna's performance that his very style amplifies the show's themes. In this regard, *Joan of Arcadia,* along with *The Sopranos,* is something like a revolution in television acting.

Joan of Arcadia attracted considerable commentary when it first appeared because of its premise of a teenage girl who speaks with God. The show's popularity inspired proclamations of an American return to religion, of American teenagers' return to religion, of the growing importance of religion in American life, and on, and on. But *Joan of Arcadia* seems more in line with the rising tide of fantasy-entertainment than a reflection of genuine religious sentiment. If, as someone once said, romanticism is spilled religion, then fantasy is spilled romanticism now that romanticism has been exhausted. Whereas romanticism once appealed to the heart, fantasy appeals to the mind at a time when the feelings have been almost wholly psychologized. Fantasy is an idea presented as a feeling. And this is where Mantegna comes in.

Long associated with David Mamet, Mantegna is the exemplar of Mamet's theories of acting, which reject the so-called naturalism of the Method. In Mamet, a transparent artificiality replaces the attempt to be true to life with an attempt to be true to an idea about life; that is, to the notion that reality itself consists of pretense, artifice, and illusion. If Mamet's actors seem at times patently to be acting, it's because in Mamet's work, the gulf between appearance and reality is so wide that the only way to capture the texture of experience is to define, at different moments, appearance as reality and vice versa. What saves this from being an easy cleverness is partly Mamet's intelligence and inventiveness, and partly his actors' seamless fusion of acting with authentic social behavior, so that the two modes of self-presentation are distinct from one another and indistinguishable from each other all at the same time. It's no surprise that these actors, so adept at playing games with appearance— William H. Macy is another Mametian who has been warmly accepted by television—are just right for a television in revolt against the reign of superficial images.

The way Mamet's actors put social life in doubt even as they are acting social is just right for *Joan of Arcadia*. Set in a small city called Arcadia, which could be anywhere in the United

States, the series is about a cop, played by Mantegna, who brings his family to the new town where he's gotten a job as a police chief. His wife Helen, beautifully performed by Mary Steenburgen, is an erstwhile artist who works as an administrator at the local public high school, which is attended by their three teenage children, implausibly close in age: Kevin, a former athlete crippled in a car accident and now in a wheelchair; Luke, a science-geek obsessed with finding the "logical explanation" for every ethical question; and Joan herself.

For network television, *Joan of Arcadia* is almost shockingly intelligent. The town's name recalls the title of a famous painting by Poussin, *Et in Arcadia ego,* which means "and I am also in Arcadia," a reminder that death is present even in an idyllic paradise. Every episode of *Joan of Arcadia* that I watched has either an instance of or a reference to someone dying. The premise of the show is that God, who appears to the sixteen-year-old Joan in the form of various types of people, has decided to teach the young girl how to live a good life, which has to do with accepting the fact of mortality, of transience, of the wide gulf between fleeting appearance and spiritual reality. She has to be instructed in the way of the world; this demands that she be constantly tested (for sixty minutes, including fifteen minutes of commercials, every week). God tells her to do something, and she, being a creature of free will, has the choice of refusing or obeying, though she almost always obeys.

Her father's name is Will Girardi, the surname meaning, in Italian, something like "the daily revolving of the will"—a good motto for the job of trying to distinguish bad guys from good guys; her kind, gentle geek-brother's name is Luke, like the gentlest of the apostles; her worldly, cynical, rebellious, mordant Jewish (natch) friend is Grace (the second Will and Grace on television). Joan's actions always lead to some measure of personal unhappiness for her and, as God sometimes reveals, a measure of salvation for those whose destinies she has changed by her intervention. This is the show's nice, surprising, ego-defying message. With its sensitive, unglamorous, modest-looking adolescents, who are smart, worldly, and hip yet also vulnerable, and self-conscious and conscientious about everything, from friendship to sex, *Joan of Arcadia* is the anti-*O.C.*, Fox's "teen" drama, whose teens seem more like middle-age Hollywood producers and agents disguised as teens.

There are plenty of criticisms to make of *Joan of Arcadia*. On one level, it's yet another empowering, self-help drama for teens, this time in the form of thoughtful dramatizations of various moral dilemmas and ethical precepts: the true nature of a gift; the meaning of obligation; the question of means versus ends. This last occurs in an episode where God requests that Joan destroy the sculpture of a dear friend in order to prevent him from dropping out of school to pursue the life of an artist, a life for which he's ill-equipped. Perplexed, Joan asks a rabbi, Grace's father, if God has ever commanded anyone to do anything that seemed wrong. No! he exclaims, as if scandalized, apparently having forgotten a little miniseries some thousands of seasons back called "The Story of Abraham and Isaac." In fact, since Joan almost always obeys God, the question of free will, which the show keeps raising, is not so much a question as an empty gesture toward The Serious. The show's deep inconsistency is that when Joan does heed God's instructions, she ends up curbing someone else's free will, like the young artist who stays in school as a result of her actions, which means that he never gets to decide his own path in life.

But thematic inconsistency is the price good television shows pay now. A good conception needs a strong storyline, but because television has to fulfill harsh demographic requirements, it has to include every type of person from every kind of group. And so good shows end up being driven by character—or more precisely, by stereotype—rather than by plot, and being plotless, they lose their purpose and their premises. Though superficially Christian—the incidental music sounds like a softer version of guitar-driven Christian rock—*Joan of Arcadia* might just as well be running for mayor of New York in the way it frantically tries to amplify its appeal by divesting itself of any religious affiliation whatsoever.

But these are petty cavils about a fine thing. A television drama about the hunger for faith, a show that is at the same time witty and moving and complex, is, well, a godsend. God tells Joan to have more sympathy for a teacher, who turns out to be as unsympathetic as she thought he was. The mayor pressures Will, for political reasons, to fire two cops for brutality before the facts of the case are known, and the mayor, though a terrible person, turns out to be right. Yet he's still a terrible person, just as the unsympathetic teacher still deserves Joan's sympathy. *Joan of Arcadia* is a teen drama for adults.

And the hub of the show is Mantegna. For one thing, his transparent artifice not only suits a world in which God keeps stripping away veils of appearance for Joan's edification; it is also appropriate to Joan's state of mind, which is a fragile balance between sanity and madness. But even more to the point is the use television has found for Mantegna's style. For his new medium, he has had to tone down his deliberately stilted, artificial manner, and what is left of it seems to be embedded in his character as an idiosyncratic quality that belongs to that character—a mark of Will's originality. It's like a beacon of hope for Will's children, who might see in their father's originality the eventual ripening of the "weirdness" they keep decrying in themselves into their own rich particularity. Hollywood has always made thematic use of the tendency that famous actors have to play their specific roles and their larger screen persona simultaneously. Nicholson, for example, was always the insolent, rebellious Nicholson playing an insolent, rebellious character. Now television is using the detached, cerebral manner of Mantegna to fill out a detached, cerebral character. That's as good an indication of television's creative allure as any.

JUNE 9, 2004

22 Revelations

After weeks of the media pandering to the Christian right *in re* Ashley, Terri, and John Paul, there suddenly comes *Revelations*. Or, to be more precise, NBC's broadcast of a miniseries based on the last book of the New Testament, in which the world crashes to an end, good triumphs over evil, and Christ begins a millennial reign. And I started to feel pretty good about the future. (The immediate future.) It became clear to me that the almighty dollar was going to keep the country from being delivered over to some people's idea of the Almighty.

The assimilation of avant-garde aesthetic and philosophical values by the middle class is an old story—and an obsession of cultural conservatives, who can't seem to decide which is worse, the caricature of modernist heroics or the loosening of middle-class mores. Whether Rimbaud, Jarry, Picasso, et al. are behind high rates of divorce and cable television is highly debatable. But there's no doubt that commerce can eat up radical subversions as fast as you can make them.

Life magazine put Pollock on the cover almost as soon as he displayed his confounding abstractions. Reproductions of the European modernist creations that shocked Americans at the New York Armory Show in 1913 now look back at you, trapped in their own bland horror, from the walls of your dentist's office. You can catch scenes of violence on television at any minute, day or night, that make Artaud's Theater of Cruelty look like *The Song of Bernadette*. Godless modernism was soon forced to bend its knee to Mammon. And now the God-intoxicated reaction—that is, Christian fundamentalism—to modernism and modernity is, maybe, about to go the way of its adversaries.

Revelations' plot centers on two figures, a Harvard professor of astrophysics named Richard Massey (played by Bill Pullman) and a Catholic nun, Sister Josepha Montafiore (played by Natasha McElhone). Massey has just returned from Chile, where he's tracked down and brought back to American justice the Satan-worshipper who murdered his daughter and cut out her heart in a ritual of devil worship. Sister Josepha, with the aid of a wealthy religious fundamentalist, is documenting a sudden spate of signs and wonders signifying the coming of the apocalypse, and she's returning from Mexico where she's just filmed a vision—witnessed by thousands of people—of Christ on the cross.

Superficially, at least on the evidence of the pilot, the series presents a balanced argument between the skeptical nonbeliever Massey—ensconced at Harvard, the world headquarters of liberal, secular values—and Sister Josepha. But *Revelations* is really wholly partisan to Sister Josepha, since we see and hear every miracle that she herself claims to see and hear. Against the shadow of Christ moving his head, and a brain-dead girl quoting Scripture in Latin, Massey's scientific explanations of biblical miracles don't stand a chance. Like the television newspeople's submission to religion in the stories about Ashley Smith and the Pope, *Revelations* is a sop to the fervently faithful. Yet it's also a kind of mickey slipped into the communion wine.

There's something strange about the special effects: a divinely aimed lightning bolt striking down a young girl; a giant shadow on the side of a mountain that looks like Christ moving his head as he hangs on the cross; the lightning-felled girl, now in a coma, suddenly drawing apocalyptic pictures and uttering Latin phrases. On one level, to be sure, the camera is giving the lie to Massey's skeptical arguments against religion. But on another, subtler level the generic quality of the special effects—their exciting screen-familiarity—gives the lie to their function as religious evidence. You are watching the very mechanics of cultural assimilation.

Before long, the plot itself falls back into the established pattern of just about every drama on television. It becomes a crime drama. Massey (who is more and more convinced of the presence of the divine in earthly affairs) and Sister Josepha embark on a quest for the Christ child. This involves being pursued by bad guys, jumping off a bridge in a dramatic escape, and trying to avoid the vindictive rage of Massey's Satanist, now locked away in prison but busily whipping up prisoners—his colleagues in evil—into an Attica-type rebellion. It's Sunday school meets *Rosemary's Baby* meets Gene Hackman and Anne Archer in *The Package*. And if those secular, crowd-pleasing antics don't take the edge off the coming apocalypse, the lengthy commercial breaks will. My favorite was the one for the new Jaguar. (What an advertising campaign that could turn into! "In the coming apocalypse, you'll need a car that gives a faster, smoother ride than any Beast.")

Whatever were the Jewish producer and the three Jewish directors of *Revelations* thinking? A few weeks ago, a fascinating article in the *New York Times Magazine* by Jonathan Mahler described how Christian "mega-churches" are going beyond providing a place for worship and prayer and offering their congregants services ranging from aerobics to psychotherapy.

One conclusion you can draw from that development is that fundamentalist religion is responding to the many needs created by modern, secular life—needs experienced by religious people alienated from modern, secular remedies. The result might be that fundamentalist religion itself will become modernized, even secularized to some degree, and have its fervors cooled.

In the same way, cultural representations of religion might have to satisfy the very secular thirst for inane, innocuous entertainment that has been instilled even in the most religious people. In the process of doing so, religion might experience another degree of cooling. In the end, so to speak, maybe all religious fundamentalists want is a safe, unhumiliating way into the crazy, self-centered cornucopia of modern life. So, as *Revelations* may very well demonstrate, if the faithful won't come to the limelight, the limelight will go to the faithful.

APRIL 18, 2005

Drama

㉓ *Rescue Me*

Whither the American imagination? Few novelists nowadays seem able to imagine anything that doesn't already exist. This might account for the fact that just about everybody in the fiction business is writing a historical novel. It's as if they needed something real to lean their weary imaginations against, as if they couldn't envision something new without having a picture of real events in their mind to refer to as they invented. For decades, professional hand-wringers warned that visual mediums like television and movies would impoverish the use of language. But it could also be the other way around. It could be that the rise of visual mediums reflects not an impoverishment but the evolution of a new form of the imagination. Either way, there's little doubt that visual images and music have overtaken literary art in modern culture.

More and more graphic novels are being written as more and more novels falter on self-conscious language that is divorced from experience. Movies are slowly becoming more complex. And television is picking up the general imaginative slack—it's getting better even as the multiplying reality shows and so much else on the air are making it worse. It will keep getting better as it keeps getting worse because of its peculiar hybrid nature. In 1949, the U.S. Department of Commerce reported that "television's combination of moving picture, sound, and immediacy produces an impact that extends television as an advertising medium into the realm of personal sales solicitation." The key word is "immediacy." The fact that television is right there, in your home, smack in the middle of your everyday life, makes it irresistible to avid commercial interests. But the fact that television is right there, smack in the middle of your everyday life, makes it possible for screenwriters to treat delicate subjects with an intimacy and complexity unavailable to the movies, even though filmmakers increasingly have one eye on the small screen as they make their pictures. Ironically, the difference between television and the movies is like the difference between the intimacy of the novel and the broad public meanings of film. Good television is assuming the role of the page even as it replaces the page with the screen.

The device of the therapist or analyst teasing out the inner life of a character is one way television is trying to achieve the intimacy of the novel. The introduction of fantasy characters is another. In *Joan of Arcadia,* Joan tells God private thoughts that she would never divulge in a social interaction. The same goes for FX's new series, *Rescue Me,* which employs the Elizabethan convention of having its protagonist, a divorced, depressed, wry, witty, alcoholic New York City firefighter named Tommy Gavin—played to perfection by Denis Leary—talk to the ghost of his cousin, Jimmy Keefe, who died in the attack on the Twin Towers. Tommy's hallucinated conversations are a vertical, rather than a horizontal, technique. They deepen the story rather than propel it along. These days, serious television drama is a lot more vertical than horizontal.

Rescue Me is something like the firefighter counterpart to *The Shield,* FX's other hit drama where the kinds of complexities and contradictions that you usually find in a novel have made it to the small screen. In *The Shield*, brutal, corrupt cops act with honor and courage, even as they're bashing heads and stealing drug money. In *Rescue Me*, you get this humanizing multivalence in the very first minutes of the show's first episode. A young firefighter is complaining to Gavin about the changes in his social life as 9/11 recedes into the past: "Hey, Tommy, it's gettin' slow out there pal. All that pussy I was gettin' after 9/11, now nothin'. People forget." Tommy (caustically): "Yeah. Sad commentary." This is not a grim revelation or a glib deconstruction. It's a dignifying honesty on the part of the show's writers, an honesty that's only been around on television for the past few years. It occurs again when Tommy talks on the phone with his father, played by the marvelous Charles Durning. Subtitles suddenly appear, revealing the true, desperately loving meaning underlying the banal-seeming phrases that these two tough, emotionally closed men use with each other.

Of course, this kind of innovation can quickly become patented as a standard style. It then gets reiterated to the point of caricature, and ends up blocking what could be further artistic permutations of psychological and social truth. *Rescue Me* rises to the level of art in its first episode when Tommy's children, in brief, subtle moments, ask him for water, thus casting a poetic illumination on this firefighter's conflagrated marriage and shattered family life. The second episode, entitled "Gay," is as masterful as anything I've ever seen on television. It recalls that episode of *The Sopranos* in which the psychopath Ralphie's son lapses into a coma after an accident; the entire hour rang changes on the theme of people lavishing tenderness, and pouring out grief, and wreaking brutality all out of the same wound to the ego.

In "Gay," a firefighter leaks to the tabloids the names of twenty firefighters killed on 9/11 who were secretly homosexual, and the show takes off from there, spinning all manner of variations on sexual union: from firefighters who despise the idea of gay marriage to the man who sets his wife on fire because she talked too much; to gay couples who can't escape the deadening jealousy and ennui that plague heterosexual marriages; and on and on until the attempts of men and women, and men and men, and women and women to make a life together fuse into a universal comitragic (again) conflagration—the metaphor of things on fire is a gorgeous, moving poetry in this show.

But in later episodes, the blessing of television's immediacy starts to become a curse. For it can make television writers feel that they have to become more "immediate": that is to say, more adept at grabbing the attention of home-ensconced audiences surrounded by so many distractions. The emphasis on verticality creates an anxiety about narrative momentum. Tommy's very funny jealous revenge on his ex-wife's banker boyfriend, Roger, involved getting his dead cousin's teenage son to hack into all the computers at Roger's office. Whenever one of his colleagues booted up his or her computer, an image of Saddam saying, "Good morning, Roger," appeared on the screen, giving the impression that Roger had chosen this little desktop image for himself. In a later episode, though, Roger hires guys to beat Tommy up. The violence is as gratuitous as it is unbelievable.

And in the episode "Gay," another young firefighter saves the life of a man who seems to be gay, and who is so moved by the young hero's kindness that he falls in love with him, visiting him at the firehouse and trying to appeal to what he senses is something kindred and receptive in the firefighter. But in a later episode, we learn that the man who'd been saved wants to have a threesome with his girlfriend and the firefighter, eventually tricking the firefighter into bed and handcuffing him to the bed frame. What might have been an original story about the true configuration of love and eros behind appearances, in which sex would have appeared naturally, becomes an appeal to the attention span, in which sex comes mechanically. It seems almost inevitable that in even the most serious television dramas, a beautiful complexity sooner or later gets caricatured into a senseless plot twist that leads to shooting, or punching, or screwing. The novelists have history; the screenwriters have violence and sex. It makes you want to shout "Fire!" just to wake everybody up.

SEPTEMBER 7, 2004

(24) *Deadwood*

With the debut of HBO's *Deadwood*, a Western series no-table for its violence, sex, and dirty language, there is a lot of talk about how the new show "shatters" the tired old genre of the Western, that hackneyed American invention, we are told, in which evil is purely evil and good purely good, the difference be-tween them usually indicated by sneering, black-hatted villains and tight-lipped, white-hatted heroes. Except, that is, for Clint Eastwood's *Unforgiven* and Larry McMurtry's *Lonesome Dove*, made way back in 1992 and 1989, respectively, both of which, we are further told, also shattered the tired old genre of the Western. Such hysterical proclamations of cultural revolution happen at least once a month—will football or television or breast-feeding ever be the same after Janet Jackson?—but they have everything to do with a restless appetite for something new and not much to do with something that is, actually, new.

As far as the Western goes, the genre was from the beginning an attempt to idealize a period in American history that existed for only about twenty years—Tom Mix served as a pallbearer at the fu-neral of Wyatt Earp, who spent the last years of his life working as a consultant to Hollywood filmmakers devoted to transforming the early years of his life into a legend. Because the Western began as an ideal, the slightest gesture toward actuality always seemed revolutionary: Anthony Mann and Sam Peckinpah spring to mind. The seeming paradigm-bursting change introduced by *Deadwood,* however, is really no more than an extra-emphatic expression of a single element. Which in the case of *Deadwood,* and so many other so-called innovative shows, is the seamy, sordid side of life.

Dissolve from the saloon in Deadwood to the tavern in Greenwich Village—the Cedar Tavern, that is. The late art critic Clement Greenberg famously theorized that painting evolved through progressive stages, in the course of which the illusion of depth disappeared until the forms in a painting lay entirely on its surface, flat and one-dimensional—abstract expressionism. This was, Greenberg believed, the final phase of Western painting. In this abstract expressionist phase, the meaning of a painting resided in its formal perfection, not in its mimetic power. For many abstract expressionist painters themselves, however, the meaning of their art lay less in formal purity than in visceral, emotional intensity. They considered their paintings representative of shared reality, but it was a psychological, internal reality, not a visible and external one. Now, abstract expressionism came and went in the late 1950s and early 1960s, but television—this is almost an iron law of the medium—is always about a generation behind the candor of "high" culture, and with *Deadwood,* and similar shows, it is now entering its raw, emotional, abstract expressionist phase, in which the sex, violence, and obscenity that lay buried in earlier Westerns have risen to the surface.

Based loosely on historical facts, *Deadwood* takes place in a mining camp of that name which once existed in the Black Hills of Dakota—an anarchic settlement that was not part of any state or territory at the time the series opens, in 1876, two weeks after Custer's massacre at Little Big Horn. Mixing real historical figures like Wild Bill Hickok and Calamity Jane with fictional ones, the series has a godsend of a situation, one in which, as a character informatively declares in the first episode, there is "no law at all." That's the wide-open backdrop of Westerns in general; its capaciousness is what makes every mundane incident in a cowboy movie a high-stakes dilemma resolvable only by violent action. *Deadwood* crafts lawlessness as an explicit, self-conscious principle; the people at HBO know that the simplest contexts have the capacity to contain the largest situations: four single women with different personalities in *Sex and the City* or a crime family riven by domestic conflict in *The Sopranos*. A screenwriter can ring endless changes on such simple, plastic unities, the unifying principle of *Deadwood* being naked appetite and greed.

The setting itself has a premise that endows the action with a very particular clarity. The premise is formulated by the basically decent camp doctor, played to near perfection by Brad Dourif. (As the asylum patient Billy in *One Flew Over the Cuckoo's Nest*, Dourif was the holy autistic outsider who had the power to heal; as *Deadwood*'s doctor, he is the—somewhat—holy, artistic, mysteriously impaired outsider whose power to heal is derived from his inner Billy. Thus do American actors play their larger screen persona and their particular roles simultaneously.) As Dourif's Doc Cochran puts it: "I see as much misery out of them movin' to justify themselves as them that set out to do harm." In other words, *Deadwood* is going to tell human experience like it is: every person a mingled yarn, good and ill, not a black- or white-hatted caricature of pure evil versus pure good.

The phrase "mingled yarn, good and ill" is Shakespeare's: Television's new style of complexity has been around for a long time. To read a lot of the current commentary on *Deadwood,* one would think the idea that a person can be good and bad at the same time is a secret that popular culture has only recently pried from the clutches of high art. In fact, such "complexity" has also been part and parcel of the Western for a long time, but it was an integral mingling of opposite moral qualities, not a self-consciously constructed "complexity." Consider the subtle undermining of a living legend—Jimmy Stewart's Senator Ransom—in *The Man Who Shot Liberty Valance;* or the deconstruction of gender roles in *Johnny Guitar;* or the dissolution of ethical categories in *One-Eyed Jacks.* Even Howard Hawks' *Red River* possesses depths of nuance and ambiguity, though it has the reputation of being so much the archetypal old-fashioned Western that McMurtry made it the last picture—the last cinematic example of bygone heroic grandeur—in his *The Last Picture Show.* But the struggle between John Wayne, the brutal father, and Montgomery Clift, the soft, vulnerable, almost feminine son, implies all the murky libidinal and egoistic conflict a jaded palate could hope for. And it's set against the background of the cattle drive, which enveloped the "old" cowboy movies with the very theme of appetite and instinct running up against civilized boundaries that you get in *Deadwood.* Back then, however, viewers had to apply their imaginations to the themes, like miners prospecting gold with pick-axes and pans.

So though *Deadwood* is all about digging deep for treasure, its own depths are right there, strewn with blood and guts and Mametian "fucks" all over the surface of the screen. Yet it's hard to understand why so many people seem startled by the grit—especially when *Homicide* and *Glengarry Glen Ross* are right there on your cable menu, nestled up against *Deadwood.* After all, aggressive seaminess is one of HBO's trademarks: think *Oz,* think *Sopranos*. Or recall the 1999 HBO cowboy movie *The Jack Bull* with John Cusack, which was based on a story by the nineteenth-century German novelist Heinrich von Kleist about the perverted consequences of a fanatical quest for justice, an adaptation that proved how easily the Western genre accommodates muddy, mingled yarns, even from the hands of a German romantic who probably never laid eyes on a pair of chaps or a Colt Peacemaker.

Take away the show's moderate (by current standards) sex and violence, and its immoderate cussing, and *Deadwood* is really a very enjoyable, good old-fashioned cowboy series whose characters are, in the end, no more discomfiting than the characters in more conventional-seeming cowboy movies. If anything, the show's violence rules its plots with an iron hand; your senses get addicted to the extremity, and you find yourself in something like a state of withdrawal as you patiently absorb the subtle, sensitive character studies. Like most serious television drama, the series is driven by characters rather than plot, and you occasionally get the former stopping to recap storylines that get tangled and obscure as they hurtle along in their violent direction while the writers follow a different direction and concentrate on developing their fictional people. But though these figures often unfold with great psychological nuance, their yarns don't stay mingled for long.

For now, the show's chief villain is Al Swearengen (yes, he swears a lot), who runs the Gem saloon, a bar, restaurant, gambling hall, and bordello. (The show has frequent funny moments, which are almost never played for laughs, as if its creators didn't want to seem to be taking their own violent atmosphere lightly—one of the funniest and bawdiest moments is when the all-male jury is sent to deliberate in the bordello.)

Swearengen is a wholly amoral, ruthless, cold-blooded killer, but in the end he is no less reassuring than the almost wholly good and decent Seth Bullock, a quick-drawing former Montana lawman who has ridden into camp to open a business with his Jewish partner, Sol Star (the latter is shrewd with money and nervous with a gun—so much for innovation).

Swearengen (superbly played by Ian McShane) doesn't commit a single infraction without a practical purpose that is rooted in his rational apprehension of his environment. Unlike the motive-less Iagos or the solipsistic Raskolnikovs of literature, knowable, understandable, self-explanatory villains like Swearengen are popular culture's gratifying gift to the sleepless. They are not malign; they are quantitative. They proceed, as we like to say, "pragmatically." We can grasp their nefarious purposes over lunch. And just in case the illusion of knowable evil isn't sufficient to calm viewers excited by all the violence and bad words, McShane and the other actors play their characters theatrically rather than, as on *Sex and the City,* naturalistically, or, as on *The Sopranos,* a combination of the two styles. So, in the end, the "shattering" grittiness of *Deadwood* creates the illusion that the most extreme violence is distinguished by outsized dialogue and a controllable cause. *Deadwood*'s real pleasure comes between extremities: the drama of how people live when they're not being shot at, beaten, or stabbed, but simply under pressure of the nakedly human.

MARCH 29, 2004

25 *Revenge of the Middle-Aged Woman, Suburban Madness,* and *Desperate Housewives*

Where is the great essay on the Young American Woman? I mean that young woman in her late teens or early twenties, with the low-riding jeans, and the little tattoo, and the apparently knowing air, and the seemingly confident openness about what she wants, whatever that might be. She's certainly on everyone's mind. She's on the minds of marketers, and advertisers, and book publishers, and magazine editors, and movie and television producers, and Internet adventurers (and creeps). Most of all, though, the Young American Woman is on the mind of the Older American Woman. And yet so far as I know, no member of the latter group has ever expressed herself significantly on the mighty consequential fact of the former—not in fiction, non-fiction, art, or journalism.

The most famous desperate housewives are Anna Karenina and Emma Bovary. The great novels of adultery are European, and like Kate Chopin's *The Awakening,* a minor American novel of adultery, they were written in the nineteenth century. They concern a young attractive wife's betrayal of her older, more or less ineffectual husband. Anna and Emma take up with younger, stronger, more virile men, relieve their frustrated desires, and then destroy themselves in accordance with society's wishes. Written as the Industrial Revolution was completing its transformations, the novels reflected the anxiety of men contending with a new type of naked competition, men whose social orders had suddenly become perilously fluid. The outsider possessed more power than ever before. Appetite and ambition were less obstructed than ever before.

Popular culture today is also obsessed with infidelity—the "new infidelity" as an excited *Newsweek* cover called it. Two new television movies, *Revenge of the Middle-Aged Woman,* broadcast on CBS last night, and *Suburban Madness,* to be shown on CBS on October 3, take the subject up. ABC's surprisingly fresh new series, *Desperate Housewives,* also set to premiere on October 3, deals, in part, with adultery as well. In all three of these shows, it's the husband—not so ineffectual, but not as strong as his spouse—who betrays the wife. And he betrays her with a younger, more powerful woman, usually someone who is as much a presence in the wife's workplace as she becomes at home.

In these shows, the marital crisis is no longer caused by a society that represses women's instincts and keeps them confined in punishing unions. Rather, it's the result of a society that tells women to go out and seek their hearts' desire and that privileges younger, fleet-footed, and ambitious women over older women who are constrained by children, husbands, and the task of juggling family with career (or slowed down by the melancholy of having sacrificed career to family). These pop culture events portray the dark side of feminism, implying as they do that the idea of a mutually supportive sisterhood of women free from old-boy networks and demeaning male quid pro quos is as chimerical as the classless society. They suggest that woman is as much a wolf to woman as man has always been to man—maybe even more so.

The desire for a bigger life that was a fatal weakness for Anna and Emma has become a fatal strength for women youthful and autonomous enough to assert it. On television, anyway. The housebreaking (as they used to call it) receptionist in *Suburban Madness*—based on a true story—who works for both wife and husband in the orthodontic practice they share might be in her thirties, but she's unattached and prettier and blonder than the wife who ends up mowing down and killing her philandering spouse with her Mercedes. (Although the wife isn't the unfaithful one, she gets twenty years in jail and punished like some modern-day Bovary. In these shows, even the older woman's strength is her weakness.) The lissome blonde culprit in *Revenge* is young enough to be the betrayed wife's daughter, and in this case she's also the wife's own assistant. For both movies, the destructive younger, or unencumbered, woman is a new kind of social force that sweeps away stability in the workplace as well as in the home. The proverbial enchantress-secretary has become a lethal ubiquity.

Maybe this new social wrinkle accounts for ABC's new reality series, *Wife Swap*, in which wives from disparate backgrounds, and with disparate temperaments and tastes, trade places and live with each other's families for several weeks. The show presents the usual lazy voyeurism, offering to audiences reality TV's easy resentments, and outlets for envy, and fantasies of social superiority. But though *Wife Swap*'s premise is silly and degraded, the fact of its existence is an illumination. At a moment when the culture is simply swimming in representations of sex, and talk about sex, and new types of access—that is, the Internet—to sex, this latest example of the brave new genre of reality television has committed an astonishing omission. The new wives don't have sex with their "new" husbands. Here they are fighting with their substitute spouses over raising the kids and household chores, yet erotic attachment, its quality, or frequency, or even the fact that it once existed—if the reality of sex is no longer there, then the fact of sex is very much there—is nowhere to be found. If it were, the quarrels would be of a whole different species.

And you have to ask yourself (I mean, if you have nothing better to do) if this absence of sex isn't another disempowering of the older, married woman, as if only younger, unattached, and unencumbered women are allowed to threaten the household—as if being married, and older, and a mother, *and* sexually potent were just unfair. You can't have a little tattoo and a substantial self too! You can't copy your genes while you're packed into your jeans! Replaceable sexless wives; mighty amoral single sylphs; the "revenge" of the middle-age married mother rather than the "happiness" of the same—fluidity is the key element in these cultural constructions. Fluid people indulge a wider range of appetites—families save money—and this is what the sponsors like to see. And anyway, a married older woman with a cute tattoo and lots of bare skin wrapped slightly and tightly in denim would be a demographic hybrid. The people in the marketing department would go nuts.

This is why *Desperate Housewives* is so refreshing. Though its middle-age married or divorced women (mostly mothers) are types, they also defy their types. Or the show's writers are allowed to get so wicked that the types the show represents are pushed to satirical extremes until their typicality bursts and we get revelations of their inner lives. In the way the show grants its women interiority, it's a sort of anti–*Sex and the City*. Yet it has elements of that series as well as of other HBO creations.

In the show's first few minutes, one of the wives kills herself, and she becomes established as the show's narrator, in the manner of Carrie Bradshaw. There are four principal characters, as in *Sex and the City,* each of whom is a distinct personality: the perfect WASP falling to pieces behind her flawless façade; the exhausted mother of four, who's given up a high-powered career to raise her family; the Latin bombshell—the youngest of the quartet—married without children to a banker; and the freshly divorced single mom (she's the one whose husband left her for his secretary). *Desperate Housewives* is, for network television, sexually explicit, about as morbid as *Six Feet Under,* and thick with a gathering atmosphere of *Sopranos*-like dark violence.

But these aren't crime families whose pathologies seem to resonate symbolically with run-of-the-mill family dysfunctions. These are real families with real problems that are deliciously exploited for the most comical effects. "Mom," (I'm paraphrasing) says the son of Bree, the perfectly controlled WASP, as he sits at the perfectly laid dinner table, bathed in classical music, surrounded by gleaming china, eating osso buco and "basil puree" soup—"Mom," he says, "Mrs. Hooper just goes home and opens a can of pork and beans for everybody, puts it on their plates, and they're all really happy. Why can't we ever eat normal food like that?" His mother shifts her perfectly coiffed head, levels her brilliant blue eyes at him, and smiles coldly. "Dear," she replies, rising to dignity as she expresses, in full awareness of her particular fate, her particular absurdity, "are you on drugs?" These housewives are as dangerous as they are desperate. In other words, they have inner lives. Some of them are even allowed to look their age and still be attractive, sexy, and sexual. Britney, look to thy laurels.

SEPTEMBER 27, 2004

26) *Huff*

I wonder what future historians will make of a time, our time, in which no sooner is a figure granted authority in some walk of life than that person is deconstructed and annulled. The influence of such de-authoritizing on everything we do is incalculable. One effect must be to make every feeling, every impulse, we have absolute. We feel something, we want something, and our emotions and desires go on and on, with no authority to check them, to make us think twice about what we want. So we are frustrated, inevitably, not by a "norm" but by life itself. Perhaps we no longer hate only authority. Perhaps some of us hate life for depriving us of what we believe is ours simply to take from life.

And now this. It had to happen sooner or later. With Showtime's *Huff*, the psychiatrist, the last figure of secular authority in our modern God-bereft, God-searching, God-hating (Western) world, has been utterly canceled out. (Yes, I'm referring only to the so-called educated classes, not to Those Others Out There Whom Everyone Is Now Trying to Figure Out.) The politicians are a mess, the priests are unholy, the doctors are hypocritical and un-Hippocratic, the cops are lawless, the athletes are really bad sports, the sleazy celebrities are not to be celebrated—only the shrink has remained to be definitively shrunk.

You have to emphasize definitively. Intellectual culture has challenged and sometimes ferociously attacked the very idea of psychoanalysis almost since Freud started turning Viennese neuroses into a universal paradigm for the human mind. Indeed, no one has been as adversarial toward particular psychoanalytic ideas as rival analysts themselves. For some reason, no serious fiction that I can think of has taken up the figure of the shrink. Popular culture, on the other hand, has been too broad in its myriad swipes. Until recently, the irreverence usually took the form of caricature—the doctor with the funny name and the funny accent and the funny-sounding diagnoses. This had the effect of leaving the psychiatrist's inner experience untouched. His or her authority was mocked but not devalued.

All that has changed, obviously. *The Sopranos'* Dr. Melfi, to take just one example, is a wincingly realistic portrait of the therapeutic figure from the inside. Watching Lorraine Bracco's extraordinary Cubist-like portrayal of simultaneous inner and outer experiences—the confident professional; the private person disintegrating under the pressure of her profession—made me recall a story a friend once told me about his uncle, a psychiatrist in Connecticut who had a nervous breakdown and cut his wrists but continued to see patients while wearing long-sleeved shirts and a sports jacket to hide the bandages. (Connecticut readers: Don't worry. This was many years ago.) And here was Melfi, turning what had lodged in my mind as a private, isolated memory into a full disclosure, as it were. Her performance is not a caricature of the shrink that merely grazes appearance and leaves the authority of the shrink intact. What Bracco gives us is a real crisis in authority.

The effect of such representations resembles Ravel's operetta *L'Enfant et Les Sortileges* ("The Child and Sorcery"), about a little boy who maliciously breaks all his toys and then suffers the terrible consequences. We break our authority figures and then issue grievances about the quality of social life. Every episode of *Huff* ends with a cry of grievance. They end with Huff the psychiatrist going to visit his brother, a paranoid schizophrenic who apparently has been committed to a mental hospital. Huff seeks solace and strength, even advice, from his brother. It's not at all that the doctor himself is sick and thus impotent as an authority figure; it's that sickness itself has become the source of authority. Like the glass jar that held the Delphic oracle who had been shrunken by age, illness is the vessel that holds Huff's brother, whose very pain is the truth of Huff's life.

Huff is a very touching, occasionally deep show with some self-conscious, pretentious attempts at being "serious" but many more authentically serious moments. Ultimately, it's not so much despairing of psychiatry's efficacy as reflective of one by-now antiquated strain in psychiatry—the school of thought that probably began with Thomas Szasz, who was once psychiatry's greatest foe. "If you talk to God," Szasz once complained, "you are praying. If God talks to you, you have schizophrenia." A great deal of American culture, in fact, depends on the assumption that "normal" and "abnormal" are arbitrary categories imposed by social convention. In this sense, *Joan of Arcadia* and other television shows whose characters communicate with the deity are very close to the spirit of *Huff*.

And yet *Huff* resists this facile reversal. It is not, as critics have been saying, the walking, self-canceling paradox of the shrink who is himself a nutcase. On the contrary. As played by the gifted Hank Azaria—his sad, tense, expressive eyes are avatars of Buster Keaton's eyes—Huff is kind, and confused, and strong, and weakened, and highly reflective and self-aware, even as he finds all his certainties dragged down into the mud. His life is sent reeling by the suicide of a teenage patient who kills himself in front of the doctor, in the middle of a session, by putting a gun in his mouth and blowing off the back of his head. Perversely, that death—an absolute contradiction, which is what a suicide is—brings to life countless other contradictions.

Huff is sued by the boy's parents for malpractice. He begins to doubt himself, and he seeks validation through acts of random kindness that also are possibly dangerous and self-destructive. For instance, he is starting to get more deeply involved in the life of a homeless man who says that he is a composer from Hungary but who may be a fraud. He may even be Huff's delusion. But the suicide of a patient, in a place of healing, in front of a doctor who might have saved him if the doctor himself had not been afraid of being shot, throws into jeopardy all the fundamentals.

What is real about *Huff,* though, is that the show doesn't do anything as trite as try to make health and sickness, real and unreal, into interchangeable terms. Though Huff's very sense of himself, his identity, as the ultimate boundary that kept him sane, has dissolved—making him vulnerable to his destructive mother, his destructive lawyer friend (a breathtaking Oliver Platt), and others—he still creates his own comprehensible meanings. Now, however, he has to create them minute by minute. All of life's goodness is still there—it's just been scattered by the sudden de-authoritizing of Huff's own professional self. The really beautiful and moving thing about the show is that, by having Huff commune with his brother at the end, *Huff* is not making the brother's psychic pain into some absurd sentimental wisdom. It's making Huff's kindness toward his brother a constant in a world where diagnoses change by the minute, and where no one seems sane or irreproachable enough to tell you or anyone else to behave and be good.

NOVEMBER 22, 2004

[27] *The O.C.*

Anyone who works in the so-called media has been hearing for years that the marketers' Holy Grail is readers, listeners, or viewers between the ages of eighteen and thirty-four, though the true commercial quarry is usually people in their teens and twenties. The idea is that economic growth in the realm of leisure and entertainment depends on getting new audiences beyond the loyal ones already devoted to a particular venue. Since the devoted audiences are older, having stuck with said venue for a long time, the new audiences by definition have to be young—and the younger these "target-groups," the more audiences to be had, and the more profits to be made. To paraphrase that British arch-imperialist Cecil Rhodes, the marketers would colonize the cradle if they could.

And so teams of marketing gurus have been, and are at this very minute, running around trying to figure out just what it is that these coveted young people want. One entrepreneurial supposition is that, like everybody else in America, it's themselves they want to see portrayed on the big and small screen, except that marketers assume young people crave the representation and resolution of conflict and crisis even more than older people. The question is, how do the marketing shamans perceive the lives of young people, or do they perceive them at all?

The O.C. is FOX television's new hit drama about high-school teens and their families in California's Orange County, and it's the most popular teen show on television right now. The series is just one more contribution to a genre, or rather to a demographic niche, that has been growing for decades, and that includes movies and television series like *Fast Times at Ridgemont High* and *Beverly Hills 90210* on one side, and more eccentric cult favorites like *Rushmore*, (the wonderful) *Igby Goes Down,* and *Freaks and Geeks* on the other. According to *The O.C.*'s creators, their series has a new twist (the "new twist" is an old tradition). This time the innovation is that in *The O.C.,* the adults are treated as complicatedly as the teens. "The parents were essentially there to service the plot in *90210*," said Josh Schwartz, *The O.C.*'s creator. "In our show . . . we want the parents' stories to drive themselves." But a parent-driven plot is nothing special: WB's *One Tree Hill* and the far superior *Everwood,* to take two current series, also intertwine teens' stories with those of adults. *The O.C.*'s real innovation is that, according to FOX, the twenty-seven-year-old Schwartz is "the youngest person ever to create his own one-hour drama for network television." The word "own" has a dubious ring in that sentence since the network quickly brought in the fifty-six-year-old Bob de Laurentis, plus four other older producers, to guide Schwartz's hand. So Schwartz's own story is being considerably driven by older guardians of the network's money.

Yet Schwartz's emphasis on the relationship between young people and adults in any story where the former are the protagonists is certainly to the point. It's the barometer by which you measure the honesty of such a story. When Dickens wanted to expose the cruelty and hypocrisy of Victorian mores, he set children named David Copperfield and Oliver Twist and Little Dorrit against very particular adults. The novels' existential clarity depended on the stark difference between corrupt maturity and vulnerable youth. But these coming-of-age tales concluded with the protagonists emerging at the end as enlightened grown-ups. In that sense, they are worlds away from the two most famous American novels of youth.

Huck Finn and Holden Caulfield never enter the adult world. At the end of their stories, they are still teenagers, the adolescent state being one of permanent hopefulness and becoming, which is something like America, or the way America likes to think of itself. In Dickens, innocent youth, after suffering at the hands of cruel maturity, ripens into wisdom and kindness by means of its ordeal. In the American novel of youth, youth is all there is. Ripening into maturity and entering society mean the death not only of innocence but of wisdom and kindness. The hostility between Huck and Holden and their social environments—that is, adults—is unrelieved and unending. Yet the beautiful quality of these books is that their adolescent heroes are adults, of sorts. They are ideal adults, people who lead with their imaginations and feelings rather than with a calculating, acquisitive intellect. In full possession of their feelings, they don't need, as grown-ups often do, status and possessions to compensate for an adult estrangement from feeling. Like adults, they're able to fathom other people's motives; unlike adults, they are at the mercy of unruly feelings and lack the will to protect themselves from other people's plans for them until it's almost too late.

But in *The O.C.* there is no similar boundary separating the teens from the adults, circumstantially or emotionally. The grown-ups are as quick with their fists or their impulses as the kids. They're as unable to hide their feelings as the kids. They're even as unable to keep themselves from getting into trouble as the kids—and I mean trouble on the same level. Ryan, the outcast delinquent teen from a broken, lower-class home who is taken in by a prominent Newport Beach family, punches people out. Jimmy, the defrauding investment counselor and father of Marissa—Ryan's girl—punches out Caleb, the rich, cold-hearted father of Kirsten, Ryan's angelic heiress of an adoptive mother and wife of Sandy, the Bronx-born public defender who married up, way up from where he came from, when he wedded Kirsten. Sandy keeps telling Caleb to his face that he's a shit, which doesn't have much effect on his relationship to either Caleb or Kirsten. Ryan alternates telling Luke, his romantic rival, what he thinks of him to his face with punching Luke in the face, which only results in a mutually supportive friendship between the two of them. Julie, Marissa's mother, sleeps with Luke, Marissa's previous boyfriend, which has the effect of making Marissa and her crowd go, like, what a bitch, and roll their eyes in annoyance. And Cindy, Julie's sister, gets up at the engagement party for Caleb and Julie—she's divorced Jimmy—and describes Julie's many sexual exploits and acts of bad judgment and bad taste to the assembled guests. This has the surreal effect, when Cindy apologizes, of strengthening the bond between Julie and Cindy, and between Cindy and Caleb. And this is what FOX calls a "drama."

Now, you can say that portraying adults as children is just the way it is in a country famous for its childlike attitude toward life; or in a country where adult appetites are constantly stimulated by commercial appeals, thus keeping grown-up people in a perpetual state of adolescence. But anyone who thinks that adults who act like children are the moral equivalent of children needs to be strictly supervised for at least a few months. By real adults. *The O.C.*, like so much else on television these days, is a fantasy about life masquerading as an "honest" portrayal of life. It's a marketers' wish-fulfillment of what they would really like the relationship between teens and adults to be.

Once you get commercially obsessed with attracting ever younger audiences, you turn those audiences into objects of desire long before they get represented that way on the screen. *The O.C.*'s young actors, who portray high-school students, are fetching indeed (and I'm not projecting). With her very thin upper body yet wide hips, big warm brown eyes, and cold chiseled features, Marissa seems like some digitalized creation aimed at pleasing every possible male taste and female sense of recognition. But in *The O.C.*, the marketers have projected their desire for young viewers onto the show's characters themselves. The series alternates between the most unreal scenes of self-sacrificing generosity, presented like the products of a guilty conscience—Seth, Sandy's son, actually adores and constantly defends Ryan, even though Ryan has displaced Seth in Sandy's feelings—and scenes that are like the results of bad faith, which revolve around little narcissistic dramas of gratification: Will Jimmy hook up with Kirsten's much younger sister? Will Julie hook up with a beefy male stripper? Will Ryan hook up with an older model while he waits for Marissa to respond to his overtures to her?

The only excuse for writing a novel or making a movie, or even a television series, about a teen is to make him or her a special, sensitive teen, whose efforts at self-preservation expose all the meanness and hypocrisy with which he or she is surrounded. Such a teen romanticizes and idealizes where other teens simply desire; sex is a problem, not a casual incident for this kind of adolescent, who represents the essence of adolescence. But when the marketers look at adolescents, they see sex-obsessed sybarites where there are really sex-baffled naïfs striking one worldly pose after another.

Ryan, the disenfranchised outcast, who should be the moral center of the show, ends up wanting what everybody else wants: to belong to the group—Huck, where art thou?!—to get laid, to have Gabriella, the older model, go down on him while he's waiting for his true love to see the light. Never mind that because he's from a lower class—like Sandy, his new guardian—Ryan is crudely portrayed as a belligerent, streetwise guy, who is fatally drawn to waitresses from his background, and who (maybe) qualifies for the school soccer team but nothing more mental than that. Never mind that the very talented Peter Gallagher plays Sandy, with probably deliberate sly irony, as an earthy, near-simian instance of physicality, as if "Bronx" meant "zoo." The rotten upshot of the show is that Ryan, rather than being the outcast who exposes his environment by surviving it, or who transforms it by shattering all its assumptions, à la Nick Nolte in *Down and Out in Beverly Hills,* becomes, despite his own weak ambitions, an ongoing source of gratification for all of *The O.C.*'s inhabitants.

Ryan is the marketers' projection of the young objects of their desire. An outsider, he becomes the accepted insider only to the extent that just about everyone uses him to gratify their desires. The lonely Seth uses him as bodyguard, romantic adviser, social escort, and in-house companion; Marissa elevates her status by pulling the exotic outsider to her when she needs him and pushing him away when she doesn't; Summer, Seth's sometime girlfriend, and Seth pull Ryan out of an all-important, life-changing high-school entrance exam because they need his help; Ryan saves Luke from being shot. And Ryan serves as a buddy for Sandy, who is somewhat alienated from all his wealthy new neighbors; and as a cause for Kirsten, whose sponsorship of Ryan carries her way beyond the status conferred by ordinary "giving"; and on and on. Ryan becomes a one-man service industry. For FOX's marketers, being an outsider means gratifying the insiders' needs.

There is something depraved about Ryan's role in the world of *The O.C.* You wonder about Josh Schwartz's original intentions. Sure, he's making a bundle, but is this the show he wanted to create? Schwartz has said that Seth, Sandy's maladroit son and Ryan's best friend, is the character he most closely resembles. After watching a season of this show, you just can't believe that. Rather, it seems more likely that Ryan is actually Schwartz himself, now at the mercy of five older producers and a giant network not known for its emotional sensitivity or refined taste. Marcy Ross, FOX's senior vice president of current programming, said this in response to a question about Schwartz's inexperience as a scriptwriter and producer: "I mean sure he's lost a lot of weight, he's falling apart, he does nothing but work. But he was born to do this." Somebody had better recruit some detectives and S.W.A.T. guys from other shows and get to work on a new series, and as quickly as possible. They can call it *Save Josh*.

MAY 10, 2004

28 *Lost*

There are two sensationally popular new network television series at the moment, one being *Desperate Housewives,* and the other *Lost,* which so far has avoided all the heady speculation about the future of post-feminism, the paradoxical preferences of red and blue states, etc. etc. That's too bad. *Lost* is about a "combat" with "secrecy and complexity"; that is to say, it is about a complex secrecy. This country is obsessed with secrecy.

In fact, those quotes are not from the show. They're from the 9/11 Commission's report, which made recommendations "to combat the secrecy and complexity we have described." *Lost,* with its secrets multiplying minute by minute, episode by episode, in twisting, turning, multilayered plots, is like a metaphor for a country that feels it has suddenly dropped out of halcyon, ahistorical skies into a mysterious, alien, menacing world.

On September 11, 2001, Americans realized, for the first time in a long time, that the world keeps secrets from us, and that some of these secrets are very dangerous indeed. And so secrets are everywhere, culturally speaking. Just take a look at book publishing over the past year. There are the tell-all memoirs by Joseph Wilson and Richard Clarke, as well as Ron Suskind's account of Paul O'Neill's disclosures of the Bush administration's private doings. In fiction, Philip Roth's *The Plot Against America* unfolds an (imagined) secret conspiracy; and John Updike's *Villages* is about the secrets people hide from each other in small towns; and Nicholson Baker's *Checkpoint* is about a man speaking in secret to another man about his wish to kill the president; and Marilynne Robinson's *Gilead* has at its heart the secret of a prodigal son. Even this year's biographies of George Washington, Alexander Hamilton, and Benjamin Franklin are notable for representing the obverse side to the secret-shattering trend in the way that they eschewed the despoiling, exposing tactics employed by so many biographies of the recent past. These Founding Fathers had no secrets for their biographers to expose because they were portrayed as having nothing to hide. Their characters were as cathartically transparent as their noble intentions.

But the books that were the most expressive of our obsession with secrets were the books about sex. Though radically different from each other, Toni Bentley's *The Surrender* and Jenna Jameson's *How to Make Love Like a Porn Star* were both intense, prolonged disclosures of sexual acts. Sex is the most intimate and concealed thing humans do, and our utter fascination with sex is like an ongoing symbolic ritual of secret-busting. Finding out about other people's sexual operations can be an empowering, cathartic event.

Lost is a hatchery, a greenhouse of secrets. The story of a predictably diverse group of people who survive a plane crash on a deserted island, the series has a pregnant woman with a secret (she is carrying inside her some kind of evil being); and an escaped prisoner with a secret (what was in the briefcase of the federal marshal who was transporting her to prison when he was killed in the crash?); and a violent, dangerous passenger with a secret (is he really a passenger, or was he already on the island when they slammed into it?).

And is Boone just a lifeguard, or is he the possessor of a great fortune? Why does Locke seem so relaxed? Does he know something about their predicament that the others don't? In fact, just about every character has secrets, which surface in one episode and usually are divulged in the next. And along with these individual secrets, as it were, there are the impersonal secrets: Who is the monster-like creature running around the island and wreaking mayhem? Are there other people on the island besides the survivors?

Finally, there are the more prosaic-seeming secrets. Why does everybody on the show look so fantastic every week? They're on a deserted island, for heaven's sake. I mean, you can't keep spending four hours a day in the gym and still look desolate and stranded. And once in a while, *someone* has to be more concerned with finding food than running away from some exotic danger. I'd rather find a good substitute for mayonnaise to put on all the delicious mahi-mahi than go see what was On the Other Side of That Mountain. And I accept that they've made tools to cut each other's hair. But I do not accept that they've made tools to *style* each other's hair.

Lost is popular for a lot of likely reasons, not least of which is that it's a way back from reality crap like *Survivor* to good old-fashioned television storytelling. *Survivor* is about "winning" on conventional, game-like terms; *Lost* is about preserving your fragile mortality beyond the conventions of mere "winning" and "losing." In that sense, the new series, for all of its glossy close-ups, soap-opera contrivances, and self-conscious acting—sometimes it's like *The O.C.* out to sea—is a healthy development in television land.

But the show inevitably resonates beyond the screen. Few things are more revealing than how a culture represents the experience of being lost. Frank Capra's classic *Lost Horizon*, made in 1937, was about a plane crash and the survivors' discovery of Shangri-La in the snowy Himalayas. It submerged the personal stories of its characters in an uplifting vision of tranquility and spiritual fulfillment at the height of the Depression, a time when people yearned to be distracted from their particular distresses. For all of our fears nowadays, however, most of us are untouched by what we think is lurking in the far corners of the alien world. And so *Lost* emphasizes, through flashbacks, the past stories of its characters' lives over their present plight, as if implying that the world's unknown dangers—those secrets hidden in the shadows of mosques, in the back of dark caves, in the cries of the *muezzin*—are nothing compared to the entanglements of our everyday lives. All the really important secrets, the show seems to say—the "secrecy and complexity"—are here, at home, in our hearts. What a relief.

DECEMBER 13, 2004

⟦29⟧ *Invasion*

Invasion, ABC's new primetime drama about the arrival on Earth of mischief-making aliens, reminded me that the new TV season is full of shows about the supernatural. You've got, well, *Supernatural,* and then there's *Surface,* and *Threshold,* and *Ghost Whisperer.* The Emmys were in fact dominated by *Lost,* ABC's cash cow, a frenetically popular series in which plane-crash survivors stranded on a deserted island are, maybe, being stalked by something not human. A few months ago, the network also broadcast a "news" special that made a case for UFOs. Another big Emmy winner this year was NBC's *Medium,* a show about a woman who talks with the dead, reads people's thoughts, predicts future crimes, and so on. As for the movies, two recent films, *White Noise* and *Birth,* are about the possibility of life after death; Steven Spielberg's *War of the Worlds* is about big-time alien visitation. And if you still haven't had your fill of the supernatural and the occult, you can transubstantiate yourself over to the Metropolitan Museum of Art, where starting next week you can see "The Perfect Medium: Photography and the Occult," an exhibition about photographers at work from the 1860s to the brink of World War II who attempted to catch ghosts on film.

As the catalogue for the Metropolitan's show observes, the rage for photographs revealing the living presence of the dead began in France after its defeat and brief occupation by Prussia in the 1870s. In this country, occult photographers grew popular following the Civil War's unprecedented savagery and mass destruction. That period saw the rise of theosophy, a mystical system formulated by Madame Blavatsky, who established the Theosophical Society in New York in 1875. In the aftermath of World War I, and during the rise of fascism in the 1930s, Blavatsky's ideas seized the imaginations of countless artists and intellectuals. It almost goes without saying that at a time of unforeseen, unfamiliar, and invisible dangers, people seek both to embody and assuage their fears in visions of a fourth dimension outside the pale of the quotidian, and beyond life itself.

So thanks a lot, Al Qaeda, for, among other things, ruining the fall season. We now share with Islamic fanatics an all-consuming desire to escape into fantastical imaginings of the Beyond. *Invasion,* however, is by no means inadequate entertainment.

Like Spielberg's *War of the Worlds, Invasion,* premiering tonight, opens with a weather event, in this case a hurricane—the pilot was written and made long before Katrina—and the show moves swiftly and suspensefully as it portrays the small south-Florida town of Homestead, located on the edge of the Everglades, slowly falling into the hands, or whatever, of the new arrivals. I would watch it every week if I weren't so busy stockpiling food and weapons. Our hero is Russell Varon, the divorced father of two, the husband of pregnant Larkin Groves Varon (I can barely imagine making a woman named Larkin pregnant), and the ex-husband of Mariel Underlay, who is the current wife of Sheriff Tom Underlay. Mariel is the extraterrestrials' first victim; I guess the show's writers are having a little fun with the Mariel boat lift, which brought to Florida Cuban criminals (that is, dangerous intruders) along with refugees.

Sound familiar? It should. Anytime aliens take over the minds and bodies of friends and family, they are indebted to the plot of the granddaddy of all paranoid supernatural thrillers, *Invasion of the Body Snatchers,* the 1956 classic that alluded to the perils of both communist and McCarthyite conformity. (Did the producers of that film relish making its star Kevin McCarthy, who also happened to be the brother of Mary McCarthy?) The difference between that earlier *Invasion*—and its later remakes—and ABC's *Invasion* is a précis of cultural change.

For one thing, the celebrated 1950s flick depicted the havoc wreaked by aliens on stable civic and family structures. In the course of the movie, the nice little town of Santa Mira, in southern California—aliens have an eye for valuable real estate—with its nice little families, slowly has its structures of normalcy dismantled and destroyed. But Russell's family has already been deconstructed.

The good sheriff is actually bad—on the emotional level, cultural representations of stepparents are traditionally scary; on the political level, Florida's forces of law and order haven't recently inspired confidence in their legitimacy. Even before the aliens hit town, there's a tension between Russell and Tom. In *Invasion of the Body Snatchers,* the disruption arrives from the outside. Like so much else in popular culture now, *Invasion's* strange intruders seem partly to sprout from bad psychic seeds planted long before their appearance on the scene. You're not surprised to discover that the aliens' first three victims are figures of authority: a doctor, a cop, and a priest. Alongside good-old American impatience with authority is the good-old American reassurance that the problem lies in a faulty system that can be fixed.

But the real difference between the two *Invasions* is the ideological nature of the enemy. Whether as a result of communism or McCarthyism, the inhabited Americans in the first *Invasion* are transformed into conformist zombies. They turn suddenly cold and unfeeling, they all think alike, and they take instructions from some sort of central intelligence. What a difference from today.

Even after they've been commandeered by the aliens, Homestead's victims retain their specialness as distinctive personalities. Mariel has to be encouraged by Tom to stick to their nefarious task once she's been taken over by another form of life. She also retains the appearance of warmth and intimacy. And alien-inhabited as she is, she has a very different "personality" than the alien-possessed priest. The danger in the 1950s *Invasion* was mass conformity. The danger in our *Invasion* is individual malevolence. Mariel and the others are free agents, not fellow travelers. For people who like to make analogies between the terror haunting us now and the menace that faced us during the cold war, that offers some food for thought.

SEPTEMBER 21, 2005

③⓪ *Alias*

There should be daily reports on the status of the individual in America, the way there are hourly reports on the weather and the stock market. By "status," I mean the extent to which the individual is made the touchstone for every kind of experience. You could simply show, on some kind of graph, the degree to which characters in various art forms—novels, plays, movies, television dramas—refer to themselves whenever something happens around them. If there's a movie coming out about an earthquake in California, you could compare it with a movie about the same subject that appeared ten years ago. You'd look at similar characters in both films, a young couple, say, and compare their responses when they felt the quaking commence. Did one of them turn to the other and say:

1. "What was that?"
2. "It's an earthquake, let's get out of here!"
3. "Does this mean the beaches will all be closed?"
4. "Let's get one last smoothie."
5. "Why was my mother so cold to me on Thanksgiving?"

Depending on the answer's SAL (self-absorption level), you could then gauge how much the IRR (individual: reality ratio) has changed over the past decade.

I did my own little comparison, between ABC's new spy drama, *Alias,* and the old *Mission Impossible* (I had to summon the latter from the depths of memory). According to my findings, there was a dramatic, no, an astounding increase in the SAL. This has had the most drastic effect, of course, on the IRR. I don't want to alarm anyone, but this has driven the GSM (general sanity meter) well into the RZ (red zone). The results could well be catastrophic, if not downright soporific.

Ten years ago, when a bomb exploded near one or more of *Mission Impossible*'s agents, their reaction was to take quick action and find the people who were trying to kill them, or something like that. Their response to any event, was to directly address themselves to the event. You barely knew anything about these people. They never shared their secrets with each other. This strange impersonality of the show's characters is what made the series so bracing and what made the characters so intimate and familiar. The fact that their inner life was so tightly sealed and protected against events seemed to be, like Popeye's spinach, the force that nourished their strength in the face of dangerous events and enabled them to prevail. The fact that they were never explicit about what was going on deep inside them allowed each viewer to have his or her own private notion of who each character really was. The characters' lack of publicly delineated individuality accentuated the viewer's imagination and own individuality.

Alias, now experiencing its fourth season, is something like *Mission Impossible*—at moments, its music even campily alludes to the earlier series' famous theme song. There's a spymaster and his perpetually changing multicultural team of operatives: its central character, Sydney Bristow, played by Jennifer Garner (a made-for-TV Julia Roberts), who may very well be the first actress to die from collagen poisoning if someone doesn't do something fast; Vaughan, her handsome former/sometimes/ like, whatever, boyfriend; an Argentine female agent; a black male agent; a short, unglamorous head of technology—performing the same function as Q in the Bond movies—who has most of the show's best (if you can call them that) lines.

Like *Mission Impossible*'s mysterious spymaster Jim Phelps, the team's boss in *Alias*, Arvin Sloane, explains a new assignment at the beginning of each episode as his agents sit around in a chic, bright office somewhere way underground. This is a lot like homeroom in high school, and in fact, the issues that confront the show's characters week after week have less to do with the international terrorists they are always pursuing than with their own personal development. Just about everybody is emotionally entangled with everybody else.

Allow me to take a giant cultural leap. At the heart of two great spiritual cornerstones of Western culture, the Hebrew Bible and ancient Greek tragedy, is a movement out into the world, away from the starting point of family. The Hebrew Bible begins with something like an incestuous relationship between Adam and Eve and ends, with Kings and Samuel, in a vast panorama of protagonists and antagonists unrelated by blood. Aeschylus' *Oresteia* begins with bloodlust stoked within the family, and concludes with the rule of reason and law imposed by the community outside the family. The motion in both these masterworks mirrors the development of the individual, away from parents and siblings and out into the world of strangers. That's pretty much the way things have gone in modern serious and popular culture, too.

Alias, however, is an example of a growing trend, which is to resist the motion into the strange, indifferent world and to substitute family issues for worldly situations and events. One of Sydney's colleagues is her father, though Arvin Sloane, her boss, thinks that he's her real father. Her mother was killed by her father because, as he solemnly explains to Sydney, "your mother was a security risk." (I know exactly what he means.) She put a hit out on Sydney, too. Bitch. Another of Sydney's teammates is her half-sister. A lot of the bad guys themselves are unhappy siblings, murderous spouses, and suchlike. So even the world outside is ruled by the same intimate-emotional dynamic as the emotionally intimate world the team inhabits.

What all this means is that *Alias* is not really about, as its title implies, changing identities. It's about holding onto your groovy little self no matter where you are or what you're doing: running around Moscow looking for an electromagnetic device that will kill hundreds of thousands of people; crashing through a North African bazaar as enemy agents chase you; etc. etc. Even while they're torturing you, you're going to be wondering why Mom and Dad split up.

JANUARY 31, 2005

War

31 *The Hamburg Cell* and *Dirty War*

The speed at which popular culture now dramatizes actual events is extraordinary. I'm not sure whether a movie was made about Kennedy's assassination not long after the event, but it was decades before a film appeared that portrayed Kennedy's murder with real provocative detachment, Oliver Stone's tendentious *JFK*. Two years later, Hollywood finally applied itself bigtime to the Holocaust with *Schindler's List*. There were previous Holocaust films, obviously; but Hollywood gigantism in the treatment of the subject had to await Steven Spielberg. His expertly done movie was thoroughly formulaic, and thoroughly, if understandably, reverential before its subject; and yet it was so unthinkingly arrogant at moments—Spielberg took his imperial camera all the way into the showers themselves—that it could only have been made after nearly two post-Holocaust generations had come and gone.

Indeed, the commercial representation, on the big or small screen, of the Holocaust—of any unspeakable historical tragedy—entails a paradoxical requirement with regard to its intended audience. For the sake of financial success, the film must not primarily address itself to the people who have survived the real historical catastrophe that the film is attempting to depict.

Few of them would accept the reflection of their experience through commerce-warped formulas. *Hotel Rwanda* is an American product, not a Rwandan one, made primarily for American audiences. *Schindler's List* was not made for the Jews who had survived the death camps, and *The Killing Fields* was not made for the Cambodians who had lived through the genocide organized by the Khmer Rouge, and the several films about the genocide in Bosnia—*Welcome to Sarajevo, Harrison's Flowers, Behind Enemy Lines*—did not have in mind an audience of Bosnians. Whatever their emotional or intellectual strengths, those movies could not be profitable unless they hewed to certain movie conventions that refine horror into bearable, even comfortable sadness, and unless they ended on some kind of improving, affirmative note.

In doing so, however, they end up harrowing the memories of the people who were there, and violating the reality of the people who have been violated. *The Killing Fields* was about a brave American journalist who returned home alive to tell the world his horrible tale. A Cambodian film about the genocide would not finish like that, nor would a Bosnian film or a Rwandan film conclude with the image of a foreigner who survived, who will go on with his life. No matter how sensitively done they are, no matter how committed to truth and justice, the only justification for these movies that appear while their subjects—the ones who survived or escaped—are still living is that they are made for people who had no connection to the historical tragedies they portray.

Three years after September 11, 2001, the representations of that day and its consequences in the new world that we now inhabit are starting to appear, and as movies they raise interesting questions. Unlike *Hotel Rwanda* and the rest, they are not about historical tragedies that have taken hundreds of thousands or millions of lives, and whose survivors are still living, in many cases with their agony fresh in their minds. The September 11 films do not, therefore, fall helplessly into that unwitting erasure of experience, into that marginalization of the dead and the near-dead of the other movies. On the contrary, the audience they want to reach is made up of potential victims and survivors, people whose very lives depend upon the outcome of the circumstances that the movies depict—in a word, us. And we have too much of a stake in the subject to be merely entertained. Yet can such movies be anything more than entertainments when they have to follow the formulas and conventions of any movie produced for a mass audience? And what kind of entertainments can they decently be?

Two films that premiered on HBO deal with the attacks of September 11 and the radically new situation left in their wake, and they seem like impossible undertakings, each one beset by its special impossibility. *The Hamburg Cell,* based on "known facts and actual events," as the movie tells us, portrays the hijackers and their accomplices in the years and months leading up to September 11. *Dirty War,* on the other hand, is wholly fictional, though also a fact-based scenario of what might happen if a so-called dirty bomb—low-grade radioactive material dispersed by an explosive—went off in the middle of a workday in the center of London.

One way these movies might have eluded the compromising neutrality of entertainments would have been for their makers to take a crude ideological turn. Such crudeness might have been, at least, a saving authenticity. *The Hamburg Cell,* in particular, must have been vulnerable to that temptation. It could have denied the Al Qaeda members human dimensions and portrayed them as cardboard villains, the way the Germans and the Japanese were depicted in American and British films during World War II. Yet the Final Solution, the Nazis' treatment of their conquered populations, and the Japanese atrocities in Manchuria made the one-dimensional representation of German and Japanese soldiers an ironically full disclosure of their humanity. Crude and flat was what the killers had become as people. (This didn't mean that fuller, more empathetic portraits were not possible; but they started to appear once the conflict with Germany and Japan had settled back beyond the horizon, into history.) And we were at war, a concrete war with known enemies, whose intentions and capabilities were also known.

Or *The Hamburg Cell* could have shown the hijackers as tortured and misguided, manipulated by their environment and by Western exploitation and neglect; and it could have represented their Western targets as being driven by all the corruption and the evil that the West attributes to Islamic militants. The Germans and the Japanese were sometimes depicted in this way long after World War II in American films such as *The Young Lions,* which were sentimental attempts at expanding common human sympathies that the war had contracted. In the current context, such moral equivalences would be the sharpest kind of anti-war propaganda. But *The Hamburg Cell* is neither anti-war nor pro-war. Its attempt at ethical sobriety and narrative poise is proof of the absolute strangeness and tension of this moment in history.

We are at war, and yet you can hardly imagine a movie during World War II depicting a German soldier as anything but one-dimensionally evil. It is proof of the profound ambivalence attending our current conflict that *The Hamburg Cell*—a mostly British production, bought by HBO, an American company—presents the hijackers and their cohorts in a full human light. It is certainly proof of the opaque, somewhat confused nature of the war against terrorism. At the same time—and this is sort of remarkable—the film's terrorists are fully, and humanly, despicable. They are human, but they are monsters. And the cause they slaughter for, their immensely destructive and self-destructive jihad, is depicted with a steady, penetrating, analytical eye as a fundamental—and fundamentalist—deformation of humanity.

In a sense, *The Hamburg Cell* has something of the calm balance of the better World War II films made many years after the war, in which Nazism is not presented as a supernatural force, or as an evil latent in human nature, but as a very particular evil rooted in particular individuals. Watching this film, you realize that what is unique about the war against terrorism is that the terrorists' campaign against the United States consists, in the public mind, of a single assault. The attacks on September 11 have been so often memorialized and commemorated that their singularity has been hallowed; they are often made to seem like flukes of history rather than, as we are constantly being warned—or assured—the first tragedy in a long onslaught against us.

And so there exists alongside all the calls for a resolved and relentless war against the jihadists a popular feeling that the wrenching emotional loss of war is over. Nothing we hear now about the fight against the insurgents in Iraq rises to the moral clarity that seemed to be produced by the events on September 11. This is why we will see more and more non-ideological artistic representations of September 11 and its aftermath, such as *The Hamburg Cell*. Though not committed to a political position, these works will probably infuriate people who believe that the war against terrorism is America's most urgent task. Certainly, both movies refuse to endorse the idea of an endless, permanent offensive against an all-pervasive enemy, and so you could say that they represent a skeptical position with regard to the war. But they are also so clear about the malevolence and the fanaticism that drive the Islamic militants, and about what calamities such emotions might lead to, that they will also disappoint anyone hoping for an anti-war statement.

The most peculiar quality of these movies about a warlike situation is that they have the detachment of peaceful times. *Dirty War*, a simple, literal, strenuously researched scenario of disaster, seems like the chronicle of a horrific event rather than the prediction of one. Its strongest note is ruefulness. It begins with a drill involving firefighters rushing to save lives in the wake of a dirty bomb attack, and then tells the parallel stories of the terrorists' organization of such an assault, the explosion itself, and the attempts to deal with the aftermath while catching the terrorists, who are still at large and planning more attacks. Yet the movie is profoundly low-keyed and sparing in its central human dramas, among them the poignant portrayal of a fire department officer and his wife. Its thrust is a documentary-like conscientiousness about the facts, as if it were not a drama at all but a clarifying supplement to confused, panic-inciting news reports. *Dirty War* is so intent on depicting techniques of bioterror containment and control, so detailed in its enactment of the terrorists' apprehension or destruction, that it has the soothing effect of making you feel that the worst is over. PBS's rebroadcast of the film scheduled for late February, accompanied by a panel of experts on bioterrorism, will doubtlessly reinforce the feeling that *Dirty War* represented a real event, now safely past. Given the hysteria that the Bush administration likes to provoke with its politically timed terror alerts, all this reassurance is hardly a complacency. It is something of a public service.

The term "therapeutic," as applied to any organized experience that is not actually therapy, immediately makes that experience suspect. With regard to a work of art, whether popular or serious, "therapeutic" falls upon it like a doom. But television has always straddled the boundary between popular art and therapeutic consolation. You watch it at home, in your familiar, intimate surroundings; maybe you are not even fully dressed; maybe you are not dressed at all. You could be eating dinner, or relieving yourself, or getting drunk. Until the advent of television, there never was a mass medium for entertainment or information that had such intimacy.

It became inevitable that television would address life's mundane problems because television itself is so mundane, part of the ordinary flow of time the way those problems are. Television has to reflect back to you your own sense of security. It also has to mirror your sense of your own decency and your own limitations. It can't leave you ready for bed with your adrenaline racing, or your thirst for justice unslaked. You cannot be unsettled, shaken, in your own home. Perhaps, very slowly, DVDs—not to mention HBO's raw pioneering dramas—are changing all of that, and creating a new type of nervous system that goes to bed excited and wakes up agitated. For the most part, however, television is a patronizing narcotic, and for all the junk a most respectful medium.

The terrorist threat is so cloudy, faceless, and vague, so manipulable by political purposes, so definitely present but indefinitely manifested, that it sometimes feels interchangeable with everyday dread itself. In other words, the terrorist threat operates on the most intimate level imaginable. The aspect of it that makes the mind complicit with unseen dangers is what makes it so hard to prove, so hard to refute, and so serviceable to so many interests. Its battlefield is, in fact, our familiar surroundings.

The attacks on September 11, after all, destroyed people in their safe, habitual, everyday environments—the heartbreakingly ordinary office papers that floated above Manhattan for days afterward were like an image of terror's apparently enveloping presence and intimate battleground. What better medium, then, exists for the clarification of terror, and for the consolation about terror, than television? Tom Clancy's irresponsible and demented *The Sum of All Fears,* in which a nuclear device is exploded on American soil—not a dirty bomb, a nuclear bomb, which is extremely unlikely—could not have been made for television. The movie would have violated and then burst its medium.

At the heart of both *The Hamburg Cell* and, to a much lesser extent, *Dirty War* is the relationship between two people, a man and a woman. This time-tested Hollywood convention of reducing every type of conflict, even actual historical conflict, to a romantic relationship is often the worst kind of cop-out. (It would make more sense to reduce romantic relationships to historical conflicts.) But given the intimate nature of the terrorist threat, the decision of *The Hamburg Cell*'s creators to center their true story on the courtship and marriage of Ziad Jarrar, the Lebanese dental student who hijacked one of the planes headed for Washington, to Aysel, a Muslim Turkish student he met while studying in Germany, makes sense. It puts a human face on all the talk of the war on terrorism, which sometimes rises to the level of the supernatural, or occult, or begins to echo dialectical materialism's absolute certainty of final, resolving, historical conflict.

The Hamburg Cell begins and ends with Ziad standing in the terminal of Newark Airport, where he is about to board his final flight in this life. We see him on a pay phone talking with Aysel, his wife, to whom he has lied for month after month, promising her that he will cut off the murderous nutcases who are sinking into hell with him, that they will have a quiet, peaceful life, with children, in a good place, in a nice house. His almost astonishing deceitfulness runs parallel, throughout the movie, to his gradual transformation into a suicide-killer, and to his fellow jihadists' evolving plans for their attacks on the United States. He stands with the phone to his ear, refusing to answer Aysel's nervous questions about where he is and what he is doing—she has no idea—responding to her only by repeating, over and over again, the words "I love you."

For the entire movie, as Ziad has become twisted into a murderer, his sole response to Aysel's recriminations and desperate pleas has been this simple, timeless phrase: "I love you." What he really means is, "I hate you." But he has so completely identified his ideals with his motives, and his motives with the world outside him, that his feeling about another human being thoroughly absorbs that person's reality. He is too vain to nakedly hate Aysel. He has to flatter his ego by "loving" her as he is destroying her. "Do not cause the discomfort of those you are killing," one of the hijackers' handlers commands them, with outrageously self-deluded sanctimony, as he quickly teaches them some incapacitating martial-arts techniques in a hotel room a few hours before the attacks. In *Dirty War,* the chief terrorist savors his own virtue by giving his wife detailed instructions for the care, after his death, of their son.

I have no idea whether Ziad's conversation at the airport is what actually transpired, or whether it is one of this movie's modest embellishments. But it has the perfect effect. War-against-terrorism purists might fear the soft-seeming quality of such stuff. To my mind, though, it does the right kind of work. It gives evil the demystified face of (as Americans like to say) an asshole. It gives a comprehensible correlative to the self-deceit that fanaticism cultivates and thrives on. And it implies that just as "love" can be a war cry, and a free pass, to the indulgence of some deep-hidden enmity, so evil can be—perhaps is, in its essence—the putrid excess of self-conscious and self-justifying goodness.

FEBRUARY 7, 2005

The Unit

"Guys like that, I like to fuck their wives." That's from *American Buffalo*, David Mamet's classic play about three losers plotting a petty burglary. The line is spoken by Teach, an amalgam of limp machismo, brute self-delusion, and street-wisdom that undermines him and his two pals even as it clarifies the big American picture. He's talking about a successful young businessman across the street, whom Teach viciously envies. The irony is that he couldn't even get within talking distance of the type of woman guys like that marry.

Like all of this elementally brilliant playwright's best work—to my mind, some of the greatest American plays ever written—*American Buffalo* beautifully walks that thin Mametian line between celebrating maleness and deconstructing some of its more rotten hidden qualities. Maybe the quintessential hero of Mamet's world is Ricky in *Glengarry Glen Ross,* a work of art that possesses Sophoclean dimensions. You might remember Al Pacino's electric performance of this rich character in the film version of the play. For all his posturing as an insouciant Romeo, for all his ultra-smooth deceitfulness, Ricky's virtue lies not in his masculinity but in his awareness of his own inauthenticity, in his realization that putting on a show of virility is, really, the essence of what society deems to be virile. Unlike

Teach, Ricky has maintained a border between his appearance of machismo and his feline sense of life's limitations. Such self-knowledge lies behind his compassion for a colleague (Jack Lemmon, whose success as an actor was to perform failure to perfection) who is down on his luck. The tough guy as also a self-sacrificing, sympathetic guy defines one type of Mametian hero. Think Sean Connery in Mamet's *The Untouchables* or, more recently, Val Kilmer in *Spartan*.

Spartan's world of secret special-forces operatives brings us to *The Unit,* a new dramatic series on CBS that Mamet created, produced, and wrote. It is a somewhat startling but wholly predictable development that America's finest living playwright has tumbled happily into the tube. After all, top-flight Hollywood directors now make commercials for American Express that you can see on TV or the Internet. Mark my words: Soon, if you have ten million dollars to spare, you'll be able to get Ridley Scott to direct a film dramatization of your daughter's sixteenth birthday party. Unfortunately, Mamet's submersion in television has hastened a growing deficiency in his art.

Maybe putting *The Unit* on a cable channel would have provided a more welcoming artistic context for Mamet—at first glance, it's astonishing that a playwright who used to take such faultless aim at America's business culture would try to find a creative haven on a commercial TV network. But here is where the deepening flaw in Mamet's work rears its head. The splendor of Mamet's art lies in its balance of fascinated attention to the worst aspects of American character with the urge to expose and explode them. But nowadays, Mamet's fascination with the amoral pursuit of the almighty buck seems to have tipped over into mundane pursuit of the almighty buck. In the same way, his celebration of masculinity has almost completely overtaken his exposure of masculinity's pretenses. Mamet is now more obsessed with conventional, little-boy ideas of what it means to be a man than Teach was.

Both tendencies converge in *The Unit*, a show about a special strike force that is almost embarrassingly similar to last season's ill-fated series on FX about American soldiers in Iraq, *Over There*, the difference being that Mamet's soldiers fight their battles in various places throughout the world. (*The Unit*'s background music is identical to the background music for the Bourne movies. The series is cursed by derivativeness.) So far, they've been dispatched to Afghanistan to take out a terrorist; to an Idaho airport (of all places) to rescue a plane full of conventioneering Europeans that's been hijacked by more Middle Eastern terrorists; and to the Serengeti Desert to retrieve a Chinese satellite and, serendipitously, snatch a much sought-after European terrorist. *The Unit*'s main villains are terrorists, natch.

Like *Over There*, *The Unit* switches back and forth between the men fighting and their wives back home struggling to survive their husband's absence and the possibility that the men might never return. *Over There*'s portrait of life back in the States was trite and crude, but at least it lacked self-conscious solemnity about its artistic purpose. In *The Unit*, however, Mamet seems to have staked the series' artistic dimension on his depiction of the wives' embattled domestic lives. The women's problems with, for example, *The Unit*'s martinet commander—who is also sleeping with one of the wives—serve the purpose of deconstructing Mamet's old target, the American myth of manhood. Mamet used to do this with hybrid characters like Teach and Ricky, men whose leathery toughness had plentiful holes and patches. But in *The Unit* you have a bizarre sort of segregation. The combat half of the show inflates the masculine myth for all it's worth, in the manner of the standard action-adventure series. The back-home half, on the other hand, very self-consciously bears the burden of Mamet's complicating, ambiguity-making art.

What you get is a show constricted by radical artistic compromises that it refuses to acknowledge having made. The result is an expulsion of Mamet's distinctive vision into the margins of the series, where it wanders around like a director who's been fired from a movie yet will not leave the set. The dialogue in the "male" half of the show—the liberal Jewish Mamet has actually succeeded in structuring his television debut like an Orthodox synagogue—is so much a mere filler between action sequences that it's like a parody of vintage Mamet lines, which once fused bravado with infinite pianissimo cross-currents and ironies. *The Unit*'s skipper, convincingly played by Dennis Haysbert, at one point tells a comrade about an episode in Afghanistan that almost foiled an operation: "We had an incident with [a mule]—sent us back to first principles." This is not meant to be funny-tough. It's meant to be almost entirely tough—what humor there is exists between the author and himself as he laughs all the way to the bank. Mamet patented the overblown comic mixture of tough-guy talk with awkward formal language—you hear the stylized brawn of his cadences in every line of *The Sopranos*. But *The Unit* is TV doing Mamet in half-travesty of his hallmark style.

It's no better in the "women's" section. Domestic drama, and especially the relations between women, has never been Mamet's strong suit. But in the back-home segments, Mamet forces himself, to disastrous effect, to pump up the domestic stretches in order to compensate for the monolithic action-sequences. In one scene, the wife of *The Unit*'s newest member has to console a woman she knows who has just learned that her husband was killed in action. At first, the grief-struck woman is hostile. Then she collapses in tears. She pulls coldly away again. You wait, moved and riveted, for the scene to develop. Instead, Mamet fabricates another filler. The visiting consoler asks the new widow if she remembers a yellow blouse that she once bought especially to wear one evening with her now-dead husband, the other woman nods with tears running down her face and then falls sobbing into her friend's arms. It's a textbook theatrical strategy, the construction of a scene out of a brief story revolving around a memory, or an object. In *The Unit*, the contrived moment sticks out like a sore trigger-finger. The Story of the Yellow Blouse is so isolated a self-conscious device that the sudden humanity of the moment just as suddenly dissolves into a formal segue empty of even superficial emotional truth.

And then it's back to men fighting, once the subject of admiring, fascinated, skeptical, detached, amused, ironic Mametian playfulness, and now seemingly the writer's all-consuming obsession. The wives in this show, and the viewers too, really are getting you-know-what.

MARCH 21, 2006

33 Over There

There is a revealing difference between the title of FX's new war drama set in Iraq, *Over There*, and "Over There," George M. Cohan's celebrated tune, written and performed just months after America's enthusiastic entry into World War I. Cohan's "over there" is a tidy problem of a place to which we're looking forward to sending American troops in order to clear things up. The atmosphere that is waiting for us over there is characterized by freedom-starved Europeans "calling, you and me, every son of liberty," and wicked Germans:

> *Johnnie, get your gun*
> *Get your gun, get your gun*
> *Johnnie show the Hun*
> *Who's a son of a gun.*

With its image of the fluttering American flag—"Hoist the flag and let her fly / Yankee Doodle do or die"—the song evokes the American cavalry galloping to the rescue. The conviction at the heart of Cohan's lyrics is that simply going there is enough to solve what's over there—the song is so lighthearted about this certainty that it ends with a play on words:

Send the word, send the word to beware.
We'll be over, we're coming over,
And we won't come back till it's over
Over there.

Two and a half years ago, people in favor of invading Iraq proclaimed their feeling that American troops were going to be a deus ex machina warmly welcomed by a nation long mired in tragedy. But nobody is expressing that feeling now. (I wonder if intelligent adults with the slightest sense of history and human nature even believed what they were saying about liberating Americans and grateful Iraqis back then.) So the new show's title is a grimly clever inflection of the old patriotic song. "Over there" is not where we are going to rescue and rebuild, and then return home. The phrase "over there" now has the foul power of an imprecation, a mysterious, obscene euphemism for a riddle inside an enigma wrapped in a ceaseless slaughter. In this new series' idiom, you utter the words with a profane hush, the way some people used to refer to the "evil one" without ever mentioning his name. Unfortunately, this new show's title is the only worthy thing about it.

Only at the end of the Vietnam War did you get a television series, *M*A*S*H*, that obviously referred to the futility of the conflict in Southeast Asia. Yet *M*A*S*H* was set in Korea and dealt with a war America had fought twenty years earlier—you never heard the word "Vietnam" uttered in that show. And what was singular about that series was that it never showed men fighting. There was barely, if any, violence in *M*A*S*H*. Indeed, as the war in Vietnam took more and more American lives, as the television news got bloodier and bloodier, violence actually declined on television. In 1968, the year in which the

Tet Offensive took place, and Martin Luther King and Bobby Kennedy were assassinated, and police beat protesters in the streets in Chicago, *Gunsmoke* decided to drop its famous opening gunfight. Yet here we are, in Iraq for less than three years, and now we have a television war drama, which is not just set in Iraq, but whose plots bizarrely echo events reported in the newspaper you read that morning. Most unsettling of all, *Over There* is perhaps the most graphically violent show ever to appear as a television series.

The relentless dispatches from Iraq describing suicide bombings and mass shootings, limbs flying and heads bursting, bewildered American soldiers and innocent Iraqi civilians dying in great numbers—you would think Americans would be so disgusted or outraged by all this carnage that they would not want to be entertained by carnage. But in *Over There,* you witness the special effect of an insurgent's torso being blown off and his two disconnected legs continuing to run for a few more steps. I guess this just has pretty much the same emotional resonance as the camera lingering on the faces of humiliated losers on the reality shows—in which case *Over There* will be a nice big hit.

But I don't think so. *Over There* is going to be too much even for the stupid legions who sit with glazed eyes before *The Apprentice* or *Hell's Kitchen.* For one thing, the series' co-creator, *NYPD Blue*'s Steven Bochco—Chris Gerolmo is the series' other originator—has transplanted all the formulas from his legendary police show to the Iraqi landscape. But the devices that made *NYPD Blue* so gripping make *Over There* hard to take seriously. Complicated psychological conflict against the background of periodic violence is not the same thing as complicated psychological conflict against the background of constant violence. A great war movie like *Saving Private Ryan* tells simple, sentimental stories about its characters and their relationships to each other. Bochco and Gerolmo have racial tension, and gender tension, and conflicted psyches, and on, and on, and on. But war doesn't leave much time for all of that. The perpetual danger of violent death on the one hand and unrelieved tedium on the other flatten psychology.

For all their "complexity," *Over There*'s characters don't even come across as plausible personalities. Frank "Dim" Dumphy is a highly educated graduate of Cornell whom we see screaming in the show's opening sequences at his wife, who is less cultivated than Frank and from a lower class. Yet after seeing his friend's leg blown off by an enemy mine, Frank intervenes to help an Iraqi prisoner—a definite insurgent—from being roughed up. Even after the prisoner briefly breaks free and attacks Frank before being wrestled to the ground, Frank—the enraged husband—suffers an anguished conscience as he watches the prisoner getting "tortured," that is, made to stand in a "stress position." Men in war rarely react so kindly to the enemy after seeing their friend's leg blown off. Especially men with bad tempers.

As for *Over There*'s idea of torture, I have no idea what a "stress position" looks like—is it sitting up and taking notice?— but this one resembles yoga more than the organ-crushing pulverizations described by the *New York Times*' Tim Golden in his unforgettable articles on American torture of prisoners in Afghan prisons. If Golden doesn't get a Pulitzer and Bochco receives an Emmy, I'm off to Canada.

From the show's opening sequence, in which American soldiers pinned down by insurgent gunfire expound plot particulars to each other over the din, you lose the sense that you're watching a show about war. There is no utter chaos of violence in *Over There*. There is just shocking special-effects violence. The opening battle scene in *Saving Private Ryan* and the long battle sequence in Orson Welles' astounding *Chimes at Midnight*—the two finest war scenes in film—are enough to make you a pacifist. *Over There*'s re-creations of war merely enliven and then dull your senses. Partly this is because the series uses the traditional "innovative" TV camera—its jumps and swerves manhandle the violence, as it were. But there is one main reason why *Over There* fails utterly as a convincing portrait of armed conflict. Unlike *Saving Private Ryan* and *Chimes at Midnight* and just about every other great war movie, *Over There* uses music during its battle scenes. Music, fancy camerawork, and violent special effects: *Over There* wants to be a great war movie, but it has the soul and the reflexes of cheap commercial television.

As other people have pointed out, we're at war, but we don't feel like we're at war. *Over There* will only reinforce that segregation from reality. Since television in the 1960s and 1970s became less violent as the Vietnam War became more of an absurdist slaughterhouse, the fact that we now have a super-violent show about the Iraq War, as that war is being fought, perhaps means that we have a long way to go before Iraq touches the national nervous system and conscience. Until then, *Over There*'s unprecedentedly extreme violence, padded with music and a buffering camera, will serve the purpose of protecting us from the real violence.

AUGUST 3, 2005

Documentaries
and "Special
Reports"

34 *Ghosts of Rwanda*

Ghosts of Rwanda, a powerful, necessary documentary shown by PBS to commemorate the tenth anniversary of the Rwandan genocide, reminds you of the "other television" the way Michael Harrington once reminded complacent readers of the "other America," the impoverished and dispossessed one. By "other television," I mean the television of attention as opposed to the television of diversion. For we can forget, as high and popular art bend themselves more and more toward real experiences that might be familiar to us, that there are vast regions of the real that we have never experienced, and probably never will experience. To comprehend these exotic and sometimes wretched precincts of life requires a focused viewer every bit as much as a focused camera.

We can forget, too, watching so-called innovative drama on television, that as popular culture proceeds with its multidimensional project of making itself more real—that is, more documentary-like—more violent, more honest about sordid human motives and the universality of moral hypocrisy, there are moments in life—real life—that are unreal in their dishonesty, violence, sordidness, and moral hypocrisy. In moments like these, the heroism that countless advanced movies and television shows have taught us to be suspicious of becomes the only hope for people trapped in horrific circumstances. For a journalist or a historian, uncovering such instances of self-sacrifice is as much a mark of originality as uncovering base human motives has become the mark of seriousness for much television and film.

As an act of memory and witness; as historical indictment of not just the perpetrators of genocide, but also of the politicians and bureaucrats who allowed it to happen; as an illumination of the motives driving the murderers, as well as those animating the individuals caught in an unimaginable situation, *Ghosts of Rwanda* fails to tell a coherent story. It fails to illuminate the psychology of the U.N. and U.S. officials who refused to deploy troops that would have saved perhaps half of the 800,000 Rwandans killed over a three-month period from April to July 1994. It fails to offer viewers consolation for its images of men, women, and children hacked to death by machetes, or to offer reassurance that international mechanisms are now in place to prevent such atrocities from happening again. That is to say, *Ghosts of Rwanda* is a success; it is a scathing accomplishment almost on the same level of urgency as Samantha Power's vital ray of light, *A Problem from Hell: America and the Age of Genocide.*

Violent, gritty, sordidness-exposing television drama ends on a note of happiness, coherence, and illumination. But documentaries that approach evil, and that seek the faint glimmer of heroism amid carnage, if they are true to events, do not end satisfyingly. Consider *Ghosts of Rwanda*, which concludes with then President Clinton blaming his inaction on "the people bringing these decisions to me," and emoting that "I'll always regret that Rwandan thing." Honest documentaries about extreme events do not end, period.

An effective documentary has just about every medium of expression at its disposal: the interview; historical footage; written text; an avid, polished camera; fancy editing; atmospheric or manipulative music. But in the same way as great actors underplay their emotions, a great documentary has to underplay its resources. To my mind, the most successful documentary about the Holocaust is Claude Lanzmann's *Shoah*, because the film despairs of its own medium's claims to verisimilitude, a humbleness that is a near impossibility nowadays when film revels in its own Promethean capacities. But *Shoah* constrained its lens the way some mythic heroes blinded themselves to gain insight. Lanzmann's film avoided any attempt at visually representing the events of the Holocaust and relied solely on a steady camera trained on the faces of survivors and witnesses who tell their stories, thus forcing viewers to imaginatively enter a space that a filmmaker's imagination, let alone technique, is powerless to make accessible. *Shoah*'s anti-esthetic plainness is a fundamental criterion for documentaries about the operation of evil in human life. In one degree or another, such films have to obey the anti-esthetic law.

Ghosts of Rwanda is mildly obstructed by *Frontline*'s customary foreboding music, by the film's vague, visual analogies between foggy events and shots of mist rising over Rwandan hills, and by the trademark tones of its cosmically consoling narrator—as if liberal, secular public television had substituted for an omniscient God an Investigative Voice. But the film, written, produced, and directed by Greg Barker, is as subdued and matter-of-fact as its subject is ultimately ungraspable.

On April 6, 1994, the airplane carrying Rwandan President Juvenal Habyarimana was shot down—to this day, no one knows who fired the fatal missile. Habyarimana was a member of the country's majority Hutu population, and extremist members of his government used his assassination as a pretext to derail the U.N. agreement known as the Arusha Accords, which laid out a power-sharing arrangement between the Hutu and Rwanda's Tutsi minority. The two tribes had been at murderous odds since Rwanda's independence from Belgium in 1962 put the privileged Tutsi under Hutu rule, inciting some Tutsi to create a rebel army in 1990 and try to topple the Hutu regime. For the next three months after the president's death, Hutu extremists went on a genocidal rampage, whipping up ordinary Hutus with propaganda and playing on Hutu memories of Tutsi oppression. The peacekeeping forces sent by the United Nations in 1993 to enforce the accords were ordered by Kofi Annan, the U.N.'s secretary-general at the time, to limit themselves to evacuating Westerners living in Rwanda.

It is one of life's perversities that those who should forget, for their sake or for the sake of others, cannot stop remembering; and that those who should remember, for the sake of a human future, seek the solace of being able to forget. The film's title, *Ghosts of Rwanda,* refers not only to the victims of genocide but also to the images of their destruction that haunt people who were powerless to help. Indeed, a stark revelation is the difference between people-of-action whom crushing events have turned reflective and introspective, and people-of-action who refuse to own up to their actions and remain immune to self-examination and second thoughts, and perhaps also to depression and thoughts of self-destruction.

One member of the former group is Major General Romeo Dallaire, a genuinely tragic figure, the commander of the U.N. peacekeeping forces in Rwanda who was forbidden by Annan to intervene in the genocide, and from whom the film radiates outward in its various directions: personal, political, military. It is one thing to see the face of Dallaire, who looks as though he had aged thirty years since the events of 1994, and the faces of Carl Wilkin, an Adventist relief worker and the only American to stay in Rwanda after the evacuation, and Gromo Alex, a U.N. relief worker who returned on his own to try to save people, or Philippe Gaillard, who ran the International Red Cross mission in Rwanda and defied the Red Cross' insistence on its workers' silence and neutrality, and the Senegalese peacekeeping captain, Mbaye Daigne, who all alone saved perhaps one hundred lives before he was finally killed by a mortar shell—it is one thing to see these faces, worked-over, lined, worried, humanized by turmoil inside them and all around them, and the porcelain complacent face of Anthony Lake, Clinton's national security adviser, as he brightly confesses to having made a mistake and then smiles again, as though shrugging with his eyes. But the contrast between the former faces, in which experience has been forced into consciousness by a frantic conscience, and Clinton's glazed, needy, other-obsessed, eternally boylike face, which is impervious to experience, is almost ghastly. They are like two tribes, Dallaire's and Clinton's, the tribe of the sigh and the tribe of the shrug, the latter in the overwhelming majority.

Perhaps, though, the film's widest resonance is more immediate. If, during the Rwandan genocide, Clinton was afraid to act unilaterally without the other members of the U.N. Security Council, we are now living with the consequences of a president who did just that in order to act aggressively rather than defensively (though he relied on the defensive argument). Some liberals were appalled by Clinton's ass-covering postulation during Rwanda that America could not involve itself in foreign situations unless American interests were at stake, a policy formulated at the time by a special assistant to Clinton named Richard Clarke (at least he is consistent). Yet some of the same liberals, with defiant, newfound Thucydidean hardness, supported Bush's defensive rationale for the invasion and occupation of Iraq. And whereas the death of a few American soldiers in Somalia paralyzed the United States in its response to Rwanda and Bosnia, the deaths of dozens of American soldiers per month in Iraq seem only to harden American resolve to remain there. Could it be that Americans associate rescue missions with something nurse-like, something passive and therapeutic and effeminate, but support a continuing American presence in Iraq because it bears the more virile undercurrent of retaliation and revenge for September 11? If that is the case, then perhaps we need a serious television drama about peacekeepers allowed to take action, and rescuers with the capacity to strike back.

APRIL 1, 2004

35 *The Children of Lenigradsky*

Who needs the irony of twenty/twenty hindsight when you can see the present right before your eyes?

From the countless reports published after September 11 on the impoverishment and despair in the Islamic world, you can infer that anyone who observed those circumstances before September 11 should have seen the Twin Towers crumbling long before it happened. (Unless, that is, you're Thomas Friedman, and so dazzled by your own pedestrian thought processes—Look Ma! I can conceptualize!—that you are blind to the reality outside your head.) Never mind the big ideas about historical trends, and traditional antagonisms, and shifting paradigms. In the everyday life of any given place lies the shape of its future.

If you were to propose to a newspaper or magazine editor a story about Moscow's homeless children, you'd probably get asked if there was a porn angle to it, and if your answer was no, you'd probably be told to go find something more original— something, you know, with a porn angle to it. That's why Cinemax's *The Children of Lenigradsky* is such a welcome event, despite the fact that the film is yet another documentary about yet another pathology in Russian life. A decade or two from now, countless reports about some catastrophic development in Russia will provoke people into demanding to know why "we didn't see it coming." The seeds of what might be coming are right here, in this raw thirty-five-minute film.

The documentary estimates, very broadly, that since the collapse of the Soviet Union, one to four million children have become homeless throughout Russia. (According to a less alarmist recent report in the news, there are about 750,000 Russian orphans.) The *Children of Lenigradsky* takes as its subject two groups of homeless children, in Moscow's Lenigradsky and Kursky train stations. It records their stories of fleeing from alcoholic, physically abusive parents—alcoholism is the catalyst behind all their tragedies—and of living on the street and in sewers. The police catch them and beat them. Pedophiles prey on them, and in order to subsist day after day, most of them turn to prostitution to survive. While Roman Polanski slyly trades on the notoriety of his conviction for statutory rape by directing *Oliver Twist,* here is the real Victorian degradation unfolding as if in a time-warp, in Moscow, once the capital of political modernism.

Along with the heartbreaking tales of humiliation, rape, and murder is the bizarre physical background of much of the film. Built under Stalin's supervision, the most beautiful subway stations in the world are in Moscow. The escalators rapidly convey passengers up and down at what seems like an almost vertical incline. Magnificent art deco vaults adorn a few stations. Some are embellished by intricately laid mosaics—lines from Mayakovsky adorn the gaily colored tiles in one station. Leave it to the Soviets to construct deep below the surface of the earth their most enduring architectural paeans to a utopian future, avant-garde edifices roughly at the level of the gold mines in Kolyma.

Stricken lands burst with poetic ironies, so it's not surprising that the sight of these poor, dispossessed children should remind you of the slave-laborers who once worked the depths of the Soviet gulags. These brutalized orphans are the consequence of a reckless liberty that hasn't yet worked itself out into genuine freedom. But unlike the vast numbers of starving children in Africa, most of whom will die, the majority of the homeless children of Moscow will, on the evidence of this film, somehow survive. (Though the scenes that depict the death of one of the children—a hauntingly beautiful fourteen-year-old girl named Tanya—seemingly from sniffing an overdose of glue, are almost impossible to watch.) That is the point at which this chronicle of a human tragedy becomes the foretelling of a political tragedy.

As you watch some of these children fighting with each other, their faces deformed and hardened by unaccountable suffering, and then turning their feelings of powerlessness and humiliation into a merciless rage against homeless adults—"bums," as the orphans call them—whom they pummel and sometimes set on fire (a rage against these alcoholic adults that is also perhaps a displaced rage against their parents), you begin to get spine-chilling glimpses of Russia's future and, therefore, of the future of every other place Russia touches. And this is happening in Moscow; in the Russian countryside, where Western journalists rarely venture, conditions are even more relentlessly bleak and soul-hardening. A country that chews up its children is mired in a lethal self-hatred and loathing of life. It's sorrowful to know that many of these children won't make it to adulthood. It's horrifying to think that of those who will, some will flourish by means of everything their past taught them about human nature.

SEPTEMBER 28, 2005

36 *Transgeneration*

The response to *Transgeneration*—a documentary that follows four transgender college students through one year at their four respective schools—has been extraordinary. There's been no response. Not a single major news publication has reviewed the series, which has just concluded on the Sundance Channel.

Yet here is a show about young, college-age people, and no one even turns his head to see whether it's the real thing or just another sexually exploitative curiosity. And it is the real thing. Approaching it, you're ready for the usual cloying, sensationalizing camera, amateur editing, and self-centered, self-promoting subjects. Instead you encounter an ongoing drama that has the framework of tragedy, with some rich comic moments.

As in tragedy, these four kids—Gabbie and Raci are boys who have become girls; Lucas and T.J. girls who have become boys—have found their desire for happiness running up against the brick wall of a limiting condition. They are genetically destined to live as the opposite sex, just as other people are biologically fated to be the gender they are given at conception. It's incredible that in this cultural moment, when so much is being written about genetics, and about sociobiology's possible applications to various dimensions of life, no one has taken up this show as a new kind of drama. Not Sophoclean or Shakespearean, but Chromosomal tragedy. "To have the organ there," says Gabbie with distaste, the only one of the four to have a sex-change operation, graphically portrayed in the film. "To have no emotional attachment to it, to just want to get rid of it."

The scope of their alienation is staggering. They're not necessarily gay; they are not sure whom they are attracted to, or whom they should attract. The person they most desire is who they really are, beneath their antithetical biology—and yet, strangely, they are no more narcissistic than anyone else, maybe even less so. Perhaps they are so focused on growing into themselves by becoming wholly other that they've been spared the contemporary disease of self-involution. They exist in a limbo of identity, yet that limbo is their identity, which is to straddle the highly exclusive spectrum (only two members) of sexual gender.

In their rare transmigration, they recall Diane Arbus' remark, that whereas we all live in fear of some traumatizing event, "freaks" are born with their trauma; they live in it and through it. Arbus, perhaps with distasteful condescension, said this made them "aristocrats." (But she proved her sincerity when she took her own life.) The experience of living in one gender and then another confers on these four students—they are students to the nth degree, in the grip of an ultimate lesson about identity and society—the status (if not the gift) of prophets, or seers.

Though it might seem newsy and contemporary, the subject of transgendering (it's about to surface again in a feature film about a boy and his transgender mother) is a hallowed old phenomenon. One of the most interesting aspects of this fascinating documentary is that it shows the four kids researching sex-change operations, hormonal treatments, and the like, but you never see any of them reading up on transgenderism in history and myth.

They might have felt empowered by reading the story of Tiresias, or by knowing that in various ancient cultures shamans were men who dressed and acted like women, eventually marrying other men. But this is America, and their journeys are strictly fore-grounded in the medical technologies of surgery, drugs, and counseling, which has the effect of both normalizing their fate and turning it into an illness that can be cured, or repaired.

Sometimes their stories really do rise to the level of myth or fairy tale. Raci is a beautiful Philippino boy who is now a beautiful Philippino woman. So delicate and ultra-feminine was she as a boy that she would have had as hard a time with certain gay men as with certain straight men. As the show points out, no form of sexuality is as much the object of violent rage as being transgender.

Besides having to become a girl, Raci is also poor and almost deaf. There is a dark comedy to her ordeal. ("Don't flirt," an older transgender friend warns her before she goes out one night, which Raci mishears as the unhelpful "Don't fear.") In this episode, Raci has to buy her hormones illegally, from street dealers, because she can't afford them otherwise. But when she is unable to find her connection, time starts to run out. Her voice deepens, her alluring looks begin to sink back into their original mistaken form. If you could tell that story as a tale about a person and not a category, you would have a great American novel.

In the end, these kids are misfits. They are drawn to misfits, and misfits are drawn to them. Their parents themselves, mostly understanding—at least in front of the cameras—be-come misfits by virtue of wanting to love their misfit children. (The most exquisite moments of comic pathos include the al-most running joke of Lucas' father declaring, over and over, how he has come to be proud of his son, and to love his son, and to know that his son is a rare, fine, wonderful human being and then, after each time he says this, breaking down and sobbing.) In college, the four construct a sheltered world of misfits, all of them struggling to negotiate who they really are, what they have been given instead, and what society will allow them to accomplish and to have. They face very difficult lives. They deserve the utmost attention.

NOVEMBER 15, 2005

37 *The Staircase*

The Staircase—an eight-part documentary about a sensational 2003 murder trial in Durham, North Carolina—premiered over the course of eight weeks on the Sundance Channel. The film, as critics have said, is an extraordinary, and extraordinarily riveting, piece of work that holds the American judicial system up to unsettling scrutiny. In other words, it does not fail to show you what you've long suspected—or you perhaps have experienced—was there. *The Staircase* leaves you emotionally jolted, intellectually stimulated, and in awe of the filmmakers' psychological subtlety. Yet you also come away from it feeling that you have been unsettled in this way before.

The mad arbitrariness of the legal system; each side's effort to tell a more believable story rather than discover the truth; the way in which social and cultural prejudices distort a jury's perceptions; the overarching influence of ego and careerism on the part of defense lawyers, district attorneys, and judges; the media's unforgivable deformations of a trial's already warped reality—the only film I've seen that captures the justice system's Einsteinian universe better than this documentary directed by Frenchman Jean-Xavier de Lestrade is Errol Morris' *Thin Blue Line*. Morris and Lestrade, in fact, seem to have exhausted the genre. After all the questions *The Staircase* raises about the American court system—*Quis custodiet custodes ipsos?*—it raises questions about its own methods and authority. Who will film the filmmakers themselves?

For just about every public realm in American life, we've been told that there has occurred an event after which everything in that realm was never the same. Vietnam changed foreign policy, Watergate changed domestic politics, the Lewinsky scandal changed the media, the Internet changed human consciousness, and on and on. If scientists were ever able to prove that, in fact, nothing significant about the human condition has changed since Neolithic times—dinner at the White House might actually prove that—the country would experience a collective nervous breakdown. Allow me, however, to add to all this historical fictionalizing. In the realm of that favorite American obsession, The Trial, the turning point was the trial of O. J. Simpson.

Just as Watergate undermined confidence in the political system, American faith in the legal system was profoundly shaken when Simpson's high-powered and impossibly expensive defense team won him a verdict of not guilty despite, what seemed to most people, Simpson's transparent guilt in the murder of his estranged wife and her boyfriend. After that event, media and cultural representations of The Trial got divided into two antithetical types.

On the one hand, there is the reassuring pedestrian factuality documented by Court TV, and also the reassuring black-and-white certainties of stern, maternal Judge Judy. Interestingly, fewer and fewer feature films appear that deal with the legal system in the old, reassuring manner of, say, *The Verdict*—the cathartic function of these films seems to have been taken over by comforting television series. On the other hand, you have the prosecutorial commentary of talking legal heads like the demented Nancy Grace, vindictive screeds that channel the audience's resentments. These are equally reassuring. The legal system may be so corrupt that it allows rich murderers to go free, but they can't escape the cable Furies. You can count on Grace to make sure no dispensation of grace is ever afforded to a defendant in a capital case.

Films like *The Staircase* are a necessary corrective to both these television trends. Lestrade's documentary is clearly on the side of defendant Michael Peterson—the successful novelist and ex-Marine accused of killing his second wife, Kathleen, who was found lying at the bottom of their stairs, covered with blood. But as in *The Thin Blue Line, The Staircase* is neither reassuringly positive nor reassuringly negative. As in Morris' film, you are left feeling that no matter what the verdict in Peterson's case, justice will not have been served. Like Oedipus' riddle, the question of Peterson's guilt is ultimately insoluble because the human condition is ultimately incurable. Mercy, such films seem to say, echoing Brecht in *The Threepenny Opera,* is superior to justice. Mercy resolves life's ultimate uncertainty into the self-created certitude of forgiveness, while "justice" merely affirms and sustains all the confusion.

In Peterson's case, the uncertainty consisted of this: The prosecution never found the murder weapon and argued unconvincingly that Peterson was driven by two motives to dispose of his wife. The first was that he was secretly gay, she found out, they fought, and he took her life. The second was less a motive than an insidious precedent: Another woman friend of Peterson's was found, years before when he was stationed in Germany as a Marine captain after the Vietnam War, lying dead at the bottom of her stairs, covered in blood, hours after being with him. Though the German police concluded that no foul play was involved, the Durham prosecutors exhumed the body and a Durham medical examiner judged that she had been murdered. No motive was ascribed to Peterson in that case, either.

Lestrade seizes on the prosecution's weak arguments and sets out to show that Peterson was, as Lestrade told an interviewer, unfairly targeted and railroaded because "for the white establishment, [the white, politically liberal Peterson] is a traitor. In my opinion, he was prosecuted for being a danger, for the values defended by the prosecution, which match up more or less with the values defended by Bush—very conservative and religious, a narrow vision of life." In other words, Lestrade has his own values, which shaped his film—six and a half hours documenting a five-month trial—the way all the countervailing forces in the trial shaped and deformed the reality of what actually happened.

Bush's dishonesty and moral cretinism are, to my mind, by this point irrefutable. Under a better legal system, Bush would not be president; he would be captain of his cellblock's softball team. But Lestrade, who won an Academy Award for a film about a black man falsely accused of killing a white tourist in Florida, is a French carpetbagger exploiting the crudest caricatures of American life. After convincing Peterson and his showboating defense lawyer, David Rudolf, to allow themselves to be filmed—he didn't have to try that hard to persuade them—Lestrade caustically remarks that Americans come across "as actors in their own lives—characters who become practically movie characters." Unlike anyone else from another culture thrust in front of a gleaming new camera, guided by a prestigious, award-winning director? For too many of the French intelligentsia, American traits exist in a category separate from human nature.

Don't get the wrong idea. *The Staircase* is as good as it gets on television, and Lestrade is a master of his craft. But he is no less culpable than the guardians of public morality who often so capriciously judge the culpability of their fellow citizens. Unlike Peterson's defense team, the prosecution refused to grant Lestrade access to their activities. You can't help wondering whether, in return for Peterson and his team's openness to Lestrade's camera, Lestrade made crucial concessions to their point of view. For one thing, you are never told exactly what was the biological cause of Kathleen's death, an incredible omission in a documentary about a possible murder.

The impression Lestrade wants to leave you with is that Peterson was convicted on the strength of the jury's prejudice against him as a cultural subversive—a liberal novelist and former liberal newspaper columnist—and a bisexual man. Yet at a press conference held by the members of the jury after the trial—half the jury was black—they said they convicted Peterson for two very different reasons. The first was that there was too much blood for Kathleen Peterson to have died in an accidental fall down a flight of fifteen stairs in a narrow space. But the decisive factor was money. Peterson had $143,000 in credit-card debt, he was convinced that his wife was about to lose her high-paying job, and she had a life-insurance policy worth $1.4 million. Not once, in the entire eight-episode series, does the film make the slightest reference to either of these facts. And they are very important facts. With apologies to M. Lestrade, there is no end to the warp and woof of corrupted perspectives.

MAY 23, 2005

38 The History Channel's *Crusades*

Anyone who has grown tired of crude dichotomies like the "clash of civilizations" might want to repair to the television, where the "great man" theory of history flourishes, especially on the History Channel—alongside the familiar notion of a "clash of civilizations."

A new special on the History Channel claims to portray "the collision of two great faiths . . . [who] battled each other for two centuries during three crusades." For one thing, there were nine Crusades. For another, this two-parter gives an account of that historical epoch mostly with actors dramatically playing historical figures and teams of extras sensationally re-creating various armed conflicts. What with the background music, and the horses neighing, and the dying men screaming, *The Crusades: Crescent and the Cross* makes for very satisfying entertainment. I can just see Clint Eastwood writing and directing, with himself as a self-deprecating Richard the Lion-Hearted, Gene Hackman as shrewd Pope Urban, Ben Kingsley as noble Nur ad-Din, and Morgan Freeman playing Richard's sidekick—whom he has saved from a dead-end job in a harem—the kindly old black eunuch who tells the story ("Old Dick the Lion, he sure didn't look so good that day . . . ").

The four-hour documentary—it's really more of a docud-rama—wants to show that the medieval conflict between western Europe and the Islamic world lies behind today's headlines. But in fact today's headlines determine the film's deficiencies. "Heroes and villains emerged," the History Channel declares, "and acts of barbarism that cut wounds that are still felt to this day." The Crusades "still shape the Middle East and relations be-tween the two great religions in our present-day world." Having nailed that peg to the news cycle, the film sanguinely proceeds to emphasize the heroes, villains, and acts of barbarism over the historical background, which was a lot more complicated than the battle between "two great faiths." The film seems to consider its contemporary relevance as sufficient historical context.

It's pleasant and fun to hear the colorful stories of Urban, and Richard, and Louis VII, and Nur ad-Din. It would have been nourishing, however, to hear that the context for the Crusades was that the two great faiths were not in such great shape. We learn that the Muslims were broken up into isolated principalities, with no central political authority—like the Church in western Europe—to unify them against their ene-mies or arbitrate among them. But the film is, understandably, so careful not to offend that it never spells out Islam's inability to pry politics free from religion, a quality that has made Is-lamic countries both socially inequitable and vulnerable to outsiders. There is an elemental difference between religion getting entangled with politics, which is the Western situation, and religion incapacitating politics, which is the Islamic one.

On the Christian side, the film is better about laying out all the dysfunctions of medieval society—the feudal strife and gen-eral lawlessness. But so intent is it on staging battles and drama-tizing personalities that it leaves out historical details even more engaging than *The Crusades'* game British actors, who seem to associate medieval speech with an irritating emphasis on sibilants. For instance, the violence between feudal lords had gotten so wild that local clergy in France established what it called Truce of God, an organization dedicated to enforcing the priests' proclamation that fighting would be forbidden between Thursday evening and Monday morning. (Thank God It's Thursday.) It wasn't a *huge* success.

More important, the waxing and waning schism between the Western and Eastern churches got neatly sublimated into a fanatical emphasis on the schism between Christian and Muslim. The Byzantine emperors had always been a thorn in the papacy's side. It was fitting that the Crusades, begun in 1095, effectively came to an end with the Fourth Crusade, when not Muslim Jerusalem but Eastern Orthodox Constantinople fell to a French and Italian army in 1204.

Though the film is earnest about exposing religious hypocrisy, it never captures the ribald feel of medieval crusading Christianity, in which—as in Chaucer and Dante—religious belief can be splenetically or comically subjective. It tells the story of Peter Bartholomew, who at one point inspired beleaguered Crusaders by claiming to find the lance that pierced Christ's side as he hung on the cross. It moves next to the solemn testimony of a contemporary Catholic priest, who speaks of the authenticity of sacred relics.

What the film doesn't say is that half the Crusaders themselves laughed at Bartholomew and accused him of lying. For months, Bartholomew's supporters fought with his detractors—each group was loyal to a different Christian general— until Bartholomew offered to walk through fire to prove that God would protect a truthful man. He died a few days later. His allies claimed that he'd been manhandled by an excited crowd; skeptics insisted that the flames had killed him.

The film conscientiously emphasizes the irreligious greed and lust that animated the Crusaders' professions of piety, though this is not exactly news. And it conscientiously shifts back and forth between Western and Middle Eastern historians, a careful attempt at balance that has the unsettling effect of reinforcing the cultural divide that the film wants to expose as the tragic catalyst for today's events. At one point Tariq Ali, the author of a novel about Saladin, the Muslims' legendary leader, responds to an off-camera interviewer who apparently has been stepping gingerly around the question of whether Saladin could be as ruthless as his Christian enemies. "Of course he was ruthless!" Ali exclaims, with exasperation, and a touch of defensiveness.

It would have been nice to have Western historians making sympathetic points about Islamic civilization—for example, that contact with Islamic habits taught some Crusaders to bathe more often. It would have been gratifying to have Muslim historians offering the same about the Crusaders, though there doesn't seem to be anything very positive that you can say about soldiers of God who liked to warm up for their journey to the Middle East by killing thousands of European Jews on their way south. It is one of history's deeper ironies that the Jews, almost destroyed by Christian Europe, now find themselves in Israel— where Europe drove them—allied with Christendom against Islam, the Church's second historical enemy after the Jews.

Indeed, the film extenuates the Crusaders' homicidal tendencies when it asserts that escaping poverty was one of the motives behind people's decision to march on Islam. On the contrary, late-eleventh-century Europe was a prosperous place, and only rich knights had the resources to join the Crusades. (Bands of peasants tried but never made it to the Middle East.) Esurience and craving for adventure spurred them on, not dire need.

If *The Crusades* leads people to read and then reflect about the subject, so much the better. They'll have to read more about it after seeing this. The film leaves viewers with the impression that the Crusades, for all their many religious hypocrisies, were a wholly religious venture. But it presents no evidence that the Muslims fought the Christians for any reason other than defending their towns and cities. On the Christian side, the show never explains that in fact the Crusades permanently shifted power from the popes to the princes, a transformation that eventually made possible the rise of modern nation-states. Constantinople didn't fall to the Western Church; it fell to a consortium of Venetian shipping magnates. They tricked the Crusaders into storming Byzantium so that Venice could recover some vital business interests.

"Collision of two great faiths." "Clash of civilizations." How grand. Such conceptual splendor might satisfy some people's need to elevate politics with references to culture and ideas. If you tell them that you think large events are driven by colliding, clashing egos and interests, they look at you disapprovingly, as if you had just said that you didn't like poetry or classical music. As if you were a political philistine. *And we could have had such an interesting conversation.* But I wish *The Crusades* had made it clear that fire killed Peter Bartholomew, and that even the most fundamentalist faith, in the realm of politics, has equally fundamental realities behind it.

OCTOBER 31, 2005

39 UFOs

A major network is producing a two-hour special which argues that, as Peter Jennings, the show's host, gravely repeats over and over again, "we are not alone," that we get "visited" by aliens on a regular basis. Or at least since 1947, when someone who was obviously bored out of his mind, and scared witless both by the specter of nuclear war with Russia and the infinite silence of rural America at night, looked up from his cornfield or something, saw a giant dinner plate soaring through the nocturnal sky, and called his local police department to report an imminent invasion from outer space.

You thought all we had to worry about was Al Qaeda lurking behind every iPod? Think again. If you only knew the cosmic dangers that lurk above us, the green, spindly, big-headed beings that nurture dreams somewhere in their caves, spread out over billions of galaxies, of traipsing suddenly into our living rooms and, well, saying hello. And this is the least of it, only the beginning of a nightmare. What if they are not green? What if they are beige? What if they are (unreconstructed) liberals? What if they speak French? What if—please move your children away from the screen—they are *sane?*

Watching ABC present convincing dramatized accounts of UFOs flying over the country, listening to Jennings calmly make the case for a government perniciously indifferent to the threat from outer space, you have to wonder whether we are all as nuts as what we watch on TV. Or are the people who make television the true crazies? Or are they perhaps true cynics, whose desperate attempts to boost ratings, to be popular, to hold onto their jobs transform their anxiety into a kind of madness, a psychotic-commercial complex that descends upon us in the form of useless information that we have to know, or sleep-inducing entertainment to which we have to turn?

For all its perfunctory nods to skeptics, this special makes a quiet case that extraterrestrials are constantly circling our planet. Why they have never touched down to introduce themselves—landing only to abduct and then inexplicably to return people, thereby procuring for their abductees speaking engagements, television appearances, and book contracts—you never learn. Maybe they can't find long-term parking. Maybe they like to shop but not to buy, sampling an Earthling here, a Venutian there, and so on. Maybe our beloved Earth is actually known throughout the universe as "Planet Rest Room," and aliens only stop here to pee. These mysteries are not answered by Jennings and ABC.

Rather, Jennings is very respectful to the "witnesses" who claim to have seen aliens flying over their barnyards, or who insist that they've been abducted (they should be so lucky). There is something in Jennings' open attitude to all this of the new deference to so-called religious people that suddenly seized the commentating classes after the presidential election last November. These UFO true believers, after all, are animated by some kind of religious-ish impulse, some thirst for ultimates; or maybe just some wish to be jolted out of their dulled senses. In the latter sense, they are also like generations of vanguard artists, yearning to shock and be shocked.

But there is something else in Jennings' preening, solemn tones (his megalomania is extraterrestrial; so is his tendency to pronounce words like "project" two different ways). There is in Jennings' voice this surging American love for the absurd, and therefore contemptible, person. From politics to reality shows, we seem to like to be surrounded by people ruled by greed, hampered by stupidity, blinkered by obsession. These sad, bored UFOers, their faces blank, their landlocked figures full-sail with heartland obesity, their eyes shining with their earth-centric, mundane, child's fantasy of a populated universe—the spatial, secular version of the religious, temporal dream of a populated eternity—these people are easy to laugh at, and therefore easy to accommodate. In America, attention must be paid! Attention, that is, to everything freakish, inadequate, unthreatening, and thus usefully supportive perhaps of a shaky sense of worth, of identity. More and more, the spectacle of human inadequacy on television is like one long public stoning. Does not poor, war-ravaged, "dysfunctional" Iraq make us optimistic about America? Nowadays, American health navigates by foreign sickness.

It's easy to watch the special and draw pretty conclusions. Americans are escaping from harsh realities; the culture's normalization of deceit is resulting in a conventionalization of fantasy; Bush's triumphal end-of-daysism has its correlative in the UFOers' belief that some momentous figure—in one sense, the aliens are ultimate celebrities—will appear and explain everything to us. But the show's essential meaning lies in its recurrent assertion that "we are not alone." What an odd phrase—and how irresponsible of ABC not to examine it.

How could we be alone when the Earth currently holds over six billion of us? And who is this "we" anyway? Cross any border in the world and you either encounter or become an "alien," to one degree or another. There is something chilling about postulating the unknowable six billion as "we," and then wishing ardently to be astounded or shocked by company. Such mental sleight-of-hand implies the conceptual annihilation of everyone but you. If there's anything behind the UFO phenomenon at all, it's the human, perhaps all-too-human, desire to be freed from humanity altogether. Maybe someday scientists will tell us why ABC is conferring prestige upon the buried impulse to destroy everything except you and your local cornfield, or bowling alley.

FEBRUARY 21, 2005

40 Morning News Shows

To sleep, perchance to dream—but either way not to worry about having something to tune in to when you wake up. The first network morning show—the prototype of *The Today Show,* and *Good Morning America,* and *The Early Show*—appeared in 1952 on NBC, with Dave Garroway as host and with a clown covering the weather. ABC followed suit with its own wake-up program in 1975; seven years later CBS joined the game, though it had to push *Captain Kangaroo* out of its matutinal slot for the purpose. At the moment, 11 million Americans roll out of bed and flip on the three networks combined.

The rising numbers, or so the experts opine, are partly due to an increase in working hours and partly to a more health-conscious population, which awakens earlier to make time for calisthenics. The growing popularity of morning television might even be owed to the heightened American nervousness about "reality": the prospect of spending eight to ten hours with real, live, untelevised and uncontrollable humans makes more and more people hasten back as fast as they can into the tube world in which they happily concluded the previous evening. But perhaps the morning shows satisfy an even deeper need. It may be that Katie and Matt, Diane and Charles, Harry and Julie, and René and Hannah have proved Hegel right. Yes, Hegel. He said that the modern person's daily prayer was reading the newspaper. Nowadays it's the well-scrubbed, early-rising, up-to-the-minute, endlessly knowing and smiling anchorpeople who preside over matins and lead you, if you so desire, through the crosses and contradictions you may meet in the course of the day, and out of the dangers and the perils of the night before. Those last two clauses are, respectively, from the Catholic and the Anglican morning prayers. Here endeth the lesson. Now go forth and earneth and consume.

Of course, the morning programs exist on several levels: they are news; they are information; they are (even when they are news and information) entertainment. It is interesting that these programs, with their interviews and their musical numbers and their bits of comedy, resemble the kind of variety show you used to find on evening television fifty years ago, as if social life had become so accelerated that the morning tranquillity humankind has known throughout the ages had all but disappeared in our culture. Now you awake, as it were, in media race.

The morning format's latest development is to put the weathermen outside, among adoring crowds who throng the streets and the plazas outside the various networks' headquarters in midtown Manhattan, hoping to catch the camera's eye and enjoy a little apotheosis before lunch. Sometimes it seems as if the news only cares about an adoring glance from the people who watch it, and the people who watch it only care about the news when the news cares about them. People actually come at dawn and wait to shake hands on the air with Al Roker, or Tony Perkins, or Dave Price, the networks' happy-talking men-of-the-people weather guys. Roker and Perkins are black; and when you recall that during all the decades that the morning shows have been on, there has been only one black anchor—Bryant Gumbel, who flamed out some years ago—it is sometimes unsettling to watch them play the buffoon before the crowds, in this weird meteorological minstrelsy.

On the deepest level, however, the network morning shows—those on CNN and FOX are minor and relatively little-watched contributions to the genre—come as close as most popular culture does to replacing the spiritual devotions of yore. Media hipsters will roll their eyes at such an analogy, but the gulf between the mavens who write about these shows and the rest of the population who enjoy them is as wide as the chasm between black-and-white and digital television.

Consider the usual media response to the anchors themselves. Media observers remark upon the calculated largeness of personality, not to mention the obscene salaries—Couric reportedly earns $14 million a year; they sniff celebrity narcissism and lavish derision. You get sneering patter about the on-air colonoscopy administered to Katie after her husband died of colon cancer; and Katie's hairstyle; and Katie's catfight with Ann Coulter; and Katie's hairstyle; and Diane's gaffe over this or that; and Diane's hairstyle; and Matt's hairstyle, and so on. You get reports on the morning shows' competition with each other—they sometimes use helicopters to drown out each other's live outdoor concerts; and you get scorecard reporting on which anchors are in and which are out, or about to be. And of course the endless business-page obsession with shows' revenues. None of which is totally irrelevant, of course, since these phenomenally successful programs are network television's biggest moneymakers.

But Katie Couric and Matt Lauer, and Diane Sawyer and Charles Gibson, and Harry Smith and Julie Chen and the rest, have a job to do. They have to fill the role of extended family for the millions of people who watch them each morning; nothing less. And to become family, they have to construct an image of comfortable familiarity, and what makes the familiar comfortable is a reassuring imperfection, a demonstration of personal success without personal excellence. Katie, with her stiff, newly blonde hair; Matt, with his new close-shorn haircut that reveals his thinning hair; Diane, with the large mole on her knee, almost always visible through her stockings; bespectacled Harry, with his mild, ineffectual, old-fashioned banker's air and comfortingly bald head (the very opposite of Vin Diesel bald)—the flaws and the touching soft spots in these anchors' self-presentation are a special idiom, conscious self-caricatures meant to stick in the viewer's mind and to caress the viewer's ego.

Thus the shows are often studies in orchestrated humility and rigged self-effacement. Diane Sawyer is the master of endearing awkwardness, sometimes forgetting which way to walk on the soundstage. (She always remembers when to forget.) There is even a kind of daily duel between her and her office-husband, Charles Gibson, over who is a more flawed and ordinary human being. After Labor Day weekend, Gibson teased Sawyer for taking two consecutive weeks of vacation rather than spreading her time off over several weeks. As she smiled tolerantly, also seemingly a little uncertain as to whether Gibson was right—that is, as she confidently performed her little crisis of confidence—Gibson strode to a chart and stuck decals on the days Sawyer had taken off, and the decals, with an on-cue cuteness of their own, obligingly came loose and hung down on the board, causing Gibson to challenge Sawyer's uncertain smile with a sheepish smile. It was, like most morning television, a big smile-off. Sawyer frames her face with modesty the way cigarette smoke wreathed Garbo's face with glamour. Her smile disguises her condescension, but never merely that. Only someone this ordinary could occupy a position so extraordinary, her face always says.

And it's not just the impersonation of humility that seals the bond with the viewer. As the morning shows have surpassed the evening news in audience numbers and revenue, the anchor position on the morning news shows has become the most sought-after job in broadcast television, which also makes the turnover rate in that slot far more volatile than that of the evening news shows. No morning anchorperson has the decades-long run that their counterparts enjoy in the evening. This high-stakes competitiveness is what provides what must be one of the most appealing features of the morning shows' self-humbling dimension: you can actually see these people trying as hard as they can to hold onto their jobs. They are on, up, buzzed, frantic with joie de vivre, pushing themselves to the very breaking point of brightness and patter.

Matt Lauer makes Sammy Glick look like Khalil Gibran. The new haircut, revealing the thinning hair, gives his anxious pushiness both justification and pathos. His facial expression is always one step ahead of his conversation. He is a man whose eyes have never been introduced to his tongue. If he is talking with someone who just lost a child, his expression indicates that he is thinking about his next guest, who just made a new movie. On one segment, an old buddy of his, a radio journalist who traveled around with the Beatles during their first American tour and had just written a book about his experiences with the Fab Four ("they were so approachable, so special"), congratulated Lauer at the end of the interview. Lauer looked like he was about to have a heart attack. "For what?" he asked, nearly hysterical. Indeed, what might that have meant? A spectacular on-air firing, perhaps? A sort of personnel/colonoscopy combo? Congratulations, tomorrow you leave your current job to cover the civil war in Sudan, which experts believe will end sometime in 2075? But the unsuspecting interviewee had simply meant to congratulate Lauer on his anchor position, which apparently he had not had the chance to do until now.

I doubt that Lauer can perform such anxiety intentionally; he just has a natural gift for expressing—beneath the perennial smile—existential terror. And what could be better, more cathartic, than this open display of your deepest inner fears, whether you are a stay-at-home parent getting the kids ready for school and feeling consoled that you do not have to go out into the Darwinian den every day; or a man or woman drinking coffee or shaving or putting on makeup and feeling comforted and amused by this neutralizing spectacle of what could happen but should never happen and never will, not if you can help it. Matt is still there on *Today* tomorrow, after all, and tomorrow, and tomorrow, and tomorrow. *Today* really isn't another day. It is the same day, forever and ever.

Matt may not be deliberately performing his disquietude, but he is performing, as all the morning anchors perform. The show's producers and directors intend for you to see the performance, just as they intend for you to see the imperfection, and the signs of plastic surgery, and the tired faces of the anchors, who are up way before dawn every morning. The insincerity of the anchors is as transparent as Macy's display windows. Katie has a very special after-look, which the camera never fails to catch: she smiles, she communes, she empathizes, and then, as soon as the interview or the report is over, she looks down and her expression grows inward and even slightly dark, as if she is in the grip of a powerful memory, or feeling the pull of a pressing obligation. This little morning-apprehensiveness-before-the-day-begins look is a kind of boon to the viewer's subconscious. The anti-smile element is a brilliant stroke, a subtle innovation, a manageable little subversion, in the morning smilefest.

On the subject of insincerity, Diane put it one morning with striking frankness. Watching a report about the cryogenic freezing of Ted Williams, she learned that Williams' body and head are stored in different containers. "Your face doesn't even know what expression to make when you're watching this story," she confessed. Yes, especially if your chin is on one side of the room and your torso is on the other. Sawyer had finely articulated her and all the anchors' modus operandi. From segment to segment, from emotion to emotion, from news of war and destruction to news of finance, to weather, to interviews with grieving people, with grateful people, with important people, the anchors have to know what face to fit to what story.

But most of all they have to show the viewer that they are struggling to fit the face to the story. Gide said that you cannot appear sincere and be sincere at the same time, and the anchors and their bosses capitalize on this impasse. Who, anyway, is ready for candor from a stranger first thing in the morning? That comes soon enough: if you don't know the score by three o'clock that afternoon, you are in trouble. By the end of the day, you are ready for Letterman and Leno and beyond. America wakes to insincerity and goes to sleep to irony and cynicism.

And so in these morning times before the complicated day begins, as the mind is just beginning to grasp what lies ahead and what still lies behind, we are finally meant to notice that the anchors are feigning pity or compassion or happiness or reverence. We are meant to see the mental intention struggling to complete itself as an authentic feeling. We are meant to see that they are working at something, which isn't easy; that they are trying to satisfy the expectations of their bosses and of their audience, which isn't easy; that they are trying to conform their inner states to the social situation, which isn't easy—in other words, they are trying, so transparently, so deliberately, to do what most of us have to do every day.

This playacting is for our benefit. It gets interwoven through deftly chosen and balanced stories about death, and about survivors, who often thank God for preserving them and keeping them sane through the destruction of others. Those are the crosses that have to be borne, and the perils from the night before (a lot of these things happened while we were sleeping). Then there are the contradictions: drugs that might or might not work; politicians who might or might not have failed the public trust; parents who refuse to condemn their overweight hacker son, who has nearly brought down an entire industry, and who may or may not be guilty, but still deserves his parents' love. And then, too, there are the redemptions. Just about every morning show has, at one point or another, a story about newborn babies or young children, and each day's show often includes at least a reference to weddings.

In this subtle and wholly uncalculated way, the shows portray life's dangers, conundrums, confusions. They enumerate life's blessings. And like all morning prayers, which end with a direct appeal for protection to the divinity, the morning shows finish with our own version of perfect happiness: since Possibility is the American god, they conclude with an interview with a celebrity. Harmless and comforting and diverting inanity without end. Amen.

NOVEMBER 10, 2003

41 Tom Brokaw

Brokaw is leaving. Rather is leaving. Jennings is obviously about to leave. And so a question for all those professional analyzers knocking themselves out (I'm about to join them) trying to fathom the significance of The Network Anchorman, now that tonight is Tom Brokaw's last broadcast and next spring is Dan Rather's final season: Why aren't professional actors delivering the news?

This isn't meant as a sardonic lament of the performance aspect of presenting the evening news. If there's anything more tiresome than complaining about the calculated theatrical aspect of modern politics, it's complaining about the calculated theatricality of The Anchor. The essential function of The Anchor is to be almost Aristotelian in his practical effect on collective feeling. The popularity of the three network anchors, Brokaw, Rather, and Jennings, is the result of the same mechanism that produces the popularity of a film star. Let an anchor or an actor provoke your emotions long enough, and then share with you the emotions they've brought out of you long enough, and they become part of your experience. They provide the catharsis for the emotions they've aroused.

A lot of so-called experts describe The Anchor as a father figure, and then go on to present as proof the fact that Walter

Cronkite, The First Modern Anchor, ascended to magnetic authoritativeness on the strength of his (briefly) lachrymose coverage of JFK's assassination in 1963. Never mind that Brokaw et al. were in their late thirties and forties when they started out as anchors (as their successors will be) and hardly father figures on the order of Cronkite. Such a characterization ignores the more significant fact that the phenomenon of the single person delivering the news to a very large assortment of individuals began in the early 1950s, right after World War II.

It was a time when, despite the country's booming confidence and flourishing economy, many people were haunted by what had been fascism's spectacular success in Europe and by totalitarianism's continuing triumph in the Soviet Union. In America, what the sociologists used to call "mass society" met technology, thus creating the specter of a malleable population. The Anchor is one among many American phenomena—from the evangelical preacher, to the late-night comedian, to the talk-show host, to the movie celebrity, to the culture of dark anticelebrity celebrities à la Eminem and countless rap artists—that provides an outlet for feelings that might otherwise attach themselves to a political maestro of the darker emotions. Tyrannies rain events down upon their own populations; democracies feed them partially fabricated, mediocre reports of events. Brokaw, Rather, and Jennings are reminders—or chimeras—of ahistorical calm.

On the surface, they are culturally implausible. Each of them has been announcing the news for something like twenty-five years. They've outlasted the kind of seismic shifts that are supposed to drive the transiencies of American culture, and fashion, and politics. It's hilarious to hear pundits describe Brokaw's and Rather's retirements as not retirements at all, but as the extinction of a species. Cable news has made network news ob-solete, younger audiences need younger anchors, the evening slot for the evening news is hopelessly archaic given all the changes in American lifestyles and work-rhythms, etc. etc. If Brokaw and Rather weren't leaving, no one would be turning their departure into the beginning of a new historical phase—it's the kind of fake trend The Network Anchor is paid so hand-somely to proclaim. But the fact that they lasted so long disproves all the theories about why they are leaving.

Indeed, the very rise of The Anchor seems to refute much conventional smarts about the way American culture and soci-ety work. Their advancing age didn't hamper them in the mar-ketplace. Though Brokaw is boyish—his dry and removed, yet warm and obscurely engaged manner is attractive—he's no beauty. Jennings and Rather—whose rigid self-conscious mouth implies deep nervous travails—are far less comely. What held them aloft for so long was everything the American myth was supposed to exclude, even reject: their viewers' love of long-lasting continuity; and fear of change; and faith in age and experience; and comfort with The Anchors' physical shortcomings. Popular culture's mockery of them by myriad comedians, and in movies like *Network* and *Broadcast News,* just earned for The Anchors the affectionate, absolving con-tempt that protects a public reputation in America from re-sentment and envy.

In the end, it was nothing more complicated than familiarity that held them aloft for so long, a familiarity whose substance was the emotions they roiled and then relaxed. In a commercially driven democracy that depends on permanently stimulated ap-petites, and on the daily illusion of extravagant gratification just within reach, the essential question is how to manage unleashed, unmoored emotions. That heavy, therapeutic, almost expiative stabilizing is why they're called Anchors. And the stabilizing gets more strenuous as emotions become more complex. Mark my words: Sooner or later, the networks are going to bring in the real thing—that is to say, the actors—and drop all pretense of being free from pretense.

DECEMBER 1, 2004

42 Pope John Paul II

I saw the late Pope John Paul II once in Rome. I was about to cross the street when a short caravan of motorcycles and black Mercedes caromed past me. Looking at the cars as they sped by, I immediately recognized, from behind, the small figure of gigantic power, white-clad in his ceremony of innocence, sitting tightly between two men in minatory dark suits. Though he seemed like a precious historical prop, perhaps being transported from some sacred repository to the performance of a pageant, I was thrilled. The utter strangeness of this living historical person, with his aura of heavy centuries past, appearing doll-like, subject to the constraints of upholstered space and at the mercy of a speeding machine, only increased my sense of awe. I wanted to laugh, partly from the exclusive joy of the occasion, partly from the absurdity of the occasion, which seemed like a cross between the Book of Revelations and Cocteau.

The phrase "ceremony of innocence" is from Yeats, who lamented its extinction in modern life, and who—though not a practicing Christian—said that he loved Catholicism for its metaphors, for precisely its ceremony of innocence. The fascination with the Pope among non-Catholic Christians and even unbelievers has something to do not just with his charisma but with Catholicism's order and ritual. A dissatisfaction with modernity is the chief characteristic of modernist thinking, and in this sense, Catholicism satisfies the most critical secular appetite. Writing regularly some years ago for *Commonweal*, an honest, intelligent, irreverent, and pugnacious liberal Catholic magazine, I was so enthralled by the way Catholicism had created this many-dimensioned organic counterlife to modern life that I considered converting. But it was the beauty of the religion that had riveted my admiration, not its creed.

What is dismaying about the Television News Brain's fixation on the Pope's long dying and his death is not that it exists—the sacred is so rare that a crisis in the sacred has to be broadcast and commented on. And the general sorrow over the Pope's death is partly a general longing to be embraced by a beautiful mystery. What is so maddeningly dismaying is the way the cynical media's pose of hagiographic respect for the Pope amounts to an ungenerousness to the religion and to the world he leaves behind. To hear these shiny, modern, thoroughly secular talking heads speak about the Pope as though they were all sheep in his flock, as though they did not use contraception, or fornicate freely for pleasure, or enjoy same-sex relationships, or worship Yahweh or Allah or no divinity at all, was dreamlike. Their sudden, staged belief made you want to rub your eyes in disbelief. Once again, as with the Ashley Smith story and with Terri Schiavo, a story that should have been reported was being treated like an opportunity that had to be exploited.

Indeed, someone up there seems sensitive to coherent programming since if poor Terri Schiavo had not died before the Pope fell into his fatal last illness, the News Brain would have exploded in its attempts to cover both stories. The mind boggles at what would have happened if Terri Schiavo had still been alive while the Pope lay dying, and if at that very minute Ashley Smith had been taken hostage. The ensuing commotion would have made the apocalypse look like a class reunion. Instead, the television news people segued smoothly from one event to the other as if they were all covering the same story. Which in some sense they were: Religion in America, A New Market.

For beyond the Pope's integrity, and dignity, and humanity, was the simple fact that his intransigence about abortion, and science's role in modern life, and gay marriage, and contraception, had alienated vast numbers of Catholics who wanted to carry their faith with them into their modern lives. His stubbornness about contraception ensured that vast numbers of the Catholic poor, forbidden birth control, would stay poor. And John Paul's appointment of key cardinals who shared his intransigence guaranteed that the Church would remain in crisis, like the poor, for generations. You could argue that nothing except good things should be said of the recently deceased. But the talking heads are not exactly primed to reexamine Catholicism in a critical way after the event of the Pope's death has given way to the next late-breaking story. And John Paul's death was not the death of an ordinary man.

But the talking heads didn't use the occasion to hold up to scrutiny the role of the Pope in shaping people's destinies. They didn't use it to examine how this powerful, charismatic man, trained as an actor, had often used his awesome office to make the bread of words have the effect of intoxicating action, when in fact no action was taken. No one I saw on television seized the occasion of the Pope's passing to perform the necessary service of making distinctions between Protestant evangelicals and

Catholics, or between left-wing and right-wing Catholics; no one I saw remarked on the irony of the Pope, who is anathema to fundamentalist Christians, having invented the phrase "culture of life," which sets fundamentalist temples pounding.

Oh no. After performing as evangelicals in the Ashley Smith story, and after miming sympathy for the fundamentalist cause in the Schiavo case, only to turn that sorrowful tale into a version of the most gruesome reality television, the talking heads took up their rosaries for their reports on the Pope. Anderson Cooper declared that the Pope was dead, "his soul departed, his body at peace, serene." How this journalist was able to ascertain that the Pope had a soul, and that this soul had now left the Pontiff's body, let alone that said body was "at peace" and "serene," he didn't say. Soon they'll be doing exorcisms on C-Span. And they forced Dan Rather to retire because of a few faked memos!

Stories about religious belief seem to require from the otherwise toughly skeptical people who report them a credulity that verges on a religious leap of faith itself. Christiane Amanpour informed us that "the man who tried to kill the Pope a quarter century ago, Mehmet Ali Agca, is said by his brother to be extremely saddened, in grief." But she would never have reported that "Yasir Arafat is said by his brother to have said as his last words, 'I wish to be buried in Miami,'" unless she had heard Arafat utter the words themselves. Perhaps the gravest theological reflection emanated from Diane Sawyer, who recalled the Pope's election in 1978 and his first appearance to the crowd assembled in St. Peter's Square: "From the moment he emerged on the balcony, he was recognized as a kind of rock star of Popes." Not even being the vicar of Christ is enough to satisfy *Good Morning America*.

The critics of the Pope who did appear on the talk shows limited themselves to making mild criticisms of the Pope's refusal to allow women to be ordained as priests, a parochial Catholic issue that appealed to the TV news because it could also be presented as a lifestyle issue for female viewers. When it came to the Pope's tyrannical consolidation of Church power, to his suppression of liberal and dissenting voices, everyone was, well, self-suppressed. Perhaps the lowest point was on *Meet the Press* when Tim Russert addressed himself to Judge Anne Burke, who had served as the interim chair of the U.S. Conference of Catholic Bishops National Review Board, a panel that was charged with taking up the sex-abuse scandal. In the wake of the scandal, the Pope had preserved the Church's established order by making sure that no substantial reforms would be made and that no effective steps would be taken to prevent the sexual exploitation of children by priests in the future. But when Russert asked Judge Burke what grade she would give the Pope for his response to the crisis, she replied, "an A-plus." She was spared any uncomfortable follow-up questions, and like those speeding Mercedes, the news rushed on toward the next burst of silly obsession, the next empty cycle, as the soul departed from this story.

APRIL 4, 2005

Reality
Television

43 Reality in America

Four men. Four men left. These are the four finalists, the men among whom Haley must make the most important decision of her life. They are wearing masks. Haley must choose the man she is going to marry, which is the most important decision of her life, among four men who are wearing masks. She will choose, for this most important of decisions, not on the basis of looks, which is of course a superficial standard, and a standard that all the other networks are using, but on the basis of personality. Over the past few weeks, she has gotten to know these men in an incredibly comprehensive way. They have poured out their hearts, each one to the other, and vice versa. They have talked about their favorite wines, and their favorite sports, and their favorite snacks, and their favorite gift ideas. During a candlelit dinner, at a table beside a glimmering bay, underneath dark velvet skies, Haley has asked each startled suitor: "So why should I choose you?" Their answers, though they were all the same, shocked America with their straightforwardness.

And now comes the moment of truth, although there is still one episode left, the heartbreaking segment in which two contestants are suddenly disaggregated into a lucky winner and a pathetic loser who, America hopes, will bear his crippling, devastating, humiliating rejection with dignity and cheerfulness, two qualities that matter a lot more than being a "winner," which probably just means that you knew someone on the inside anyway. Standing a little behind Haley is Monica Lewinsky, who has been advising and consoling and encouraging her throughout her thrilling odyssey. Yes, Monica Lewinsky. Why Monica Lewinsky? Because NBC has people eating live cockroaches on *Fear Factor,* and CBS has people nearly killing each other to prevail on a desert island on *Survivor,* and ABC has *The Bachelor,* in which a man chooses from a group of women, and *The Bachelorette,* in which a woman chooses from a group of men. But no one has thought of getting a celebrity with a racy reputation. Not until *Mr. Personality,* one of America's newest reality television shows.

Only in America could reality become a trend. But then, only in America do we take time out for a "reality check," as if anyone so far gone as to lose his sense of reality would actually know what to check in order to get it back. I mean, get real. Of course, only in America could the admonishment "get real" be a reproach, and "unreality" be a sin. And now that we're on the subject, only in America do we say "I mean" before we say what we mean, as if it was an acceptable convention for people to go around saying what they didn't mean, and it had become another convention to make the distinction, before saying anything of consequence, between meaning and not meaning what you are about to say. Already I'm, like, getting dizzy. Which raises the question of why Americans distance themselves from what they are saying by putting "like" before the description of something, as if people are nervous about committing to a particular version of reality, or to a direct, unmediated, non-metaphorical experience of the real. "Like" is annoying, but it is a powerful tool of detachment and defense; it is verbal armor. So you see the depth of complexity. It is no surprise that "reality television" has become not just a gigantically profitable object of diversion, but also the subject of appalled concern.

The nature of reality in America has been a riddle ever since Europeans started fleeing their own literal conditions by exporting their dreams here in the form of Noble Savages, the Land of Opportunity, and *Mahagonny* (the last a shy overture disguised as a knowing sneer). Recently, the Europeans have stopped exporting their dreams over here and begun exporting their "reality": *Survivor*, the granddaddy of reality television, came to these shores from England in 2000, and *Big Brother* and *Fear Factor* came over from Holland and Germany around the same time. Or maybe these are new kinds of dreams. As the culture editor of *Die Zeit* said, "People are missing the real life in their lives."

Medieval artists and artisans staged Catholicism for the masses. The painter Jacques-Louis David helped to orchestrate the French Revolution, the Russian avant-garde helped to design the Russian Revolution, the Nazis aestheticized life to cover up the workings of evil. If Baudrillard sounds comical when he complains that reality has disappeared into folds of media-fabricated "simulacra," it is because he thinks that once upon a time, before the media, there used to be something called reality that was available directly and without the interference of interpretation, that existed in isolation, untouched by artifice. But degrees of so-called unreality have always constituted part of so-called reality. That is why reality is so hard to pin down. Which is why they call it reality.

In America, playing around with representations of reality is as commonplace as buying a pair of sunglasses, or getting a cosmetic makeover, or purchasing a cell phone with a clearer video display, or . . . well, you know what I mean. Melville's *The Confidence-Man* portrayed American reality as so malleable that, after a while, the distinction between art and life in that novel melts like celluloid in fire. In *Huckleberry Finn,* Colonel Sherburne shoots the town drunk dead in the street and the townspeople re-enact the shooting seconds after it happens; there is also the question of whether the drunk was playacting when he threatened to shoot Sherburne. Around the turn of the century, immigrant audiences watching the Yiddish version of *King Lear* jumped out of their seats and cried out, "Ungrateful child!" to Cordelia. Orson Welles got everyone hysterical by presenting H. G. Wells' *War of the Worlds* as an actual news event; and people tuning in to the final ride of O. J.'s white Bronco thought that this actual news event was a television drama.

There is more. In the 1960s, people participating in Happenings enacted fragments of life in the context of art, or they enacted fragments of art in the context of life; in the 1980s and 1990s, performance art continued the genre. Back in the 1960s, too, everyone was wringing their hands over the so-called New Journalism's conflation of fact and fiction. Remember *In Cold Blood?* Its author proudly called it a nonfiction novel, thereby setting the culture atwitter. The novel, later a movie, was not really a novel but a documentary, or a documentary-like telling, or retelling, of a real event, the murder of a family. But don't worry if you don't remember the book, or the movie. You probably recall that the actor Robert Blake, who starred in the movie as one of the murderers, was recently arrested for cold-blooded murder.

So reality television did not come out of nowhere. It is as much an exercise in restoration, an echo of the past, a piece of

American tradition, as so many other cultural events are now. American popular culture these days seems to be an endless tunnel of such derivative phantoms: revived plays and musicals, revived movies and television series, old movies that become new plays, remixed songs, the familiar-looking children of famous actors, old political speeches that make their way into new political speeches. Almost all the contestants on *American Idol*, a talent contest focused exclusively on finding the best singer, are impersonating the styles of famous singers from the past rather than creating an original style themselves.

Way back in 1980, Harry Waters, the acerbic television critic for *Newsweek*, referred to reality television's forerunners—shows such as *Candid Camera, Real People*, and *The Gong Show*—as "actuality programming." The term "reality television" was used the following year in an article in the *Washington Post* describing television news coverage of Anwar Sadat's assassination. Not only does the nature of reality representation keep shifting, so does the language used to describe it.

Television has its own internal history of changing styles of representation. In the early days of television, even scripted dramas were more "real"—forgive the quotation marks, but what do you do with this word?—than reality television, for the simple reason that they were broadcast live. Today's reality television is heavily edited, musically scored, and constructed with overlapping time-frames that present a participant making voice-over analysis as he and the viewers watch him in a situation taped much earlier. Allen Funt, the host of *Candid Camera*, created mildly embarrassing or charmingly awkward situations, let the hidden camera roll without editing, and then revealed to the subject that he or she should smile because "you're on *Candid Camera*." The contestants who struggle for dominance on their desert island in *Survivor,* by contrast, have agreed to participate in a highly structured game. They see the camera people running all around them, and they watch the heavily edited result later. A later precursor to reality television, MTV's *Real World,* flashier but similar to its own forerunner *Real People,* simply threw the camera into the participants' lives and let them do whatever they wanted. But the people on *Joe Millionaire, The Bachelor,* and *The Bachelorette* are not, strictly speaking, participants—they are contestants in highly calculated and formulaic situations. Their words and their actions are weighed after taping by a team of producers, who decide what to keep in and what to leave out. In the late 1970s and 1980s, *The Gong Show* vulgarized the old *Amateur Hour* by staging a talent show in which people were invited to debase themselves in outrageous ways. The difference between that show and its present-day descendant, *American Idol,* in which three judges decide on the best singer, is that the latter, for all the judges' near-sadistic treatment of the contestants, is much tamer, much more the product of slick camerawork and editing and a big music sound.

When the word "reality" is used as a modifier, as in "reality television," it means that the thing modified, in this case television, is being adapted to some generally accepted idea of what "reality" means, not that it is being brought closer to reality. It is like encountering a restaurant in Maryland that offers "continental dining." You know that you are not going to be treated to a dining experience of the sort that you would find in Lausanne or Baden-Baden. You are going to get the popular echo of the generic and generally accepted idea of an authentic European dining experience. And the more universally recognizable a quality is, the further it gets from its original denotation. Caricature is the price of a universal familiarity.

The question is what original element of a thing is being caricatured. Will the continental dining experience consist of waiters in long aprons, a menu in French, dim lights, or merely exorbitant prices? The "reality" in reality television is a caricature of the idea of reality.

And so the question is, what aspect of reality do the producers of these shows seize on and caricature when they confer upon it the honorific "reality"? It isn't the raw, uncut, unedited spontaneity of the original actuality programs. It isn't the banal, tedious texture of life that you find in *cinéma vérité* or Dogma 95, or in the subtle argument seeping up through the accumulation of suggestive quotidian particulars that you get in a documentary by Frederick Wiseman or Errol Morris. The quality of reality that reality television emphasizes and exaggerates exists only in the negative. It is anything that is not physically perfect, not carefully presented, not stylistically flawless, not shiningly successful—anything that is not packaged in the form of an ideal.

Reality television is a gospel of relaxation, a revolt of the *demos* against the oppressive idealizations of celebrity, and against the onerous images of perfection purveyed by commercial society. Its essential quality is defeat: it celebrates the experience of losing, of being humiliated and rejected, of having your deepest desires unrequited. These become, in reality television, superlative qualities.

It's true that audiences find themselves comforted by the spectacle of other people's rejection or, in the case of shows such as *Survivor, Fear Factor, American Idol,* and *Are You Hot?,* other people's humiliation. In the end, though, reality television consoles people for their daily failures and defeats rather than making them feel superior to other people's failures and defeats.

Reality television replaces the glowing, successful celebrity ideal with gross imperfection and incontrovertible unhappiness. In a ruthlessly competitive society, where the market has become the exclusive arena of success, reality television shames the illusion of meritocracy by making universal the experience of the underdog, the bumbler, the unlucky and unattractive person.

Consider an analogy from American politics. Bush junior, when running for president, misspoke on camera, bumbled, stumbled, got his facts wrong, and generally projected the image of an inferior, inadequate candidate. But he did so with a wink to the audience that acknowledged his inadequacy, and this conspiratorial wink perhaps empowered people by giving them the illusion that they held the secret to his self-presentation. No hidden trickery lay behind the image of Bush on television. He was not a creation of the media; his indictment by the camera was the proof. His magnetism lay in his lack of charisma. He was the antidote to sizzle and buzz, the antihero of the celebrity universe, the encouraging retort to the thronging images of perfection all around us. Who would not prefer true imperfection to false perfection? And so he made universal the viewer's experience of being the underdog, the bumbler, the unlucky and unattractive person. (Never mind that he is one of the luckiest people who ever lived.)

Doubtless people who participate in reality television hunger to be celebrities—to be beautiful, and excellent, and successful, and rich. But their motivation for being on a particular show is different from the motivation of the show's creators. Far from being real, reality television shows are, without exception, structured along the lines of a game show. A prize waits at the end of every series: a fiancée, a trip to Hollywood as the "American Idol," a shot at a career in modeling or acting as America's "hottest" physique, a cash prize. Even at the conclusion of *Extreme Makeover,* a reality show that offers three people complete makeovers at the hands of plastic surgeons, cosmetic dentists, and the like, the climactic scene consists of the participants' return home. Will their family and friends be overwhelmed with admiration for their new appearance, thus making the returning participant a winner? ("I can't believe that's my little girl. She's gorgeous.") Or will everyone draw back in horror, thus declaring the hopeful transformee a loser? Whatever happens, the bottom line of reality television's "reality" is winning or losing.

And yet these are game shows with a difference. They combine the competitive formula of the game show with the emotional and psychological nakedness of confessional talk shows—*Let's Make a Deal* meets Jerry Springer. Whatever the category—talent, physical beauty, survivalist skills, or romance (which encompasses them all)—the contestants speak throughout the series about their inner states: their anxiety, their frustrations, their hopes, their feelings about the other contestants. And as the losers are announced at the end of various segments of various series, the camera closes in on and lingers over their faces, catching the slightest signs of distress. In the case of the romantic reality shows, the rejected contestants gather together at the end to comment on the winner; in their defeat, they become retrospective judges whose acid analyses, now at an Olympian remove from the fray, have the effect of making them superior to the winners.

But if reality television de-glamorizes the celebrity aura of success and perfection by replacing it with the universality of failure and rejection, it also theatricalizes inner experience. Along with being a revolt against celebrity and commercially driven images of perfection, reality television is a revolt against the worship of "the real." It is a rebellion against the exposure of the dark, gritty side of human life that so much popular art—and "high" art, too—has devoted itself to accomplishing over the past twenty years. As Waters observed in *Newsweek* two decades ago, the advent of actuality programming coincided with—and was a kind of retort to—the rise of issue-oriented sitcoms such as *Lou Grant* and *All in the Family,* shows that grappled with burning topical subjects such as racism and abortion. The advent of today's reality television coincides with the rise of harsh programs such as *Oz* and *The Shield* and *The Sopranos,* which portray psychology as candidly as the earlier sitcoms depicted the social and political issues of the day. Reality television is a retort to this grimy, roiling psychic reality, a great respite from it.

The "real" in America now comes down to psychology, to the volatile fact that people have emotions. Feelings are the last frontier. There is simply nothing to be done with them. So much of present-day life seems organized to yield winnings and controlled to minimize loss. Why should emotional life be any different? Why should feelings be permitted to flow spontaneously and authentically? So the great project of popular culture over the past twenty years has been to unleash unrationalizable, incalculable, uncontrollable feelings into the public arena in hopes of organizing them as neatly as the other areas of our life are organized. Memoirs, talk shows, first-person outpourings of one kind or another—they all toss feeling into public view and cry, "Help! Do something about this! Arrange and order and control this mess!"

In the same way, reality television masters angry and confused emotions with an organizing narrative. Reality television applies sophisticated editing and jump-cuts and voice-overs and musical scorings of film to everyday situations, so as to give everyday life the scripted and directed structure of film. And not only does reality television organize life into a story, it also analyzes and interprets the story while it unfolds—as in *Blind Date,* where captions gloss each situation in which the daters find themselves. It is so hard to live life without help.

And it all gets absorbed into the competitive paradigm of American society. At one point in *The Bachelor,* the bachelor remarks about one of the contestants, "When she said yes, she would stay the night, I felt really good about it." Score! It is just a good move in what is only a game. And we are supposed to be comforted that this is so, that the life of feeling has been safely objectified for millions into another game of winning and losing. It turns out that there is something more frightening than the brutality of the market, and it is the brutality of the inner life. As they say on *American Idol*: "You ask an entire country to step forward and audition." Reality television invites an entire country to step forward and be calmed and stupefied and appeased.

At the same time, just as reality television turns inner experience into an impersonal game of winning and losing, it comfortingly turns winning and losing into a game with transparently arbitrary rules. Talent shows such as *American Idol* and the beauty shows such as *Are You Hot?* and *Extreme Makeover* demonstrate the arbitrariness of success based on talent and beauty by making the judges so obviously biased and cruel, by proving that all you need to transform your physical appearance is sufficient money for the purpose. And the survivalist shows such as *Fear Factor,* in which women dive underwater to retrieve dead rats with their mouths, are not about survival; they are about finding a structure to house and to console competition anxiety. The contestants break from below the rules of dignity and self-respect, in a society where, as everyone knows, the elites secretly break the rules from above. By bringing your self-respect so low and living to tell the tale, what you really do is prove that your self-respect is invincible. It is a spiteful rebuke to the lucky classes, whose existence weighs so heavily on you. And the "romantic" reality shows are not about romance at all. They are about turning the inexorable and inexplicable losses and setbacks and puzzles of emotional life into another transparent, impersonal game with winners and losers. Better to be a loser, after all, than to find yourself in something that is not a game. Because in the end Eliot was right when he said that humankind cannot bear very much reality. Enter reality television.

JUNE 23, 2003

44) *Family Bonds*

The Cuisinart coffeemaker said it all. Watching *The Apprentice* some months ago, I noticed that the coffeemaker in the luxury apartment where some of the show's contestants were staying was the very one I owned. I don't have the model number, but it's called the Classic Look, or something like that. Minimal, elegant, functional. Sort of a gunmetal gray with black trimmings. It has a timer, too. Twelve-cup capacity. Three levels of heating intensity. The whole thing.

Anyway, I noticed this tiny detail because I've been trained as a television critic to notice things like that. If a comma is missing in the credits, I notice it. It's a blessing, yes, and also a curse. Well, I thought nothing of seeing the coffeemaker and just filed this little detail away. I've learned that you never know when you're going to need something like that. And then, sure enough, last week, as I was annotating *Family Bonds* frame by frame—which is a little warm-up I like to do before I start the real legwork on a show—I noticed that there, in the Queens, New York, kitchen of the Evangelistas, a family of bail bondsmen and bounty hunters who are the subject of HBO's new contribution to the reality genre, was the Classic Look, the very same coffeemaker that sat in that very different place, high up in a glittering tower soaring above New York. And the wheels began to turn.

The theme of so many movies and television shows is that even the most extreme-seeming opposites are alike. American-style democracy seems to demand this identity flexibility. The macho guy is really a soft, feminine guy; the sheriff is a brutal breaker of the moral law within, and the bad guy suddenly throws open a window to the starry sky above; the prostitute is a self-sacrificing angel, while the rich woman is heartless and cruel; children are like adults and adults are like children; etc. In this Ovidian flux, anybody can become anything else in an instant—the pop-culture ethos is both an unsettling inspiration and a great hubris-buster. Your identity is not over till it's over. The Classic Look appearing in two radically different environments suggests that taste itself has become so unmoored from character that it is no longer any kind of guide to a person.

The incredible velocity of fashion trends has had the effect of effacing taste entirely. Brands like Ralph Lauren and Pottery Barn, among many others, specialize in a kind of prefabricated, generic elegance that provides the illusion of taste to their customers. Thus two people from two different universes could both show up at a social event and wear the same "distinctive" outfit. In this sense, everyone is walking around in disguise. I could never understand why contemporary American fiction writers still knock themselves out meticulously describing what a character is wearing. That's a literary convention from the nineteenth century, when taste really was a guide to class and/or character.

But the appearance of the Classic Look in these two reality shows was, actually, a real piece of reality in an otherwise fraudulent new genre. Because reality television is, among many other interesting and depressing things, a flight from the slipperiness of identity and the indeterminacy of taste. Reality shows simulate clashing personalities to achieve the illusion of a stable universal, which is that we are all reducible to our hungers whether we are competing romantically, or physically, or artistically, or economically, or socially. And although we all hunger for different things with different intensities, we are defined by our hungers. You may not be able to discern anything significant about a person by the Tommy Hilfiger shirt he's wearing, but once you know what he wants, and to what degree he wants it, then you know who and maybe even where in life he is. Come to think of it, the universality of desire is also what bound Ovid's transformations together.

"The sympathetic bond is broken," wrote D.H. Lawrence hysterically, "we stink in each other's nostrils." I think of that histrionic sentiment every time I turn on these reality-show outlets for the worst human feelings. HBO has yielded to the popularity of the genre while, not surprisingly for this cable channel, elevating its quality. Though like every other reality show *Family Bonds* has the music, and the careful editing, and the storyline imposed on its subjects, it's also part documentary. This dimension of the series is its most intriguing. It raises the show almost to the level of a parable by Kafka.

Indeed, in *The Trial*, Kafka portrayed the Law as arbitrarily driven by the appetites of its enforcers and administrators. Tom Evangelista and his family—the men, anyway—are the Law in *Family Bonds*. In exchange for collateral, they will give a person sufficient money for bail; but if that person tries to run away, they'll track him or her down. So what makes you free can also imprison you. Just like desire itself. The show should have been called *Of Human Bondage*.

The people on this show are fleshly, appetitive, *Sopranos*-like types, though operating in the world unaccompanied by the illuminating genius of a *Sopranos* script. Yet the show artfully works a metaphorical power out of their daily lives. Here are these incredibly obese people, both the men and the women, eating, buying, consuming, talking about sex—Flo, the wife of Tom Evangelista, who owns the family business, boasts that her husband is able to have sexual intercourse with her five times in one night; this claim is repeated several times in the series. So in thrall are they to their biological needs that even the "adults" among them seem to be in a state of infantile instability. Chris, Tom's nephew, is a very fat tough guy, brutal-seeming one minute, sobbing like a baby the next, whose possible homosexuality is hinted at more and more explicitly throughout the show. In material terms, he recalls Leigh Bowery, the corpulent model whose folds of flesh Lucian Freud obsessed over in his portraits; in this series, Chris' bountiful flesh sometimes gives the impression that he has a woman's breasts. Under every tough guy, a soprano; inside every bail bondsman, the yearning for a more intimate male bonding.

These huge people have semi-sublimated their unruly desires into making money by pursuing people who have broken the law; they pursue people whose own desires have gotten them in trouble. As you follow this family following its quarry through public toilets, and underground tunnels, and the dark side of existence, you feel you are getting a comitragic glimpse of some obscene dynamic driving the universe behind all the veils of convention that hide it. Don't get me wrong, the show is often unbearable to watch. The relentless portrait of mundane impulses and unintelligent people begins to get wearying. But *Family Bonds* at least has purpose and intelligence itself.

OCTOBER 18, 2004

45 *Growing Up Gotti*

It's rare that TV critics take up nature programs about animals in the wild, which is too bad. There is something dreamlike and weirdly resonant about being privy to the life of an untamed animal in its natural domain.

And now it's shark week on the Discovery Channel. The series is really five different documentaries, each one taking up a different shark, or a different place on earth inhabited by sharks. The first episode, produced by the BBC, is meant as an introduction to the subject: it follows a diver named Mike Degruy as he and a group of other divers and photographers explore the waters around a submerged volcano off the coast of Costa Rica. An enchanting place of "pristine wonder," as Degruy calls it, the place is brimming with wildlife, in particular, seven different species of shark. Tricked out with the fanciest technology, Degruy and his crew get inches away from most of their subjects. Not surprisingly, in a culture that is obsessed with the face—an actor raising his eyebrow in a close-up can change the course of a movie's plot—Degruy's cameramen are obsessed with the face of the shark.

Allow me to anthropomorphize. (Is there any other way to evoke an animal?) Maybe it's the implacable hardness of the face that grips you, or the unblinking, seemingly colorless eye, so impassive and lifeless. This is not the smaller, darker, warmer-seeming unblinking eye of a dolphin—or of any other kind of fish or aquatic mammal for that matter. This shark-eye belongs to a living thing that seems not to be alive. It's not that it could attack you and rip you apart that horrifies; it's that eye, which seems to look at you as if you were already dead. It appears to hold in its gelid consciousness with absolute indifference the secret of where you are going after this life. The eye expresses utter apathy. It has the same effect whether the shark is resting on the sandy ocean floor or furiously feeding in a pack on smaller fish.

Though as one of the series' narrators archly puts it, "sharks have an image problem," they look exactly like sharks. So they are pre-anthropomorphized, as it were. But for all their fabled predatoriness, they seem too lazy to do anything except prey on whatever opportunity is within reach. Their mouths are less like a mouth than an excuse for teeth; their mouth is not a mouth but a gash in the face; if they were human, this mouth could utter only obscenities or violent phrases, masticate or regurgitate, but never talk or smile or kiss. A shark that could speak would say things like, "I don't care if you set him on fire, beat him up—I don't care what you do." If it could be *Homo sapiens* for a minute, it would spend tens of thousands of dollars on a palatial, gilt-edged bathroom. It would have the painfully forced table manners of a person so lazy and self-indulgent that she wouldn't even be trying to maintain the mild discipline of eating in public if it were not for her feelings of shame and inferiority. It would prefer, on any given day, to wear clothes of the same color. This shark/person would be so angry underneath the thinly civilized exterior—the indolent brain yawning out stock phrases and clichés—that any perceived slight would provoke an enraged, abusive response. But it would be so empty of dignity and so brimming with self-loathing that anyone who slighted it would be cracking its secret, and therefore would have to be punished like a co-conspirator who might talk to the police. And so here it is, this vain, bleached creature, with the gold, and the accent like a drill in your ear, and for all the hostility, and the menace, and the brutality, also ignorant, and helpless and childlike—

Oops. I meant to put in a new paragraph somewhere up there because I've been describing Victoria Gotti, the daughter of the late mobster, John Gotti, and the star of her very own reality show, *Growing Up Gotti*, which premiered on A&E at the tail end of Discovery's sharks series. That's her, with the gold, and the anger, and the unbearable diction and language, and the even more unbearable footwear (when she dresses, she puts her mouth in her foot). She's an author, too, or a columnist or something, but pardon me if I don't look that up to be precise about it, because this person is so meaningless it was inevitable that sooner or later she'd get her own TV show. You could say that Gotti has mastered the trick of decrying the public perception of her in order to exploit the public perception of her— she's Donald Trump with little white boots—except that this is as common a strategy in American life now as sending out your (mostly fabricated) resume to prospective employers.

The public perception of Gotti, according to her, is that she shares her father's nature and therefore is dangerous, volatile, cunning, mysterious. And so her justification for doing the show, as she told an interviewer, is that it's "about showing the world that we are not a real-life Sopranos." Of course, this is carefully constructed code for saying that the show is really all about drawing parallels between her life and *The Sopranos*. It begins as *The Sopranos* begins, with a car ride—the car driven by Gotti's realtor—to Gotti's Long Island mansion. And throughout, Gotti is following some kind of script: recalling her father; threatening people; talking tough ("I don't care if you set him on fire, beat him up—I don't care what you do"); reminding everybody of the Missoni-clad sewer she comes from. At one point, she visits a celebrity matchmaker and explains that she makes men "intimidated, nervous, anxiety-ridden."

On the evidence of how she appears on her new show, it's more likely that she makes them disgusted, hysterical with laughter, or bored to tears. So here is the usual reality payoff: we see a sad, lost soul in the throes of self-delusion and have the satisfaction of knowing, as the camera focuses on her expensive jewelry, and big house, and fancy lifestyle, that such pathetic self-ignorance is the price she pays for all her ill-gotten lucre. How puritanical these sleazy shows are. But as the narrator on one of the shark episodes says, "Most species of shark are just too small to do us any harm."

Poor diminished Victoria Gotti is one of the tinier sharks. Is that why she has the limelight for a second now, to prove that we have nothing to fear from the notorious "animals" among us? All these shows like *Growing Up Gotti*, with their "cutting-edge" aura of sex and violence, are fairy tales about sex and violence. They create the illusion of having pierced the unknown. There is a horrifying moment in the Discovery series when the camera captures a shark sinking its teeth into the leg of a shark-behaviorist hired to appear on the show and then trying to tear it off. Such random catastrophes are, I suppose, the source of Victoria Gotti's success. With her carefully decorated atmosphere of "real" menace and ruthless violence, she makes you forget what's really out there.

JULY 28, 2004

46 Supernanny

Politics and society in North Korea are cruel and inhuman, but can the culture be worse than ours? I mean the real culture, the underground culture, if there is such a thing.

I ask this in all sincerity after watching reruns of several *Supernanny* episodes. The series will continue this fall, and I wanted to take stock, reruns being the perfect occasion for reflection and retrospection. Now a "reality series" about a professional British nanny briefly brought in to help and advise families whose children are difficult to handle violates some of the fundamental bonds between people. In a country like North Korea, the government violates—destroys—the fundamental bonds between people. Therefore ordinary North Koreans, assuming they can accomplish the almost superhuman task of keeping body and soul together, would not—insofar as culture secretly survives—allow such violations to occur in the cultural realm. On the contrary.

People existing under the boot of a totalitarian state that seeks to control all aspects of private life would not, for example, invite camera crews into their homes to record some of the most intimate and embarrassing moments of their private lives. The American families that invite the British nanny, Jo Frost—in D. H. Lawrence's novel *The Lost Girl*, Frost was the name of the oppressive housekeeper who sought to crush the sexual instincts of the novel's heroine—are undone by their young children's bad behavior, bewildered, and reduced to saying, in the manner of programmed robots, "Help us, Supernanny!" Supernanny then arrives in expert prearranged manner in her voluminous London black taxi, observes the situation for a few days, and then sits the parents down for a little talking-to, in the course of which the mothers usually break down and cry and the fathers look on, stiff, resentful, and confused.

The harrowing consultation between nanny and parents has the effect of infantilizing the parents and making them dependent on the nanny, while expanding the authority of the children by making them the chief occasion, main focus, and principal beneficiaries of the show's dubious energies. Indeed, the children are elevated for exposing their parents' deficiencies, and the little tykes' reward for all this incredible attention and attentiveness resembles the honors bestowed by the erstwhile Soviet state on Pavlik Morozov, the twelve-year-old boy who denounced his father to the KGB.

Mother and father are now in the thrall of Miss Frost, who goes about imposing on the subject household a rigorous new structure of activities meant to pacify and contain the rebellious offspring. The parents are reprimanded, controlled, made to recite Miss Frost's new precepts and also to perform according to the new principles of behavior under the nanny's watchful eye.

In the meantime, the wild children are having the time of their lives, surrounded as they are by parents forced by the public glare to be more tender and adoring than ever before, by a tender and adoring Miss Frost—she has to usurp the parents and win the children to her, plus she had better not do anything that might seem harmful to the children. They are also surrounded by the show's crew of functionaries, who like Miss Frost must be aware of the possibility of litigation in the wake of a false step, in much the same way as a totalitarian regime's functionaries are aware of the possibility of torture and death in the wake of a false step. After a few days of Miss Frost intervening, restructuring, and commanding, she and her lieutenants withdraw to their headquarters—we are never told where—but not before installing cameras throughout the house, enabling them to ensure through surveillance that the parents comply with Miss Frost's program of rehabilitation.

Safely situated in her anonymous kremlin, Miss Frost watches on a laptop the results of her crackdown. A solidly built woman with a hardy working-class accent—like most modern tyrants, her origins are among the people she knows best how to charm, browbeat, and control—she makes sounds of affirmation and assent when the parents abide by one of her rules. These rules usually involve acting forcefully with children, changing your tone of voice when angry, making clear distinctions between rewards and punishments, being consistent in the distribution of both, and refusing to melt in the face of your child's fits, tears, expressions of utter despair, etc.

In other words, Miss Frost's advocacy of the "naughty spot"— at the bottom of the stairs or up against a wall—and her insistence that children be told that if they're not nice to others, people will not be nice to them, offer a familiar return to old-fashioned methods of discipline. Society seems to yearn for these all the more as society is told from every corner of the culture to go ahead and indulge its every appetite and whim. Miss Frost is the congenial-seeming return of the repressed that exists like dream or nightmare in the hearts of Americans who are both besieged and thrilled by commercially decreed satisfactions.

In the end, the subject parents always do something wrong—the nice contemporary mother can't bear to see her child crying himself to death in the naughty spot, or something like that; Mom swoops in and liberates the prisoner from his dungeon; and Miss Frost, outraged by the infraction, leaves headquarters in high dudgeon and speeds toward the insurrection at high speed in her large black car. She crashes back into the house, wrests from the embarrassed mother a startling confession—*All I want is my son to be normal and successful and not a thirty-year-old man who plays with himself at board meetings and calls other people poopheads!*—shames the parents, and subdues the overjoyed children.

By the time Miss Frost is set to leave and continue on to her next rehabilitation, order is always restored. The end of every episode has the subject family standing outside their suburban house, with the parents looking dazed, weary, and beaten, and mechanically telling the cameras that Miss Frost has changed their lives, that they will never return to their discredited ways, that they can't thank her enough, that they don't know what they would have done without her, and that they can't even remember a time when they lived without her.

And all that for, one assumes, a check and to obey the culture's command to make money no matter what undignified thing you have to do to get it. And all that to obey the culture's command that You Must Appear Before The Cameras No Matter What. All that for a moment of wealth and a smidgeon of celebrity. Comrades, that is not entertainment. American society needs immediately to begin diplomatic negotiations with American culture.

JUNE 20, 2005

47 | *Thirty Days*

Is there anything people won't do to avoid having an ordinary job? Or to avoid working at a job that requires them to think about something or someone other than themselves, or in which they are not the center of attention? A lot of people now "go into the arts" the way other people go into real estate or insurance. They become novelists, or poets, or filmmakers not because they have been summoned by a vocation, but because they are taking up a career. Realtors have a passion for money, not selling property; insurance agents want to become rich, not gather up the fragile world in their protective arms. The desire of a lot of "artists" nowadays to become rich and famous makes their art incidental to the pursuit of their very concrete and practical goals.

Seven years after Morgan Spurlock graduated from film school in 1993, he came up with an idea for an online proto-reality show called *I Bet You Will*, which eventually was picked up by MTV. The premise for the series was that, as Spurlock told an interviewer at the time, "people will do anything . . . and I mean anything . . . for money." The "anything" consisted of, for example, a woman dancing in public for $150 wearing just a thong with the words "I Bet You Will" printed on it, and a man eating dog shit for $400.

Spurlock waxed eloquent about his brainchild: "People love to watch this. It's the public forum, it's the idea of seeing something new and original out there. And to see a regular person who's coming up and getting the chance to win $300 if he eats an entire jar of pigs' feet and washes it down with a pint-glass of corn oil, you know . . . it's . . . not something you might do, but it's something that somebody else might do, and something, you know what? I'd wanna watch that, too! I'd wanna watch that happen!" Other episodes had a woman drinking a can of condensed milk followed by a can of chicken broth, and then four shots of cod liver oil. Spurlock spurred her on: "Yeah! Four shots of cod liver oil. Want another one?" One of the anythings people will do for money is also to invite other people to humiliate themselves. Spurlock was a pioneer in this new public style of humiliation.

History, however, marches on. Just a few years later Spurlock, avid for his laurels, had another scintillating inspiration. In *Supersize Me,* Spurlock found that he himself could do some outrageous thing for money, though putting on twenty-five pounds by eating only fast food for thirty days wasn't really humiliating. On the contrary, Spurlock portrayed himself as a Michael Moore–like little guy standing up to the fast-food industry, exposing the way it sold the public anything, and I mean anything, just to make a buck. And having earned a living getting people to eat pigs' feet and animal excrement, and to drink corn oil and cod liver oil, Spurlock was just the guy to go after the purveyors of unhealthy food.

In *Supersize Me,* Spurlock had learned the standard trick of American self-presentation—the old fig-leaf-of-virtue gambit. In this new style of entrepreneurial creating and thinking, the important thing for artists and thinkers, as for businesspeople in general, is to hide a conniving ego behind an oozing conscience.

With *Thirty Days*, his new six-part series on FX, Spurlock—
and his anemic-looking fiancée, who gets teary-eyed a lot—
has brought his cod liver oil business, as it were, to the small
screen. The virtuous fig leaf in this little enterprise goes like
this: "So here we are, a nation of conservative, liberal, rich,
poor, black, Latino, brown, white, gay, straight people," Spurlock says, introducing the show. "Do we really know what it's
like to see the world through our neighbor's eyes?" The show's
conceit is to take people out of their ordinary contexts and
transport them into totally alien situations for thirty days, just
as *Supersize Me* took place over the course of thirty days. This
should, according to Spurlock, expand the sympathy of the
transported person. Episodes include a straight Army reservist
rooming with a gay man; a mother, who is concerned about
her daughter's wild ways, encouraged to drink heavily in order
to better empathize with her daughter; and a devout Christian
being set down among devout Muslims. In other words, *Thirty
Days* is a freak show.

Once he justified *I Bet You Will* as being part of the "public
forum." Now Spurlock has perfected the depressing art of humiliating people under the pretext of performing a public service. The first episode, in which Spurlock and his fiancée try to
live on a minimum wage (just as Spurlock took the idea for *Supersize Me* from Eric Schlosser's incomparably superior *Fast
Food Nation*, he took the idea for his debut segment from Bar-
bara Ehrenreich's incomparably superior *Nickel and Dimed*)
says it all.

Throughout the entire hour, Spurlock and his turgid fiancée
look at the camera and ask, "How can people live like this?" It's
rough all right. Rising to a mountain peak of indignation,
Spurlock—he can't stop smiling the entire time—offers this

searing reproach to society: "We're educated, articulate, white"—and they have to work at lousy minimum-wage jobs. But educated, articulate white people don't apply for those kinds of jobs. Not unless they're slumming for thirty days, followed around by a cameraman and technician, at the end of which it's back to a really great lifestyle, with a juicy paycheck and an even fatter moral payoff. As Spurlock puts it in the show's final scene, staring meaningfully into the camera (and barely suppressing that peculiar smile), "I've been affected. And I'm better for it." Supersize you.

JUNE 27, 2005

48) *The Apprentice*

Do you remember a few years ago when the crisis du jour was irony? The apprehension was that postmodernism's infinite regression of meaning had trickled down into daily life, and that everyone, from novelists to pundits, was saying precisely what they didn't mean. Self-distancing was in vogue; sincerity signaled a lack of style. Estimable people were justifiably alarmed. (I mean this seriously.) If people were not saying what they meant, you naturally couldn't trust what anyone was saying. And so symposia were organized, conferences convened, books written, experts consulted. Finally, sometime around—I'm looking at my notes— June 12, 2000, in the late afternoon, around three o'clock Eastern Standard Time, in the waning months of the administration of Bill Clinton, who people feared had become the country's first postmodern president, irony began to retreat—it sounded like a car with a flat tire, slowly thumping out of earshot—eventually to be vanquished by the attacks on September 11, which, many experts believe, ushered in a new era of sincerity.

Yes, I'm kidding and mostly exaggerating, but there was indeed a trend of irony, which incited a concerned backlash. And both cultural phases are, under current circumstances, profoundly ironic. Because not long after this superficial style of irony became an object of criticism, a presidential candidate was defeated to a large extent because the general perception of him, by people all over the country who probably had never heard about the Great Irony Controversy, was that he was too wooden, too earnest, too sincere even, to make a good leader. His opponent, on the other hand, who seemed vexed by the burden of serious thinking and serious behaving, and seemed to wink at his audience—as if to reassure people that if he were them, he'd be zoning out while watching him too—won (maybe) the election and appears to be the very type of person who habitually doesn't say what he means. Rather than being an ironist, however, it seems that George W. Bush is a liar. But what really boggles the mind is how this man, from one of the wealthiest and most powerful families in the country, could convince vast segments of the population that he was a regular down-home guy, just like them, and not blinded or biased by wealth and power at all.

If you want the mind to be a little less boggled on the subject of appearance versus reality in American politics, tune in to *The Apprentice,* NBC's runaway hit of a reality show in which the super-rich real-estate developer Donald Trump puts aspiring Trumps through their entrepreneurial paces as they strive for the show's brass ring: a real job with Trump's organization as Trump's real apprentice and president of one of his companies for a year. Devised by executive producer Mark Burnett, *The Apprentice* is yet another variation on *Survivor.* Divergent personalities from diverse backgrounds and places are thrown into a highly competitive situation, out of which only one of them will emerge triumphant. They bond and bicker, berate and betray, say nothing particularly dramatic or original, and get accompanied at every turn by something like Wagner's endless melody, rising and falling music that teases and excites the feelings in the absence of any real excitement or suspense, except of course for the final moment in which all the tedium crystallizes into someone winning and someone losing.

Just as the ill-fated *Mr. Personality* two seasons ago tried to capitalize on the notoriety of Monica Lewinsky, *The Apprentice* introduces Donald Trump to the world of reality TV. Unlike Monica, though, who mostly stood around smiling and consoling the choice-beleaguered heroine whenever she broke down and cried ("I could spend the rest of my life with him—but he doesn't like rollerblading!"), Trump stands at the center of the show. He dispenses his by-now famous judgment—"You're fired"—in a shadowy boardroom streaked with slender rays of light, into which he enters through a dark, wood-paneled door set in a dark, wood-paneled wall, seating himself in a high-backed chair at the center of a long conference table, flanked on either side by one of his real-life lieutenants, and facing on the other side of the table the contestants who've been called upstairs to learn which of them—after forays into selling lemonade, creating advertising campaigns, dealing in art, renting real estate, and so on—"goes up to the suite" and which of them "goes down to the street." The original sixteen candidates have been whittled down to two, Kwame and Bill, whose fates Trump will decide tonight, in a special two-hour show.

The Apprentice is a hugely successful series; it's reaped high ratings, huge media attention, and even a warm critical response. In the *New York Times*, Frank Rich attributed the success of the show to the fact that Trump's "brand of leadership, narcissistic and autocratic as it seems, strikes audiences as more palatable than the corporate shenanigans that have been in the spotlight on the public stage in recent years." In this context, Trump was a "moral paragon," Rich wrote, a "hero because he conducts business so transparently." He goes on: "It's the contestants, not Trump, who are the greedy ones." They are the ones who remind audiences of the smug, selfish dot-comers and the slick inside-traders. "We don't root for them to win, we root for them to be canned."

And Trump himself comes across as a charming fellow, down-to-earth, sympathetic to the contestants, generous to a fault, regretful about firing the unlucky ones. He even turns his mouth down ruefully when he issues his terrible judgment (now available on T-shirts at the bargain price of $35). He's clearly enjoying himself, and it's as irresistible to watch someone enjoy himself as it is to see someone laughing at his own jokes. Maybe Rich is right. Maybe Trump represents that good-old American entrepreneurial spirit that has been lost in corporate America, where you don't get fired by the boss with good, old-fashioned humanity but by some soulless cipher. After all, as Rich writes admiringly about Trump, "he wants, he buys, he builds, he slaps his name on everything in sight. His is the second-oldest profession in the world." Not only that, but it's "comforting" that "on *The Apprentice,* we never see Mr. Trump using a computer or a P.D.A.," unlike those slippery Enron-type guys. Now isn't that sweet.

A few weeks after Rich's encomium to Trump, who is the socially powerful friend of New York media figures and New York media moguls, the *New York Times* had a very different kind of article, a masterfully reported and constructed, an unforgettable article. It was about some very old-fashioned guys who, without fancy technology or P.D.A.'s, ripped off scores of lower-middle-class people who wanted to change their lives and get a small piece of the American dream by buying modest homes on small plots of land in the Poconos while continuing to make the five-hour commute to jobs in New York. They had been unable to afford houses in the stratospheric New York housing market, so these old-fashioned guys came along and made promises they couldn't keep and sold these people houses they couldn't afford, houses that were overvalued and falling apart. Now the bus drivers, and nurses, and paralegals—all of whom would probably love to get a high-paying job working in a Trump company, and would probably do whatever they had to do to get it—were declaring bankruptcy.

So it's odd that Rich would be extolling Trump's qualities, since the housing crisis in New York is partly the result of developers like Trump, who take huge tax abatements from the city in exchange for promises to create middle-income housing— promises that, in Trump's case, he almost always broke. It's odd, too, that Rich would root for *The Apprentice*'s contestants to get "canned" since their "greed" is a creation of the show's premise, editing, producers, and general atmosphere; but it's especially odd since people are getting "canned" more and more, all over the country that Rich likes to speak for. But the real poser is how Rich, the veteran theater critic, can actually take the Trump of *The Apprentice* for the real Donald Trump. For the real Trump, wanting, buying, and building isn't all there is to it.

The real Trump—the Trump who is now teaching America how to wheel and deal, how to turn yourself into a financial Titan, how to transform a few bucks into a fortune, how to be the consummate businessman—this real Trump, like our real president, is a rich daddy's boy, who came into the world with his real-estate-developer father's $40 million housing empire, and considerable connections to the Brooklyn Democratic Party, out of which came New York Mayor Abraham Beame and New York Governor Hugh Carey. (If you want to know how Trump has been able to build just about whatever he wants in New York City, all you need to know are two words: campaign contributions.) Trump is a creation of family wealth and affiliations, and of serendipity. He bought his first piece of property in the recession-deep New York of the 1970s when, eager to "revitalize," New York officials were almost giving property away with enormous tax abatements. From there, Trump made the fateful decision to purchase no less than three Atlantic City casinos, which shortly began to compete against each other, severely reducing profits for Trump's company.

But, then, according to a former Trump lieutenant, John R. O'Donnell, an embittered casualty of Trump's lack of business acumen whose book about Trump—*Trumped!*—Trump has never legally contested, Trump never bothered to learn anything about the casino business before he spent tens of millions in New Jersey. He never tried to pick up any knowledge about the airline industry before he tried and failed to buy American Airlines; or about the business of professional football before he purchased the New Jersey Generals and offered such exorbitant, unprecedented salaries that he helped drive the United States Football League out of business. In 1988, he signed a contract to buy a racehorse named Alibi, changing its name to DJ Trump— he has reduced the profits of his companies by spending millions to get his name on every inch of every property that he owns—and nearly killed the animal when Trump insisted that the horse continue practice-racing when he had a cold. Because of Trump's pushy arrogance, the colt got so sick he almost died and had to have his hooves amputated. He'll never race. As a result, after almost destroying the horse, Trump refused to pay the owner who had sold Alibi, even though Trump had signed his name to papers promising to buy him.

Trump, NBC's financial guru, has the Midas touch in reverse—born with a golden checkbook in his mouth, nearly everything he touches turns to shit. In the late 1990s, having built his "fortune" on massive borrowing, Trump declared bankruptcy four times in two years. His eyesore buildings are routinely criticized for their shoddy construction. In the last few years, he's made most of his money advising people on how to spend theirs. In New York financial circles, Trump is a joke. His fecklessness in business hasn't helped his character much, either. For years, he tried to drive tenants out of a building whose site he wanted to develop by harassing them in various ways, until the courts reined him in. The real Trump is not charmingly rueful when he is displeased: He fires at random, screams, barks, curses, humiliates. O'Donnell quotes Trump making this good, old-fashioned, transparent critique of some of his top employees: "You're all jerkoffs. I've never had so much incompetent shit working for me. First of all, you hired scum. I got scum working for me here. . . . Walt was in charge, and he hired scum. Walt was stupid." His attitudes toward women are crude. He doesn't like to be physically touched: walking with his then-wife Ivana through one of his casinos after an elderly customer had touched Ivana's dress, Trump exploded in public: "I told you a hundred times, don't talk to these people. Why do you let these people touch you. Forget them." He is a schoolyard bully. He is a coward. He is a creep. His hair isn't funny anymore.

Yet television is more and more becoming a willing accomplice to all sorts of power-hungry agendas—see how the comics promote the politicians, see how the politicians use the producers (for example, *K Street*). Trump, whose sole success rests on his ability to create the illusion of success by fabricating the chimera of his own celebrity, has been allowed by Mark Burnett—what else is involved, one wonders?—to turn *The Apprentice* into one long advertisement for Donald Trump, promoting, in show after show, his casinos and his other properties, not to mention his suddenly sweet nature. How can you foreclose on this guy; how can you refuse to do business with someone whose sheer visibility and universal familiarity provide his bona fides? There are plenty of shrewd, creative, intelligent, even public-minded businesspeople NBC could have turned to. But it followed its commercial instincts and went straight to the fraud whose appearance is in inverse relationship to his reality. There are more than a few television producers who love the real-life fraud. It makes them feel almost authentic. That has been Trump's secret throughout his entrepreneurial life: He makes the most vulgar graspers and arrivistes feel like Proust.

So Kwame and Bill, good luck tonight! By now, they should know that something is wrong because Trump has run his reality show with the same incompetence with which he runs his companies. Dividing the contestants up into two teams, two rival companies, he and the producers structured the show so that not only would the companies compete against each other but the employees within each company would also try to trip each other up. Another Trump strategy for success. Peter Drucker, move over. And the real kicker is that the show's winner gets to join a company whose CEO—that is, The Donald—is about to go under for a fifth time. It's right there, in the *New York Times*. It's almost beyond belief. But then you recall that irony has been vanquished, and that only the blunt, sincere, bald-faced liars, who "conduct their business so transparently," are to be believed.

APRIL 15, 2004

Games

49 *Deal or No Deal*

One thing Democrats can do in their seemingly never-ending quest to rediscover and reinvent their party is to try to learn from the phenomenon of a giant talking penis as he commands a small legion of voluptuous women, while at the same time he guides, advises, and cajoles a new contestant every week toward the goal of winning a fortune, or at least taking home enough cash not to feel humiliated in front of millions of viewers. I'm talking about NBC's new hit game show, *Deal or No Deal*.

The show is hosted by the comedian Howie Mandel, whose shaven head and tuft of hair on his chin put me in mind of a short story by Alberto Moravia, "He and I," in which a loquacious phallus tries continually to tempt its resistant owner into all kinds of carnal trouble. In Howie's case, he serves as the intermediary between the contestant and over two dozen models who stand throughout the show in tiered rows, a small, numbered aluminum briefcase perched on a platform beside each beauty. Howie tempts the contestants into all kinds of trouble revolving around the conflict between chance and free will. I'll explain the premise of the show in due course. For now, all you need to know is that the contestant chooses one briefcase after the other. Howie then orders the model to open the case, in which you see the dollar amount written against a background of sensuous blue velvet. The whole thing is almost casually sexual. Like the greatest fairy tales, the greatest game shows know how to organize the libido.

Invented by the shrewd moral imbeciles who brought the world *Big Brother* and *Fear Factor, Deal* is an international broadcasting phenomenon, different versions of which exist in dozens of countries around the world. Unlike the reality shows, however, *Deal* is a straightforward game show, and there is really nothing morally imbecilic about it. As game shows go, it is as well done and addictive as any that I've seen. You would have to go back thirty years to the genre's peak of perfection, *Let's Make a Deal,* which ruled the game-show roost on and off from 1963 to 2003.

Let's Make a Deal was in fact structured like a fairy tale—a sort of mercantilist fairy tale that mixed a mythic dimension of wish, chance, and desire with American craziness and self-assertiveness. After being chosen by Monty Hall, the show's legendary host, contestants offered to barter objects they brought from home for some of the goods Hall presented to them on stage. You could never be sure, though, whether an unassuming-looking chest of drawers presented by Hall contained an envelope with a check for several thousand dollars. When he felt the urge, Hall offered to buy back an item a contestant had acquired. Potential contestants themselves often showed up wearing outrageous costumes in hopes of being chosen for the show, thus turning themselves into commodities of sorts, too. (Isn't turning yourself into a commodity what dressing in the hippest, coolest, most cutting-edge style always comes down to?) The show's climax was the Big Deal, truly a fairy-tale-like event, in which contestants were invited to choose what was behind one of three doors. Sometimes Hall tempted the contestant with money or an expensive item in lieu of choosing one of the doors.

Deal or No Deal shares with *Let's Make a Deal* just such a ploy of offering the contestant a certain prize in place of making an uncertain choice. In the case of *Deal,* a mysterious figure called The Banker—you only see him in silhouette, sitting high up in a glass box, ensconced in a comfortable chair, sometimes with a pipe in his mouth—rings Howie's cell phone now and then with instructions for Howie to offer the contestant a sum of money; if the contestant accepts it, he ends the game.

Deal is played like this: The contestant chooses one briefcase from the twenty-six the models are holding. He keeps that one unopened on the table between him and Howie, who both stand, like the models, throughout the show. The remaining briefcases contain cash amounts usually from one cent up to $3 million—the maximum seems to be getting higher with each episode. Naturally, the hope is that the unopened briefcase contains the highest sum of money.

All sums are displayed on a big board, including whatever might be in the briefcase on the table. The contestant then chooses the remaining briefcases; sometimes a few at a time, sometimes only one, as the number of them dwindles. As the amounts are revealed, they disappear from the board. Any number that remains on the board could be either in the models' briefcases, or in the one on the table. The more low amounts of cash the contestant picks, the greater the chance that he'll have a high amount in the briefcase on the table; the more high amounts he chooses, the more likely the possibility that the mysterious briefcase will contain a low number. As the shifting numbers change the contestant's chances, The Banker calls, offering more or less money depending on the situation. As it becomes harder and harder for the contestant to decide whether or not to play it safe—that is, weighing The Banker's high offer against the possibility of a fortune, or a low offer against the chance of leaving empty-handed—some of the contestant's family and friends are invited to sit on the sidelines and offer usually hysterical advice.

So there are two kinds of economies on the show: the real economy and the dream economy. The real economy is The Banker's offer; as Mandel tells one contestant, a mother of seven who's been offered $74,000, "People work a year and don't make half that." It is almost dreamlike to hear such an accurate, down-to-earth truth on television, since television, like nearly everything else in American entertainment, is often in the business of making you believe that everyone is raking in huge sums of money except you. (Of course, such dream expectations are what make the real bankers on Wall Street rich.) In that sense, *Deal or No Deal* is a homey antidote to shows like *Fear Factor* and *Survivor*. In those decadent Roman extravaganzas, the possibility of great wealth becomes so intimate and familiar to the contestants that they can no more live without attaining it than they would choose to exist without shoes. Those shows know what tyrants know. The grossest absurdity—like eating cockroaches—becomes a desperate necessity once self-esteem is reduced to a matter of survival. *Deal* exists on capitalism's brighter side.

In fact, it's heartening to see how many contestants take the "deal" in the end. Most of them seem to realize that what the show wants them to believe is a deal—a compromise—is actually manna from heaven. Taking it certifies their sense of willpower. These contestants don't want to be rich; they just don't want to be made fools of, or to leave feeling that they thwarted themselves. And here's where the Democrats can learn something. People, like *Deal's* contestants, who have little or no money, don't want to feel or be told that their best interests are purely economic. (Tom Frank, take note.) They make up for not having money by raising families, going to church, passionately pursuing other interests; *by taking the deal and thinking that through the instrument of character they are in control of their lives.* They want to feel that, despite not having money, they can decide how to define and determine the way they live.

So what can the Democrats take away from *Deal,* this modern-day fairy tale, part of whose popularity lies in the fact that viewers can play along and win up to $10,000? They don't have to feign being religious, or travel the family-values route, or anything of the sort. What the party has to do is convince people that what is really manna from heaven—federal protections for the individual, and the community, in various realms of life—is actually a deal they've chosen themselves. Don't ask me the particulars of how to accomplish that—I'm just the TV critic. But it has something to do with sublimation, with submerging candor about "personal space" and "choice" in insinuating blue velvet. And with making people feel, as *Deal or No Deal* does, that rather than being losers who need the government's help, they are winners simply by virtue of being allowed to play the game. Even if it's not true.

MARCH 6, 2006

50 *Iron Chef America*

To understand the phenomenal popularity of the Food Network's *Iron Chef America*, you have to understand the phenomenal popularity of *sous vide*. *Sous vide*, which is French for "under vacuum" or "in a vacuum," is a culinary technique in which food is cooked in hermetically sealed, clear plastic bags at very low temperatures that allow a chef to keep his eye on precise details of the cooking process. Premiering almost exactly one year ago, *Iron Chef America* pits two world-class chefs against each other in the "Kitchen Stadium." They have one hour to make several dishes with the "secret ingredient" of the day: tilapia, tuna, chicken, yogurt, and so on. Three judges sample the results at the end of the competition and then declare the winner.

You want the connection between *sous vide* and the show now? What do you think this column is, the journalistic equivalent of McDonald's? Please be patient.

Patience, of course, is exactly what most cooking shows these days are not about. Whether it's Mario Batali or Bobby Flay slugging it out with a challenger on *Iron Chef America* or Rachael Ray's lessons in thirty-minute trailer-park delights, the idea behind most food-preparation series these days is to create the culinary equivalent of a car chase or gunfight. Yet in the case of Rachael Ray, a proud, happy amateur who engagingly drops and spills things, laughing at herself all the while, the purpose of the show is as much to instruct as to entertain. *Iron Chef* wants merely to keep you on the edge of your seat, in the style of any of the competitive reality shows.

It's hardly surprising that the trend of turning every mundane activity into a do-or-die struggle to win has now surfaced in the kitchen. Soon they'll have people on a row of toilets straining for the evacuation to end all evacuations. As the money culture grows, as competition becomes more widespread and intense, the vicarious release of seeing competition ritualized and formalized to the point of absurdity seems to be proliferating. Still, you would think that the kitchen is the last place on earth where the spectacle of competition would flourish.

After all, if home is the center of existence, the kitchen is the heart of home. The hearth was in the kitchen. Food, the basic stuff of life, comes from the kitchen. The kitchen used to be where women, the creators and possessors of life and of all the secrets of sustaining life, used to gather—in most cultures, it still is. In Soviet Russia, revolution, counterrevolution, endurance, and dissent all were hatched in the kitchen. All the warmth of the world is, in principle, in that room.

The difference, though, between *Iron Chef* and other cooking shows on television now, as well as the difference between those shows and similar programs on television years ago, is that earlier series like Julia Child's shows and *The Galloping Gourmet* really sought to teach viewers how to cook. You entered into almost an intimate relationship with these people as they chopped, diced, heated, and stirred, talking, digressing, explaining, opining, telling stories the whole time. You can certainly still bond with Rachael Ray, or with Emeril, or with the two fat ladies, when they were on (I used to love them), though the self-conscious camera and the emphasis on keeping the audience entertained put these figures at a further remove from you than previous cooking hosts. With *Iron Chef,* though, no one gains any kind of insight into the culinary arts.

For all its corny, quasi-parodic opening theatrics, the Japanese *Iron Chef* slowed down when it came to the contest itself. Fewer sous-chefs helped the famous adversaries out, and the commentators seemed more interested in the chefs' specific operations. In *Iron Chef America,* the camera whizzes from one scene to another, the different sequences separated by the sound of two knives clashing together. The show, in fact, is modeled on a sporting event—you get minute-by-minute commentating patter, and even instant replays.

There are a few reasons why *sous vide* has lately become so popular: In some ways, it's a high-falutin' version of the clear plastic pouches you get with TV dinners (remember when a TV dinner was something you ate while watching TV and not something you watched being made on TV?); the cool French words make you feel *très* special when you pronounce them; the idea of food being vacuum-sealed is appealing in this germ-conscious age.

But perhaps the strongest reason for *sous vide*'s allure is that it's a perfect reflection of a particular state of mind. On *Iron Chef America,* the most ordinary and necessary of tasks, one that is often mere drudgery after a tiring day at work, has been made the subject of American apotheosis. Cooking has become the apple of the media's eye. Which means that anyone who performs this most ordinary of functions—that is, just about every adult—is a potential cynosure of electronic attention. A potential star. And not only that, but food no longer has its dark side; on *Iron Chef America,* food is not a few hours of digestion away from waste, or a few hours of oxygen away from disintegration and stench. No, on this show, food itself is unperishable and immortal. As Brillat-Savarin famously said, you are what you eat. On *Iron Chef,* the viewer is, for one hour, vacuum-sealed against the ravages of time, ordinariness, and the outside world.

JANUARY 10, 2006

51 *Stump the Schwab*

I am thinking now of counterpoints and countermotions, of yin and yang, of inexorable dialectical movement, of stealthy Sophoclean irony, of the tendency of life to move in precise antitheses, one public and apparent, and the other hidden deep in fate to be revealed in time, all this double motion ending harmoniously or not so well. Consider Howie Schwab.

For seventeen years the head researcher at ESPN—he started out as the only researcher—Schwab is at present the centerpiece of a tremendously popular game show on that cable channel called *Stump the Schwab*. Corpulent, goateed, bespectacled, soft, and fleshy, he looks a little like Al Goldstein, the publisher of *Screw* magazine and another mighty cable presence—or rather, Schwab recalls Goldstein in appearance only to refute him in essence. Referred to by the show's host, Stuart Scott, as, among other monikers, Big Guy, Buddha, Big Fella, Stud of the Stats, Schwab—no one ever calls him Howie on the air; the addition of the first name would actually be a subtraction of identity, like going to a ball game and calling a hot dog a frankfurter; Schwab is Schwab as fire is fire, as Congress is Congress—Schwab knows everything there is to know about every species of professional athletic activity as currently practiced in this country.

Unlike the pornographer whom he vaguely resembles, Schwab is a meta-sublimator. The world of incessant motion that he has committed to memory and organized into discrete bits of disconnected information achieves, in the layers of Schwab's cerebellum, a perfect stasis. This trivia show about professional sports is actually a rebuff to anyone who has burned a single calorie by participating in an athletic competition. That is the Schwabian countermotion.

There are guys like Schwab. You know what I mean. You knew them when you were younger, but then you didn't see their type any more. When everyone else was running around being "other-directed," as the sociologists used to say—toward girls, toward cars, toward clothes, toward *immediate pleasure*—the Schwabs were staying out of the way and inconspicuously creating their own special branch of information. Not knowledge. Information. They didn't go the way of true religious personalities. They didn't seek power in renunciatory pursuits of quieter and stiller states of being. Not these guys. That's not how they got back at Captain Billy Bob of the high-school football team.

Rather, the Schwabs stayed in the world that they superficially withdrew from and mastered the easygoing, smiling, practical mysticism of sports trivia. Imagine the contents of the Kabbalah, the *I Ching*, the works of St. John of the Cross and Meister Eckhardt— imagine all these secrets bounding out of the books that held them and running around with shorts and Nikes in your local gym. Imagine, if you will, the Vedas on the Stairmaster. This is the arena that is the mind of the Schwab. Schwab and guys like him are the kings of sunny public arcana; out of the rough, obvious, unesoteric world of brute physical competition, they build a *mysterium triviandum*. They make a mentality out of a physicality and become kings of the realm that would not even have them as contenders.

And yet. And yet. There is a categorical difference between Schwab and the guys like him who come to defeat him at his own mental cannibalization of the physical game, as it were; three guys in every episode, who contend with him over multiple-choice questions in the first segment, which eliminates one of them; over various other tests in the second segment, which eliminates the other; until it's just Schwab and a single adversary in the final third of the show, face to face at either side of a table, Stuart Scott between them, asking each one questions that would have Schlegel to Hegel to Nagel for assistance like Tinker to Evers to Chance—questions like "Before being selected in the 2002 NBA draft, Yao Ming played for what team in the Chinese Basketball Association?"; and my favorite: "In 1951, St. Louis Browns owner Bill Veeck sent three-foot-seven-inch-midget Eddie Gaedel to pinch-hit. What was Gaedel's uniform number?" (Answers: The Shanghai Sharks; "1/8.")

But nearly all these guys are in some kind of shape, and seem like they could be athletic if they wanted to. This is *la différence Schwabianne.* Schwab is not in any kind of shape. He is the Fat Triviator the way that Kirstie Alley is the Fat Actress. He seems defiantly sedentary. He is one of the growing silent phalanx of personalities on television who seem . . . not to work out! And every time that I've seen the show, Schwab is wearing the jersey and number of a famous athlete from one sport or another, as if to almost parodically drive home his countermotional triumph of mentality over physicality in the very home of the latter. The thing is, these athletic guys almost never stump the Schwab. In this Cartesian scrimmage, he puts body in its place. But mind ought not to rejoice—he doesn't seem to truly know anything beyond bits of information, either. The real victor in this show is neither mind nor body. It's that quintessentially American realm which exists between the two: The Couch.

MAY 16, 2005

52 The Winter Olympics

The winter Olympics are to the summer Olympics what the bat mitzvah is to the bar mitzvah—a latecomer welcomed into an old tradition. It wasn't until 1924, in Chamonix, France, that the winter games were established, making them the modern cousin to the ancient ritual. Yet there is something also very old about the winter games. Unlike their summer counterparts, the winter competitions require the contestants to be attached to some piece of equipment that adapts them to the season's harsh conditions. In the summer games, the athletes compete against the clock or each other. In the winter, they are up against the elements as well. The great determining variable is nature—in the form of ice, snow, and wind. You can't get as vicariously close to the winter Olympians as to the figures in the summer. Something deep in your bones holds you back.

Inclement conditions also mean that in a good number of the winter games the athletes have their faces covered, and it's probably another reason why the winter games don't offer the intimacy between spectator and participant that the summer games do. It could be why they're not as glamorous, either. Certainly, ever since the end of the cold war, the winter Olympics have lost their central glamorous tension, which was the rivalry between the United States and the USSR in sports where the latter always seemed to have the edge. There were exceptions, but it was often like watching the launch of Sputnik every four years. It was a slur on American know-how. Until the American victory over the Soviet hockey team in Lake Placid in 1980, meeting the Russians in the hockey rink was like trying to take Moscow in the winter. The national rivalries in 2006, for example, seemed almost absurdly apolitical. *South* Korea?

The one event where the Americans and the Russians seemed to be going head to head was men's figure skating, which featured the reigning champ, Yevgeny Plushenko, up against three Americans: Evan Lysacek, Johnny Weir, and Matthew Savoie. Plushenko easily carried off the gold, and all three Americans failed to earn a medal. But what struck you was the difference between national styles. Characteristically Russian, Plushenko shunned the artistic dimension of the competition and executed one powerful, technically perfect feat after another. (Certain virtuoso Russian pianists used to sacrifice poetry to strong technique, too: They didn't interpret Schubert, for example, they expounded him.) Russia may be sinking, but its athletic coaches and trainers still stress might and force.

The American figure skaters, on the other hand, competed with ultra-sensitive felinity. When Lysacek suffered a mishap in an earlier event, he sat next to his coach in front of spectators and cameras with his head in his hands as if weeping. Later, you saw him sighing on his mother's shoulder. The music that accompanied his near comeback was from *Carmen,* an opera in which the protagonist's fatal vulnerability to a seductress has its roots in his helpless maternal attachment. Weir seemed androgynous as he floated almost surreally over the ice. The most beautiful performance was by Savoie, who really should have won the gold medal, and who moved around the arena with ethereal grace. The Americans all sacrificed mighty technique to artistic delicacy. Maybe being the world's sole superpower has its soulful benefits, after all.

Instead of the old cold war rivalry, the really dramatic grudge matches seem this year to be between American individuals and American commerce, or just between American individuals. First there was Michelle Kwan versus NBC. After the injured skater withdrew from the Olympics, the network shamelessly offered her what must have been a very lucrative position as commentator on the very games that were going to continue without her. A dignified Kwan turned them down. (Hollywood will no doubt offer to reward her for resisting Burbank.) Even more revealing about life back home in the States was the antagonism between Shani Davis and Chad Hedrick, two champion members of the American speed-skating team.

Hedrick had been uncollegially voluble about his contempt for Davis' decision not to participate in the team pursuit event, a choice Davis made in order to save his strength for the contests he was competing in as an individual. It seems that Davis' demurral was nothing new; members of the speed-skating team routinely refuse to take part in the group event—apparently, the team's motto is "Every man for himself." Naturally, the press took after both. Davis grew so bitter about it that after he won the gold medal in the 1,000 meters, he barely spoke to the NBC blonde sent down to the arena to interview him. "Are you angry, Shani?" she finally asked the grim-looking, tight-lipped winner, exasperated that he wouldn't open up to her. "No, I'm happy," he said. "I have a loss for words right now," and he walked away. "You sure do look happy," she said sarcastically. What thin-skinned compatriots we have. But the silver lining in this gold-medaled spat was that although Davis was the first black man to win a gold medal in an individual sport at the winter Olympics since their inception, no one made a big deal about it, though the NBC blonde tried as hard as she could, as in the following: "You are the first African American male to win a gold medal at the winter games." In a sense, it was a cheerful sign that Davis had been caught up in an unheroic, petty grudge match just like anyone else. You only have heroes like Jesse Owens or Jackie Robinson in a world that won't let them live like anyone else.

But being undramatic is the fate of the winter Olympics. The drama—and the tragedies—always happens during the summer games: Jesse Owens in Nazi Berlin in 1936; the public show of solidarity, in Mexico City in 1968, by black athletes on the American team with black militants back in the States; the murder of Israeli athletes by Palestinian terrorists in 1972; the bomb exploded by an anti-abortionist at the Atlanta games in 1996. The susceptibility of the summer Olympics to politics is predictable, since only a fraction of the countries represented in the summer participate in the winter games. If you are looking to make a political statement, the winter Olympics isn't the place. Indeed, though a war rages in the desert in the Middle East, you wouldn't have known it in Torino. Ice, snow, wind, and trivial antagonisms seemed like a blessing.

FEBRUARY 20, 2006

Politics

53 Tanner on Tanner

Tanner on Tanner peaks, as one might expect, in the third episode of this three-part Sundance series. High up in the press-box at the Democratic Convention in Boston, Alex Tanner (Cynthia Nixon) is interviewing Ron Reagan for the independent film she's making about her father, Jack Tanner (Michael Murphy), a former Michigan congressman and unsuccessful Democratic candidate for president. She bumps into (the real) Alex Kerry, who says that she's there to make a film about her father, too, and that there must have been some misunderstanding because she was the one supposed to interview Ron Reagan at this time. The real daughter of the real candidate and the fake daughter of the fake (erstwhile) candidate bicker.

Reagan arrives, and they explain to the nonplussed real son of the real former president, who was an actor like Nixon—not Richard Nixon, Cynthia Nixon, the actress who is playing the daughter of a politician, who is played by an actor (see above)—the nature of their dilemma. It is all very absurd and very funny—a press-box farce. Reagan conciliatorily suggests that they both interview him, and the two women—one real, one fake, don't forget—agree. Alex Kerry begins and asks him to explain his position on stem-cell research. But in the middle of Reagan's thoughtful answer, Alex Tanner interrupts with a question about how it feels to be the son of a former president, etc., etc. This is the sort of banal, predictable interruption the official media specialize in, the sort of focus on trivial preoccupation with candidates' personal lives that we have all come to abhor, haven't we? *Tanner on Tanner* is a very witty and sophisticated satire on just this sort of demeaning inanity, and like the best satire, it revolves through various alternating levels of irony and sincerity, sending itself up as it sends up the big-time media, while intermittently making its own political position strikingly clear. And all this artfulness, and careful orchestration, and highly wrought meaning and anti-meaning, is often very entertaining. It's also about as relevant to politics today as Alex Tanner's question to Ron Reagan.

Tanner is the sequel to *Tanner '88,* another Robert Altman series made sixteen years ago that mixed reality and fiction in order to expose precisely the same media-trivializing. Altman's evidentiary exhibits were the Gary Hart–Donna Rice scandal and the way the press jumped all over Joseph Biden for plagiarizing a speech by Neil Kinnock, the British Labor Party leader. Even then, Altman's critique of the media's banality was itself a predictable and banal response to the media. Hart was as weak in the intellectual-substance department as he was weak in the flesh, and so the press really was following the wrong path to the right destination. And even worse than Biden's plagiarizing— which was a bad sign—was the fact that he'd plagiarized Kinnock of all people. Why not Churchill? Everyone else does. But Altman did his conventionally adversarial thing, introduced a funny new wrinkle into film by mixing reality with fiction (if only he had a crystal ball), and created a pleasantly entertaining series, which had the added virtue of introducing Cynthia Nixon, a superb comic actress, to audiences.

Sixteen years later there is bad news and there is good news for the official anti-media, which includes Altman, whose mission is to pursue the official media. The bad news is that over a decade and a half of raising the public consciousness of media shenanigans has had the result of making everyone so cynical and apathetic that, somehow, no one noticed the barely perceptible stages by which the country was delivered over to a gang of crooks. The good news is that such a dire situation has produced an election year in which the political discourse is more serious, more elevated, and less trivial than it has been in years. Even Bush has started to lie in complete sentences. The disclosure and clarification of such distinct national disagreements is thrilling.

But the good news is also bad news for politically committed movie people, who are left dangling by their camera straps. Themselves in the business of representation, they are at their adversarial best when they are criticizing other representers. Fancying themselves the makers of honest images, when they find that they lack calculatedly dishonest images to attack, they're at a loss for a target. Altman and Garry Trudeau—the latter wrote both *Tanner* series—trot off to the Democratic Convention in Boston to find American politics, but they find only the reflection of the earlier show. They also find that they've become less relevant to political critique than ever before.

Their response is to try, in some subtle way, to show how the politicians they filmed in 1988 have had their ideals compromised through time. In the first episode of the new series, called "Dinner at Elaine's," famously soulful Mario Cuomo— who finally decided not to run in 1988—sits at a corner table talking with Murphy about the Bush administration's various depredations. Later, we see Nixon running out of the screening of her film about her father to buy a pair of shoes at Kenneth Cole. Altman and Trudeau aren't just sending up their independent filmmaker. For Maria Cuomo, Mario Cuomo's daughter, happened to have married Kenneth Cole. From soul to sole, you see—how the mighty have fallen! Later, at the convention, Madeleine Albright speaks seriously to Murphy about Bush and Iraq and then answers Murphy's question about what her plans are for that evening by saying that she's going "to party." People are dying, you see, and these big shots are having fun.

Indeed, the show presents its own candor about the war in Iraq as far superior to what it pleases itself to see as the politicians' smooth equivocations. Murphy, as Jack Tanner, blasts Kerry for having virtually the same position on Iraq as Bush— this is absurd. Murphy then faces the camera and delivers a heated tirade against the president and his cohorts, "who hijacked this country and drove us straight into hell." The show doesn't want to lose its ironical remove, so it has Murphy make his brave speech while standing sweating on a racquetball court at a tony health club. But it's clear that they want us to think that none of the countless real and famous political and cultural figures Murphy has spoken to in the course of the three episodes have the guts to declare themselves so bluntly.

No one, that is, except Michael Moore. We see a clip of Moore speaking—he doesn't appear in *Tanner on Tanner*—in the climactic final episode. Altman and Trudeau obviously consider him the truth-telling center of the film, a figure representing an ideal of really committed independent filmmaking, the opposite number to poor Alex Tanner. In fact, *Tanner on Tanner* is really an attempt to share, or perhaps to steal, a little of the limelight Moore has won for himself with *Fahrenheit 9/11*.

Moore's clip is not a flattering moment for *Tanner on Tanner*, however. Moore may well be everything his detractors say he is, but one thing he's not is a star-fucker who stocks his films with every cultural or political celebrity he can lure in front of his camera. Altman, however, has peopled his film with everyone from Martin Scorsese to Steve Buscemi to Robert Redford to Dick Gephardt, to mention just a few among many. All this to "send up" the empty trivializing and celebrity-hunting of the official media. It's like going on a sex tour to Thailand to prove the importance of sexual abstinence. And anyway, we have been here before, with *K Street*, another nervously self-indulgent disaster. All these "committed" filmmakers mixing reality and fiction to critique political dishonesty. It's beyond me that the thought has never occurred to them that mixing reality and fiction is, in fact, the very nature of political dishonesty.

OCTOBER 11, 2004

54 Jack and Bobby

A common reaction to psychological trauma is the construction of what psychologists call an "ego-ideal," a kind of counterself, grand, inflated, magnificent, free from imperfections, and impervious to the kind of injury that created it in the first place. *Joan of Arcadia* features a teenage girl who believes that she is involved in a private dialogue with God, and who—possibly—exhibits all the signs of having fabricated a counterself in response to some shock to her psyche. And the deceased George who comes back to life in Showtime's *Dead Like Me* could very well be the self-protective daydream of the real George. After all, Showtime describes the series as being about people "who died with unresolved issues." (I swear that's what its website says.)

Other shows don't offer characters who re-create themselves as immortal or divinely connected: the show itself is a fantasy of escape from the nightmare of mortality. *Six Feet Under* sometimes begins with a person speaking from beyond the grave, and the dead father often returns to visit with his children. *Rescue Me*'s main character has extended conversations with his cousin, who died in the attack on the Twin Towers. *Desperate Housewives* is narrated from the afterlife by a character who killed herself in the opening minutes of the first episode.

The classic children's stories usually begin with the child's parents absent or dead, and such eternity-obsessed shows— many of which are directed toward teens—present a variation on that premise. Not just parents, but the entire world is conjured away before an omniscient ego. Rather than the parents abandoning the child by dying, in some of these shows it is the dead or prophetic child who has abandoned the deeply flawed and impossibly needy mortals who remain alive. Thus Joan and George can hang onto their parents and be solitary and apart from their parents all at once. And they have enormous power—a child's buried wish come true. Even adult dramas like *Six Feet Under* and *Desperate Housewives* have, at their heart, a fantasy of power and omniscience. Their adult immortals take a childlike satisfaction in the eternalizing of their egos.

The latest television series to embody an ego-ideal is WB's *Jack and Bobby*. There are no undead or FOG (Friends of God) in this very original show. The conceit is even more potent than that since it introduces the fiction of immortality without resorting to the reality of death. In this family drama, a single mother, played with perfect pitch by Christine Lahti, raises two boys in present-day America, one of whom—Bobby—grows up to be president in 2041. We know this because although the family's story unfolds in our moment, it is really one long flashback recalled by various friends of "President McCallister," who are speaking to the camera in 2049 about McCallister's various character traits. These are then illustrated, sometimes very obliquely, by scenes from the president's life when he was a young boy. In this way, the show grants viewers themselves an all-powerful, omniscient perspective. We can feel like God as we watch Jack and Bobby while knowing what they don't know, which is what the future holds for them. Time distinctions vanish in our viewers' omniscience.

So *Jack and Bobby* exists in an eternal present, which is the all-American temporal ideal. The show twists and bends past, present, and future into a single dimension like a balloon shaped into an adorable animal. And this space-time sunniness has an interesting bearing on the show's political aspect. Though the two boys have famous Kennedy names, there really isn't anything Kennedy-like about them. They're of modest means, living with their mother, who's a radically left, pot-smoking professor of, I think, sociology at a nearby university. (Most exciting moment: She writes the name "Vilfredo Pareto" on the blackboard. My eyes grew moist.) If anything, they're more like the young Harry Truman. The show, in fact, is set in Missouri, where the boys attend "Truman High"—the names "Jack" and "Bobby" just add a little allure. (Indeed, one could imagine a Comedy Central parody called "George and Jeb," in which the two youngsters sell off parcels of playground to developers; tell the school administration that the Science Club is in possession of dangerous firecrackers [they're never found]; attempt to install pay-toilets in the lavatories.)

But the two boys certainly don't have Truman's fabled recalcitrance. Bobby, we learn, becomes a Republican, but a Republican so liberal that his own party tries to destroy him. Apparently, he makes Nelson Rockefeller look like Barry Goldwater. After three episodes, we're still not told what kept him from switching allegiances and joining the Democratic Party, but we find out that he ran for president as an independent—though he's not at all a lone idealist like Ralph (*dans la lune*) Nader. In a three-way debate—we never see these events; they're related to us—Bobby is about to self-destruct before a lowdown question when he's suddenly, inexplicably saved by the Democratic president, who at that moment feels sorry for the fiery asthmatic boy from Missouri. The show is about politics, even if its politics are reduced to personality, American-style, and its vision of politics is summed up by the (plagiarized) thesis of one of Grace McCallister's graduate students, who stole from a distinguished essay the idea of a "joint contribution of liberal monarchists and socialists."

My history isn't good enough to say whether such collaboration ever existed (perhaps in Italy in the decades before World War II). But if it did, it had a mayfly's duration. The show's space-time sunniness has its parallel in this kind of delusional politics, which is like the ego-ideal for an entire country gone crazy with distraction. And this fantastical political syncretism is matched by an intellectual and emotional kind. Grace—the third Grace on grace-obsessed television—makes an incredible stink when her son doesn't get admitted to a program for gifted kids. Yet a few scenes later, she's giving a speech to a college audience, exhorting everyone to cherish failure and setback as boons to character.

She really believes that. And an A-type Mom wouldn't. These aren't shrewdly orchestrated scenes, integrated into some portrait of hypocrisy, or self-contradiction. They're just there, unassimilated to the story's logic. So is the scene in which Grace catches the same graduate student plagiarizing, fires her as her research assistant, tells her that she was an affirmative-action admission whom Grace only hired because she needed help, and that she, Grace, would now rethink the whole premise of affirmative-action policy. But when the girl is about to leave her office, Grace startlingly adds: "Next time you meet a woman who needs help, make sure you give it. Who knows, maybe she'll even deserve it." Yet Grace has just said that thanks to her error in judgment, she would probably never again admit someone on the basis of need. The narrative has the soul of a weaseling politician.

For all the lamentations over the climate of divisiveness in America, that divisiveness produced, in last Thursday's debate between Bush and Kerry, one of the most strenuous political debates in decades. The worldviews of the two candidates, which reflect the nation's general rifts, were beautifully clarified. And they were often irreconcilable. Seeing this so frankly and rationally delineated in public was the political version of allowing nudity on television. The country is growing up. Yet popular culture remains mired in a hatred of politics as intense as Marx's hatred of the state. Embedded in *Jack and Bobby* is the hope that politics will simply wither away, and that we will exist—as so much pop culture does now—in a dictatorship of feeling, where the present abides eternally, and no one disagrees for long because ideas are so silly (Pareto notwithstanding) and everything, emotionally, politically, and through time, makes sense. No wonder so many people rush to instantly gratifying extremes in their politics. Their favorite TV shows make them feel bad about having any kind of conviction at all.

OCTOBER 4, 2004

Personalities

55   Greta Garbo

Watching Turner Classic Movies' wonderfully done documentary about Greta Garbo—part of the channel's Garbo festival—I recalled my favorite story about the legendary actress. One evening, Garbo entertained a small group of friends in her apartment with a private screening of Cocteau's *Beauty and the Beast.* At the end of the film, Beauty gets her prince, who has been transformed from the Beast, and the kingdom springs back into shape. In Garbo's lair, the camera stopped rolling, the lights came back on. Rising in a slow, silky pout from the back of the room came Garbo's unmistakable voice: "Give me back my beast."

Garbo was built of strong contrarian stuff. She became famous, of course, for the way she reviled her fame. Her most celebrated line—"I want to be alone"—from the 1932 film *Grand Hotel,* got taken up by MGM's publicity people and then by posterity as the synopsis of an enigmatic desire to withdraw from her admiring public. But as the documentary points out, the studio discouraged Garbo from giving interviews and the like because she wasn't a team player. She resented the studio's efforts to cheapen her gifts, refusing to show up at the set for one film because the role that had been imposed on her travestied her talent. She held out for leading men she admired rather than box-office leads that the studio prescribed. She didn't even make the required appearance at Louis B. Mayer's annual birthday party. Her so-called reclusiveness was really her assertion of dignity in the face of the studio's bottom-line depredations and celebrity's leveling blandishments.

Born Greta Lovisa Gustafsson in 1905 to working-class parents in Stockholm, Garbo made *The Torrent,* her first American film, in 1926, barely survived the advent of sound in movies, and starred in her last movie—*Two-Faced Woman*—in 1941, retiring from film for good after the war. There was no mystery about Garbo's decision to give up acting, though the persistence of her myth has much to do with the illusion, conjured by time, of some unfathomable implosion in Garbo's psyche that forced her to de-screen herself and inhabit the life of an ordinary person. But that wasn't the case. Despite a few great "talkie" roles like Anna Christie, sound never suited her, and the characters that she felt most comfortable playing—Anna Karenina, Camille, Queen Christina—were willful, complex figures who had a European impermeability, rather than the blithe glamorous transparencies American audiences expected. Americans want movies to suddenly light up their darkened theaters, as if being alone with your imagination were an untrustworthy enterprise; Europeans like (or used to like) dark-hued films that keep their imaginations glowing in the dark.

Before Garbo, erotic feminine sexuality on the silver screen was for the most part represented by the figure of the vamp, for whom sex was a special event: theatrical, fraught with danger, a romantic finality that spelled the death of romantic feeling. With the vamp, sex was obvious, in other words. It was also, for all the vamp's perilous seductiveness, a fateful, singular act between two people, the temptress and her victim. Garbo's sexuality was a whole different story. Watching her, you feel that sex is not some climactic, so to speak, moment of existence but a seamless part of her everyday life. Garbo's evocation of sex had the most subversive connotation imaginable: *It was no big deal*. When she embraced or kissed a man, you didn't get the feeling that she was sexually focusing on that particular man. Rather, it seemed that the man in question was bobbing about in the indiscriminate waves of her abundant desire.

So easily, luxuriously, sensually physical was Garbo that her face had the evocativeness of a voice. When the talkies came, Garbo's words seemed to interfere with her acting. She didn't need the mentalness of words; her intellect was in her eyes. What was physically irresistible about her was that she promised complete sexual gratification, yet also rationality and sympathy in the emotional realm, two qualities that rarely exist alongside unyielding erotic happiness.

Garbo's ordinary gestures on the screen—picking up a glass, turning her back to the camera, leaning on a piece of furniture—seemed, uncannily, to be the very same way she would move in the midst of the sexual act. Her physical motions reflected her native candor. People have often described her soft-focus face, filling the silver screen, as the epitome of glamour. Yet her glamour really lay in her unconsciously sexualized ordinariness. Such a quality is why men leave their rich, elegant, proper wives for the waitress who serves them lunch in the diner. The transfixing soft-focus wasn't some contrivance of Hollywood magic. It was the revelation of sexual chemistry latent in every individual, sprung from the recesses of personality by a fateful encounter with the right—or wrong—person.

Until Garbo—and even to this day—sex appeared in American movies as a hidden destination, lying teasingly below the surface. With Garbo, sex is out in the open; something is hiding below the surface of sex—you can see it in her eyes, which possess a clarity that floats above her sexual allure. The concealed meaning was not just, as the film implies, the possibility that Garbo was bisexual or a lesbian. Perhaps, as with Brando, as with Marilyn, Garbo's secret was her conception of sex as a comic absurdity. Indeed, Garbo, Brando, and Marilyn all finished their careers as great comic actors, as if in the end their sexy, secret indifference to sex had burst through to the surface. That sex might not be a Crisis, or a Dilemma, or an Enigma, that it might be as funny and as natural as a fart at the opera, is still a novel idea in American popular culture. We have yet to feel comfortable with our beast.

AUGUST 31, 2005

56 Lauren Bacall

Hybridity is the secret essence of American culture, and Lauren Bacall is one of the culture's more original hybrid creations. Born Betty Joan Perske to Jewish parents who divorced when she was six—she was raised by her Romanian-born mother—Bacall had Katharine Hepburn's implacably confident chiseled features. She was a mid-twentieth-century American-Jewish girl's dream of the ideal American-looking girl. The creators of *The African Queen* must have been playing with the resemblance when they cast Hepburn in that film as Humphrey Bogart's romantic interest. Bogart was Bacall's first husband and her great love. She was Bogart's fourth wife.

But not only did the Jewish Bacall's WASPish physical presence and sangfroid seem to spring from the socially insecure minds of certain Hollywood Jews during the 1940s. Her husky voice and tomboy aspect played subtle havoc with conventional appearances. It's strange to watch so much television and film now, and to realize that over sixty years after Bacall taught Bogart how to whistle in her first starring role in *To Have and Have Not,* male and female stereotypes still persist on the big and small screens. In ads for the movie, Bacall was billed as the "only girl who could stand up to Bogart," or something to that effect. Her character in the film is that of an adventuress, a kind of female roué, who often favors pants that hide her curves under a sleek arch toughness that hints at sex the way a bow hints at being strung.

Bacall was also only nineteen at the time. Bogart was in his mid-forties, and the two began an affair while the movie was being made. And Bogart was married. So at the same time Howard Hawks' masterpiece was projecting yet another romantic myth about men and women—Bogart breaks through Bacall's tough façade eventually; everything works out, don't worry—the film's two stars were shattering the conventional mores that such myths keep afloat. To complicate matters, Hawks was also pursuing her, as the famously brassy, laconic, wisecracking Bacall reminisces in *Private Screenings: Lauren Bacall*, a pleasant, breezy, hour-long documentary about her life. The reality of Hollywood, more than the reality of any other place, is antithetical to the creations of Hollywood. It recalls Dostoevsky's fable of the Grand Inquisitor, who spins a lie about Christian love and redemption to keep people in their place.

After Bogart died in 1957, Bacall seemed to lose herself, briefly getting emotionally involved with a compulsively faithless Frank Sinatra (as Ava Gardner once said, "Frank was only 120 pounds, but 110 of it was pure cock"), never making a great film again, emigrating to Broadway, and then to television, and to more mediocre films. You can only admire her grit and persistence in an industry that has less place for elderly people than it does for any other human type. The high point of Bacall's life seemed to be her marriage to Bogart; the high point of her art was certainly the movies she made with Bogey: *To Have and Have Not, The Big Sleep, Dark Passage, Key Largo*. On stage, where she had a huge success in *Applause* in 1970, her lostness seemed to work for her. The live audience found her, and not only revived her, but seemed to make her a person for the first time. Perhaps Bogart had been, most of all, her ideal audience, and after his death she rediscovered Bogart's spontaneous, rewarding emotional warmth—or adoration (he was so much older)—in the live audience's spontaneous stream of affection. "Applause" indeed.

Sitting in her majestic chair across from her interviewer, the attentive and affable Robert Osborne, playing the grande dame, deploying her side-of-the mouth sassiness and savvyness while predictably insisting that she really isn't like that, Bacall makes you realize that she most certainly isn't like that. She relates that she spent her early years in Hollywood, before fame emboldened her, ashamed of her Jewishness, which she hid as well as she could. Hawks was anti-Semitic, she said, and she was afraid to tell him about her religious origins. Living with her mother when she first came to Hollywood as an adolescent—after being discovered by Howard Hawks' wife, who saw a photograph of Bacall the model on the cover of *Harper's Bazaar*—Bacall apparently was afraid of a lot of things, one of them being Bogart himself, who Bacall says terrified her when she first met him.

No wonder, then, that Bacall's screen persona came to her so early and so precociously in *To Have and Have Not*. Her tough-girl act was wholly a reflection of Bogart's own persona, which she perhaps used to mask the shame she felt about her own identity. It's revealing that in her two greatest roles, in *To Have and Have Not* and *The Big Sleep*, Bacall's Bogart impersonation—which, after all, is what really attracts the Bogart character—sooner or later breaks down, and the naïve, embarrassed, insecure girl emerges, needing Bogart's help, protection, and love. In those two unforgettable films, Bacall seduces Bogart by becoming Bogart, and she holds onto him by bending entirely to his will. It's like one of the less lovely types of cultural assimilation. On stage, however, Bacall came entirely into her own, and she did this by immersing herself in the large group of people sitting just beyond the footlights. There is something more than a little sad about Bacall's glamorous and exciting life.

JULY 27, 2005

57 Steve McQueen

The title of the Turner Classic Movies' documentary of Steve McQueen is *Steve McQueen: The Essence of Cool,* and the film tries to take up the theme of "cool" as often as it can. McQueen, after all, in movies like *The Cincinnati Kid, Bullitt, The Thomas Crown Affair,* and *The Getaway,* belonged to that American royalty, the bourbon-drinking Bourbons of cool, whose line ran from Gary Cooper (high cool) and Humphrey Bogart (low cool) to Brando (something of both) through James Dean and Paul Newman and Jack Nicholson and Warren Beatty—whose cool was so invincible it stayed with him even when he was being victimized in *The Parallax View* and deceiving himself in *Shampoo.* Pacino and DeNiro run too hot to be cool; even when Brando lost it, he was full of ice. The only cool actors today are Samuel L. Jackson and Nicholas Cage. Everybody else is either too knowing or too self-conscious. It could even be that the popularization of "hot," meaning "in" and "eagerly marketable," has melted cool—meaning "outside" and "indifferent"—into a fine mist and made it disappear.

In the manner of such projects, *Steve McQueen: The Essence of Cool* is too busy keeping the myth of McQueen alive—while exposing just enough tattered underside to seem skeptical—to get very far into the business of definition. The closest it gets is an ironic quip from Alec Baldwin, one of the documentary's handful of famous reminiscers and commentators, though it's not clear whether Baldwin knows he's being ironic. In Baldwin's whimsical perspective, what makes McQueen and certain other actors cool in the roles they played on screen was simple: They knew that the script had them win in the end. They could afford to stay calm and unflappable no matter what happened.

As the descriptive term for an existential condition, "cool" has been around for a long time, and it seems to be permanently fixed in American speech. Its various essences seem to be walking slowly; speaking in a measured, unexcited manner, and usually in a deep voice; treating people who have greater power or authority somewhat haughtily, not to say insolently, while treating people with less power or authority as equals; refusing to act the way other people tell you to act; living unaffected by external forces or circumstances; preferring to be solitary rather than joining the chorus of other people; and speaking in your own original idiom, to the point of even seeming to have your very own vocabulary.

Those qualities are the rudiments of cool. In fact, I've taken them straight out of Aristotle—his definition of the "great-souled" man—Epictetus, and Montaigne. You can find similar prescriptions throughout Western culture—throughout world culture, actually: quiet, composed Buddha was quintessentially cool—in Machiavelli and in Castiglione's famous Renaissance guide to being an effective courtier. You could say that cool reached its apotheosis in Enlightenment rationalism, disappeared in Romanticism's raptures and stayed absent during Modernism's frenzies, finally surfacing in postmodernism's paeans to the death of feeling and personality—with the critical

exception that postmodern irony, or any kind of irony, is anathema to profoundly cool people.

I say people, but being cool in the American sense is not a
quality that any real person possesses. It's a fantasy of immutable
individuality; it's an aesthetic masquerading as an ethos. That's
why the icons of cool are almost all actors. Andy Warhol might
have pushed cool into ironic, cool-destructing postmodern waters, but he was "on" all the time. If our Cool Figures are not actors, then they're musicians. Miles Davis, John Coltrane, Charlie
Parker, Dexter Gordon, and all the other creators and inventors
of cool jazz were cool only when they were playing music. Music,
in fact, is the true essence of cool because cool is essentially non-
verbal. Words attach you to feelings, people, and things, and cool
is an essentially unaffiliated state. Rap is cool because it burns
words up in rhythm without emotion. Cool's orthodoxy of silence makes it an aesthetic with religious moods.

McQueen's cool lay in silence. When he acquired the control-
ling power of a star, he often gave his lines away in paragraphs to
other characters in the script. "I can do that with my face," he said.
He mastered the Method's reliance on the marriage between the
camera and facial expression. Where Brando spoke softly—he
never mumbled—McQueen just didn't speak. His favorite character was the action hero with ineffable psychological depths; his
most expressive gesture was the car-chase. The genre of the car-
chase reached its peak of perfection in *Bullitt,* and you realize as
you're experiencing every stomach-heaving rise and drop of that
unforgettable ride over San Francisco's hills that what made Mc-
Queen so riveting on screen was that he acted every scene in the
spirit of a chase. He was in slow, deep-down pursuit of everyone
his character encountered, either out of love or hate, simply for
the sake of visceral motion with a self-created purpose. That's

why he had that caught-in-the-headlights look even when he was mastering the situation. His screen persona was afraid of getting what he wanted because then he would be in danger of losing it, and he would be at loose ends once the chase was done.

Like all great American actors, McQueen was not really "in the moment" as the Method famously prescribed. Rather, he distilled his life into the moment of the scene. He was an orphan with a violent, lawbreaking past, who was saved by serving with the Marines and getting a new lease on life with the GI bill. All his life, we are told, even at the zenith of his success, he was afraid that everything he had won for himself would be taken away. In McQueen's case, it turns out, Baldwin was wrong. McQueen's cool came not from his character's sense that the script guaranteed a happy ending, but from his private experience of how easy it is for good things to suddenly slip away. The essence of Steve McQueen's cool was that he knew that nobody wins in the end, but that you have to learn to play your part in life as if you were indifferent to the final outcome. Epictetus would have understood.

MAY 31, 2005

58 Elvis Presley

Elvis Presley was born in January and died in August, but for some reason CBS has decided that this is Elvis week, airing the first half of a biopic about the singer last night and the conclusion this Wednesday. On Friday the network will broadcast *Elvis by the Presleys,* a documentary consisting mostly of interviews with Priscilla Presley, Elvis' wife—from whom he was divorced—and his daughter Lisa, along with recollections of Elvis by various other family members and friends. And just in case some viewers were still yearning for an exploration of some aspect of Elvis' life that the network left unexplored, the local CBS News affiliate in New York followed the biodrama last night with a segment examining Elvis' "spiritual side."

Since there's no apparent reason for an Elvisfest at this particular moment, you could be forgiven for making a cynical speculation. It could well be that CBS turned hungrily to the Mississippi-born singer after feeling bereft of—you should pardon the crude category—the "red state" demographic it had enjoyed drawing with stories like Ashley Smith, Terri Schiavo, and even the Popes (late and current).

Elvis, after all, was not just a good ol' boy; he seemed like a pretty good guy. He loved his mama, gave millions of dollars to charity, was a God-fearing Christian, and doesn't seem to have hurt a fly. Though he was notorious—among people who knew—for entertaining groups of very young girls in his emperor-sized bed at Graceland, women said that all he really wanted to do was kiss and cuddle. All the sex came out on stage, as the crowd fed his ego, and his eyes glazed over, and he went into a demon-trance, swiveling, sliding, and somersaulting around the stage, kissing women in the audience on the mouth when they approached the edge of the stage (all Franz Liszt, music's first superstar, had to do was lean back away from the keyboard while he was playing and wink and women went nuts). So Elvis makes for a nice, wholesome icon at the present moment, when "moral values" are touted like a new detergent. Even the drug habit that killed him gets wholesomely qualified by Priscilla, who stresses that they were prescription drugs that he needed to lull his beleaguered spirit to sleep at night. Which is true. Aside from the drugs his doctor supplied to him, Elvis didn't drink anything stronger than a Coke.

And, to its credit, CBS is not trying to have its Coke and snort it, too. It goes out of its way not to pruriently play up Elvis' attraction to young girls. But this maybe is one case where the sexual life of an icon should be made explicit. The unsettling thing about this aspect of Elvis' life is that it resembles that of another pop icon, Michael Jackson, now the subject of possibly the sleaziest criminal trial in the annals of legal history.

The parallels are eerie. Like Jackson, Elvis was an overgrown child who felt more comfortable in his Neverland-like compound—he called it Graceland—than anywhere else. He liked to "cuddle" young girls in his bed. The documentary gets darkly funny when the subject of Priscilla's first sexual encounters with Elvis come up between her and her father, Paul Beaulieu. She was fourteen when she met Elvis, and he was twenty-four.

Priscilla's father makes you recall the mother of Picasso's teenage lover, Marie-Therese, who advised her daughter, after being told that the rich and famous artist had asked Marie-Therese to be his mistress, "Go to him immediately," or something to that effect. Mr. Beaulieu, obviously pleased as punch that the young millionaire had come a-courtin' to his daughter, disarmingly confesses that he "acted old-fashioned," the way he thought a father should act. No, Daddy, you were strict, protests Priscilla, and father, mother, and daughter enjoy a moment of rural, faith-based, sophisticated irony.

It's odd that the juvenescent objects of Elvis' desire—whatever it was—including Priscilla, are treated as just another of the singer's eccentricities, like using joy-buzzers when he shook a stranger's hand. Is it because death sanctifies the objects of popular adoration, or is it because Jackson is the anti-Elvis? In many ways, Jackson presents a grotesque parody of Elvis' quintessentially American appeal. The great American icons are racial, ethnic, and sexual hybrids, hybridity being an American purity. Brando had a woman's face buried in his features (Elvis idolized him)—so did Miles Davis and James Dean. The macho Pollock's gossamer skeins of color have a feminine delicacy. Even Marilyn Monroe had a hybrid quality in the way she seemed both absolutely corrupt and absolutely innocent. American energy has a miscegenational source.

In Elvis' case, he had the face and movements of a woman— what upset some people was that he gyrated his pelvis like a stripper; he didn't thrust like a copulating male—and the voice and stage-presence of a black man. No wonder CBS got for the role of Elvis the Irish actor Jonathan Rhys-Meyer, who played a bisexual David Bowie–like rock star in Todd Haynes' 1998 film *Velvet Goldmine.* (Alas, he doesn't play Elvis; he plays a vacuity pretending to be Elvis.) A country boy, Elvis had the wild, boundless diversity of a city. He translated urban energies into a rural idiom, and vice versa. Spiritually, he was in a pure state of unaffiliated receptivity; his audiences were homes and he was a hotel room. That's why they needed each other so desperately.

Michael Jackson, on the other hand, has turned himself into a macabre inversion of American hybridity. His mixtures and blendings are not organic; they're Frankenstein creations—or, rather, he's a cubist painting gone awry. His whiteness is an attempt to cancel out his blackness; his blackness is like a shameful secret; his femininity is cruel; his masculinity is injured. He is the pathological underside of America's historically unique fusions and conjunctions; such a creation is what would happen if America's original experiment became an absolute failure. I don't like Elvis' hankering after young girls; it gives me the creeps. It's not really "just one of those things" (Sarah Vaughan sang that song with masculine undertones). But it lets me sleep. Jackson, the face of a dysfunctional American future, keeps me awake. He's not even a hound dog.

MAY 9, 2005

59 Charles Manson

Three cheers for the "remake." Comparing the new version of an old film to the original is one of the most vivid ways to take the social pulse. Or at least to take the measure of the people in the entertainment biz who believe that they have their finger on the social pulse. The question is whether their fare follows the public taste, or whether they create a chimera called the "public," pretend to follow its lead, and then give this public such a narrow set of entertainment choices that audiences have no other recourse than to take whatever they are presented with—thus giving the impression that these limited choices are the public taste.

In the eyes of the producers of *Helter Skelter,* a remake of the 1976 miniseries of the same name, the time was ripe for another movie about Charles Manson and several of his followers, who were convicted in 1970 of mutilating and murdering seven people the year before. "Just what we need," you say, when dozens, maybe hundreds of Americans and Iraqis are being butchered every month, when this country is being shaken by revelations of American torture and murder of Iraqi prisoners, when a group of Iraqis cuts off the head of a seemingly poignant young American in revenge. But you don't really mean that.

No, what is really going on inside your mind is this: According to Vincent Bugliosi, now a successful crime novelist but formerly the crack district attorney who successfully prosecuted Manson and his group (both movies are based on his book, *Helter Skelter*), "the nation continues to be fascinated with the Manson murder case." This is because "Manson's name has become synonymous with evil," and "there's a side to human nature that's fascinated with pure, unalloyed evil." Not only that, but "Manson got many other people to murder for him, making the possibility of death far greater and making Manson much more frightening." According to executive producer Mark Wolper, "America is still intrigued by this man. Every time he comes up for parole, people go crazy. What kind of guy has that kind of power over people?" Are you scratching your head, trying to remember the last time you threw yourself under the bed when you heard that Charles Manson was coming up for parole? You might want to look into your capacity for denial, because according to *TV Guide*, circulation 9 million, "even after decades of escalating violence and horror, America is no less terrified and fascinated by Manson's evil persona."

Well, America is terrified and maybe fascinated by many things at the moment, but Charles Manson isn't one of them. What is fascinating is that Manson saw himself as precisely this kind of fascinating, fear-inducing phenomenon; he saw himself in the same absolute, mesmerizing terms in which he is now being portrayed to attract viewers. So what was once the pathological hallucination of a deluded, pathetic con-man named Charles Manson has now become established as the real quality of true evil, and one that might entertain large numbers of people to boot.

But it's not just the new *Helter Skelter*'s promoters who have assimilated Manson's deranged idea of himself. It's the movie's creators, too. The difference between the two versions isn't just the difference between two sets of cultural attitudes. It's a difference in perception of reality—the difference between a time when high and popular art set their stories in broad social and political contexts, and a time, our time, when a ferocious, bewildering context gets reduced to a set of personality profiles (Jessica Lynch, Lynndie England, Thomas Hamill, Nicholas Berg) so that there is not even the hope of seeing the burning forest for these strangely familiar trees. The first *Helter Skelter* didn't emphasize the story of any single character in the Manson case. It was about the interaction of people with their circumstances, about the influence of various external conditions on people's lives, and about the confluences and consequences produced by all these people and circumstances tangled up together. This latest movie is all about Manson.

The 1976 film made clear from the very beginning that there was the real person called Charles Manson, and the idea of himself that this real person had; and that the latter had nothing to do with the former. You learn within the first half-hour that Manson was born without a name, that his father abandoned him and his mother when he was a baby, and that his mother took him with her from one cheap hotel room to another, where she drank and drifted from man to man. From the age of thirteen on, Manson journeyed through reform schools and prisons; by the time he was thirty-four, when *Helter Skelter* takes place, he had spent half his life, seventeen years, in prison, where he was brutalized and raped. By 1969, the year of the murders, Manson had made his way to Haight-Ashbury, headquarters of the 1960s drug culture, where he recorded a song for a Beach Boys album (he'd been taught guitar in prison by the last living member of the Ma Barker gang, a criminal family notorious for practicing incest), and then failed to advance his musical career. Next he attracted a large group of followers to live with him on a deserted movie set, Spahn Ranch, where he handed out drugs and organized orgies. Around that time, he began to claim that the Beatles were sending him messages through their songs, and he appropriated the "White Album" song "Helter Skelter," whose title he used to refer to the war he said he wanted to start between blacks and whites, which would result in mass destruction, allowing him to rule the world. Somewhere along the line he convinced some of his followers that he was Jesus Christ, and also the Devil.

The 1976 movie keeps Manson in his place, as it were; its emphasis is on the process of tracking him down, collecting evidence of his crimes, bringing him to trial and convicting him. By the end of the movie, he's raving in the courtroom, hurling himself over tables at the judge, being dragged out and back to his cell by the bailiffs. When we last see him and the three women who stood trial with Manson, all four of them, their heads shaved, are pathetic and enclosed in their private mental hell. The contrast between them and their deformed ambitions is so vast it is almost embarrassing. Throughout the movie, the voice of the actor playing Bugliosi narrates events like the reality principle itself. For all of Bugliosi's transparent vanity—which guided the script—the device works. The story of Charles Manson is not the story of his crimes, but the story of the price he paid for failing as a human being. Up until now, it was only in the mind of Charles Manson that Charles Manson loomed larger than the world around him. Manson was at war with humanity but he barely touched humanity. Humanity, however, in the form of the law, vanquished Manson absolutely.

I say up until now, because this recent *Helter Skelter* makes Charles Manson loom larger than the world around him. It opens with the Beatles' "Helter Skelter" playing against a montage of iconic events from the 1960s: the war, the riots, the assassinations, the civil rights marches. This little Ipod-fantasy has the effect of taking the song that Manson believed expressed the apocalyptic spirit of his age and making it actually express the apocalyptic spirit of the age. It is a very glamorous, pounding, exciting beginning. From there we see Manson playing a gorgeous-looking guitar in a recording studio, talking with a Beach Boy, getting dissed by a glamorous music producer, and vowing some kind of revenge. In other words, the movie begins with Manson's own reference points: the image of himself as a powerful libidinal force, a would-be star.

And it continues to be steered by Manson's self-conception. Not once does the movie tell the viewer anything about Manson's life, about his mother, or his youth, or his experience in prison. He is presented as self-created, in the same way as he thought of himself. In the first, fact-based movie, the police find Manson at Spahn Ranch hiding underground like a frightened animal. This is what he looked like in the eyes of the larger world around him. In the second, fictionalized movie, when police raid the ranch, he strolls upright, with casual, insouciant dignity, between two sheriff's deputies to the patrol cars. This is what he looked like in the crooked corners of his own mind. Even the process of catching him has been removed from this updated version; the process of catching him is made to seem as fateful and inexorable as the spell he cast over his followers. In reality, the police made one mistake after the other; in dramatizing that, the first movie made it clear that Manson's criminal "genius," as Bugliosi calls it, was the result of countless unfortunate circumstances.

This time around, Bugliosi seems to have a lot invested in turning Manson into another Hitler, a figure of evil whose powers of persuasion should still make us all tremble. The movie asks over and over again how one man could have convinced so many people to follow him, and to stay with him, and to kill for him. The answer is easier than the movie wants you to believe. Most of the people at Spahn Ranch were there for the free drugs and the easy sex. It's doubtful that many of them, beyond the small hardcore group that did the killings, believed that Manson was Christ, or that he was about to set in motion Armageddon. As for the hard core, they were lost, damaged people; but even more significant, they had taken LSD, which in large quantities produces psychosis, numerous times. And Manson gave the orphans and displaced souls who came to him concrete assistance: food to eat and a place to sleep. There was nothing Svengali-like about Manson. His "magnetism" was a product of his moment, and of the services he offered. Jeremy Davies, in a shallow, glib performance, might play Manson as a cross between Jim Morrison and Rasputin, the movie might never show him to us with his head shaved, but if one of Manson's victims hadn't been the beautiful young actress Sharon Tate, the wife of Roman Polanski—the questions, the suspicions, the titillation that followed!—and if his disciples hadn't killed her in her glamorous Bel Air mansion, no one would even remember him today.

Instead, the promoters of the latest *Helter Skelter* want to persuade America that Manson is a dominating, irresistible, evil genius, in the same way that Manson wanted to persuade his followers that he was a dominating, irresistible, evil genius. The movie itself presents him as a figure of endless fascination and menace, an uncontainable force of nature larger than life. Again, that's how he thought of himself. And that's what got him into trouble in the first place.

MAY 14, 2004

60 Johnny Carson

With his small eyes, modest features, and boyish face, Johnny Carson, who died yesterday from emphysema at the age of seventy-nine, looked like a prototype for Tom Brokaw, as if Brokaw himself had been manufactured along the lines of Carson, just as Hollywood keeps turning out some version or other of Marilyn Monroe, or Cary Grant (e.g., Hugh Grant) and countless other bankable film icons. Carson and Brokaw both hailed from the Midwest, and Carson's heartland decency, his All-American Everyman quality, had everything to do, we are being told by panegyrizing obituary writers and commentators, with his popularity.

Well, Carson's distillation and refinement of averageness, his seeming modesty and good will, had a lot to do with the warmth with which, for thirty years, Americans welcomed him into their homes before hitting the sack. The last, or second-to-last, face you see before going to sleep is a significant existential fact. That this face now often appears as the remote, electronic image of a face is a significance no one has really fathomed. Carson gave up his show over twelve years ago, but for all the velocity and instant forgetfulness of American culture, he's being mourned as if he had still been on the air. Part of his currency is the lingering electronic bedroom intimacy of that face. Part of it is that television caters to our pleasure; that is to say, to our appetite for pleasure, which is ruled by our id, which—as Freud said—exists in an eternal present. Popular culture is our eternal present, our illusion of deathlessness. Its constant recycling has about it the tinge of a religious thirst for the eternal. We don't really mourn the death of a pop-culture icon. We use his extinction to resurrect his life. In America, the death of an American star is really the occasion for a garrulous, obsessive, round-the-clock denial of death.

Carson was indeed self-effacing, and much is being made of the way he turned a joke that bombed into a hilarious joke on himself. But this was hardly Carson's invention. Lenny Bruce was doing it in the 1950s before Carson started doing it in the 1960s. And before either of them, Jack Benny—Lenny was the antithesis of Benny—patented that affronted, slightly repelled look at an unresponsive audience, or at an unseemly or too-strange situation. It was, to a degree, an affirmation of the audience's own estrangement from anything outside their ordinary experience. But it was also a lethal put-down of anything that tried to interfere with the operation of the comic's ego, as well as of anything that might be bigger or better than the audience.

Carson—nice, modest, decent Carson—perfected this deadly deflation. He refined into a smoothly running machine of comic devastation all the elements that late-night comedy had adapted from stand-up nightclub routines. He understood that with the advent of television, Americans had started to sour on Hollywood glamour and larger-than-life exceptionalism. Late at night, he came to Americans as a kind of celluloid Aristophanes, determined to diminish and deflate anything that made members of his audience feel small and insignificant during their beleaguering days.

The formula that Carson perfected was beautiful. First came the stand-up routine, in which, as the audience sat at home, he stood erect as a needle, puncturing presidents, public figures, and celebrities. He was the Midwestern needle in a haystack, which no one could find and blunt, who emerged from the haystack every night to lash out at large, impersonal forces and then withdrew as sleep and morning beckoned. But he couldn't remain standing. Aside from the uncomfortable impracticality of it, if Carson had remained standing he would have soon become the deflating and diminishing, large impersonal force his audience expected him to bring low. So he repaired to his desk, and from that lower vantage point he proceeded to lampoon Ed McMahon, as if allowing Carson to deflate what had become in the course of his monologue his own stand-up authority.

Now Carson was sitting, just like his audience at home. (I bet adults didn't start lying down to watch television until the 1970s.) He had the authority of the desk, but now he was no longer a needle-puncturing authority. He himself was an authority figure, recalling most of all the boss or job interviewer who receives you from behind his or her desk. But he was a boss who was working for us. For all his warm repartee with his celebrity guests, he never failed to put these mostly inflated figures in their place, lest they forget that, just as you work for your boss, they—for all their wealth, and glamour, and cultural power—are working for you. Carson's revelation of this fact might even make you feel better the next time you were summoned by your own boss. And just in case the guests ever forgot that they were in the employ of Carson and his audience, Carson would often give them the same look of slightly repelled disapproval and estrangement that he gave to any overbearingly odd situation when inhabiting one of his many personas.

With animals he was always more respectful. That's why he liked animals. Their vulnerability and straightforwardness kept the professional dissemblers honest. He sometimes pretended to fear an animal, or perhaps really was afraid at times. He never gave the appearance of fearing his guests. On the contrary. Unlike the animals, he held them, sometimes with reproving glances, in the palm of his hand.

It wasn't his modesty, it was his gently punitive awareness of the electronically inflated size of his ego and his guests' egos that made Carson so popular. He refused to be complicit with his chosen medium's outlandish magnifying sorcery. Rather, he set himself playfully against it. He was the last big little guy on late-night television. Whatever his successors' charms, they have gotten so large that they couldn't even touch the top of his shoes.

JANUARY 24, 2005

Inside the Actors Studio

Bravo's *Inside the Actors Studio,* the ten-year-old smash series that reaches 40 million viewers every week, in countries all over the world, is about acting, which means that it is about a class of people who make their living by dissolving their personalities into imagined characters. As Jeff Bridges tells James Lipton, the show's host and interviewer, "First I'll look into myself to figure out different aspects of myself that I might want to use, or kind of lay aside." That's a frightening capacity. The last thing you want is to meet someone in a social situation who has Bridges' gift for pretense and for manipulating appearances.

The possibility of such an encounter is a special nightmare in a thoroughly commercialized culture like ours, where just about everyone is playing with truth and appearance to try to sell something, including themselves, and make a buck. It's one of the origins of reality television, which on one level is a response to this kind of general anxiety about being duped by someone's fiction, or performance. It's one of the reasons why Americans love film stars who reassuringly play themselves while playing their character. And the fear that people might not be what they seem is why, in so many television shows and Hollywood movies, actors rarely perform characters who are themselves capable of performing like actors. Rather, they play people of absolute consistency. They play people with invincible, immutable personalities.

Inside the Actors Studio, which takes as its subject a famous movie star every week (and enjoys reruns of different past episodes throughout the week), has drawn the derision of a lot of people on account of Lipton, who is also the dean of the New School University's MFA program in acting and directing. He is probably one of the most vilified figures on television. A critic for the *Dallas Observer* declared that "James Lipton is so obsequious, it's astonishing the man does not conduct his interviews from his subjects' anal cavities." (Oh my.) And Lipton certainly is shameless in the way he unctuously compliments his celebrated guests, refers to his relationships with other famous people—"that is so Steven" was how he responded to an anecdote about Spielberg's generosity—and flatters his own attempts at making a bon mot.

Worst of all is that Lipton seems unqualified for his position. Though his acting credits consist only of a ten-year-long gig on a soap opera, he heads the Actors Studio, once the most prestigious and influential acting school in America. About Val Kilmer, Lipton effused that Kilmer was "that rare breed of actor who vanishes into each character he plays." Well, that's an accurate yet oddly naïve thing for the dean of the Method-dominated Actors Studio to be saying. The Method has always been about actors building a character out of pieces of themselves, but there's nothing rare about actors who vanish into their characters, either: In England, all you have are actors who vanish into their characters. The dean of the New School's MFA program in acting and directing doesn't give the impression of being equipped to make such distinctions. That's the underlying reason why his critics regard him as an operator, a huckster, and a little bit of a fraud.

Which is to say that actors, who love to detachedly observe hucksters, and frauds, and outrageously transparent operators, truly warm to Lipton (except when he is fulsomely praising their worst movies, which makes you wonder just how starry-eyed he really is). Lipton is, in fact, a very canny fellow. He knows that in actors the universal human need to be loved attains the intensity of a vocation—the root of charisma is the desperate need to be loved—and so he alternates overwhelming praise with cold, stern, impassive stares, the latter most often deployed when the famous subject has just made a joke or come up with an insight. Divorced parents are a "theme of the series," Lipton likes to repeat again and again, referring to the backgrounds of many of his interviewees, and perhaps—and obnoxiously—to what he believes is the origin of their hunger for affection. Sitting behind a small desk on a stage in the New School's Tishman Auditorium, Lipton has his star sitting in a chair across from him, but without the protection of a desk. This makes the New School dean part psychoanalyst, part school principal, part father, part studio executive, part confident director—actors love confidence in a director and some go haywire if it isn't there. Having turned himself into some archetypal authority figure with who-knows-what associations in his actors' sensuous memories, Lipton gets them to open up to him. They are fatally drawn to this reassuringly ridiculous, subtly manipulative figure. The question is, what are they opening up about?

Lipton is not the problem with *Inside the Actors Studio*. By harping exclusively on his seeming thralldom to celebrity, his critics put themselves in thrall to the famous Lipton. The celebrities aren't the problem, either, because the celebrities are actors, and the actors are famous, and often witty, gifted raconteurs and mimics, and it's not just fun but satisfying to learn about the trajectories of famous people, like seeing an X-ray of someone's destiny. And who can deny the magic of a star, a movie star, stepping out of the screen, as it were, toward you in the form of what seems to be his or her ordinary self?

As that declension into ordinary life unfolds in a long interview, though, the famous actor can either become a disappointing regular person, or an egotistical bore. Lipton doesn't "gossip" with his subjects in order to avoid the first outcome, and he tries to stay away from discussing the trappings of stardom—houses, cars, salaries, vacations—in order to elude the second. Indeed, he edits his subjects' answers so that they never elaborate on any thought or sentiment that might embarrass them when they watch the show later, and he never follows up after he poses even the most artful question for the same reason. When Jeff Bridges, for example, mentioned that his parents had both studied at UCLA with the famed acting teacher Michael Chekhov, and that he learned some of Chekhov's technique from them, he was presenting Lipton with an opportunity for the kind of insightful discussion about the art of acting that the show, and the New School's program, is supposed to be offering the students who pack the auditorium every week. Instead, Lipton smiled knowingly at Bridges and uttered the term "psychological gesture," which is Chekhov's fundamental concept. Bridges good-naturedly said, "Right," and Lipton dropped the subject without even letting this extraordinary actor tell the avid student-audience if or how he has used "psychological gesture" in his work (it means the distillation of character into a physical gesture).

Lipton's lack of passionate engagement on any level is a shrewd preservation of the actors' screen-persona even as they are moving away from the screen into your living room. That's how he wins their trust and keeps the parade of stars coming. But he could still keep the actors coming to talk with him about their art. Few celebrity-actors would feel diminished by being treated as artists rather than as pretty presences. But what Lipton ends up doing is talking for the most part about the drab and neutral business of acting—how did you get that role; what made you choose that role; do you like (this, a favorite) doing nude scenes—rather than the art of acting, except, and very peremptorily, for basic Method-related questions with obvious answers like, Do you do research to prepare for a role? (What actor doesn't?) The reason for such bland conversation is that *Inside the Actors Studio* pitches itself to a television audience that is mostly composed of non-actors who would grow bored with too much shoptalk. And this has the shameful effect of leaving the show's alleged audience—the students sitting out there in the auditorium—out in the cold. It's an almost grotesque parody of the original Actors Studio's purpose.

The Method style of acting taught by the Actors Studio has many forebears and disciples and Method-trained dissenters— Stanislavsky, Richard Boleslavski, Stella Adler, Michael Chekhov, Sanford Meisner—but the most influential Method figure in America was Lee Strasberg, who directed the Actors Studio from 1949, two years after its inception, to 1982, the year of his death. Strasberg was fanatical and tyrannical, but he was also a great teacher. He structured the Actors Studio around scenes that the students would perform; then the other students would critique the performances; and finally outside observers invited to the closed sessions would make comments.

The beautiful thing about it was that the foundation of the program was work. Even when famous film stars (Marilyn Monroe most famously) took a break from Hollywood and enrolled in the Studio, Strasberg, though not averse to exploiting the stars' power for his own purposes, treated the celebrities not too much differently than he treated the students. He barked, berated, stripped bare.

The current Actors Studio, having moved to the New School in 1995, has turned the original program on its head, though its board of directors is made up mainly of actors who have the most honorable intentions. The program still uses Strasberg's—and every acting teacher's—structure of scenes and critiques, but the Bravo series has become the centerpiece of the academic course of study. Yet the visiting stars, who come only to appear on the show, don't speak the common language of work with the students. On the contrary, they loom above and beyond the context of work, the context of acting, as static personalities. Lipton does make mechanical nods to the show's putative educational purpose (allow me to paraphrase): "How did you prepare for this role?" "I put on forty, no, thirty-seven pounds." "Do you rely on your instincts when inhabiting a character?" "Yes." "How much of *you* is in the parts you play?" "Oh, a lot. A lot." But his favorite question is, "How did you get that role?" referring usually to parts and movies that have become episodes in American folklore, and the poor students have to listen not to actors exploring their art, not to artists examining, say, the technical difference between what the character wants and what the actor wants, but to savvy little sagas of insider maneuvering.

Struggling to pay their tuition, they have to listen to Russell Crowe talk about how easy it was for him to become a working actor, without even having to go to school for it—"not like you guys"—which was good because he thought academic training not very worthwhile anyway. Living in cramped apartments, waiting tables, tramping from one unsuccessful audition to the next, haunted by failure—is there a harder vocation than acting? Is there a worse time to be taking a chance on some marginal profession than in the shadow of this careerist, conformist, all-encompassing business culture?—the students have to sit and listen to Dennis Quaid turn to them and ask if they don't agree that this job, their job, is a great job, and with "really good money," too. Having painfully to explain to worried mothers why they're not pulling down a solid salary in a stable position like their cousin Alan, who graduated from college when they did and is *making a nice living in the bond market,* they have to sit there, forcing a smile for 40 million people all over the world—at least they have an audience—while Lipton, referring to Gwyneth Paltrow and Ben Affleck, declares that "sometimes our guest could be sitting out there, among our students, they belong in the same age-group." This is not to say that the students are so fragile that they all walk out crushed and despondent after each show—at the end of which a group of them is allowed to ask five minutes worth of probably carefully vetted questions. But at the very least, it's hard to imagine that they leave feeling uplifted, encouraged, or inspired.

This is all too bad because, as Willem Dafoe once said, going back and forth between film and theater allowed him to "examine what I really think about acting and to cultivate a beginner's mind about what I do for a living." To cultivate a beginner's mind. What a nice thing to say, and how nice it would be for the students, all beginners, to hear that even an established, famous actor has to draw from precisely their own growing stock of riches; that is, the secrets of craft. (Alan, keep your bonds and enjoy *Fiddler on the*

Roof.) But Dafoe didn't say that on this show. Most actors want desperately to break out of the empty shell of celebrity, return to fundamentals, and talk about the authenticity of their work. That's what the students are hungry to hear; that is the language artists share, "stars" and aspirants both. All through *Inside the Actors Studio,* the camera pans over the star-struck, star-stricken audience to keep alive the virtuous pretext of the glamorous series being all about them. But it's not.

The final sad irony is that by using established "stars" to pitch the show to the non-actor television audience, and by emphasizing star-power over craft, Bravo and the New School are deadening those very audiences to the art of acting that the Actors Studio's students are trying so hard to master. Once the Actors Studio offered a refuge, a family, a community for people struggling to perfect themselves in an impossible, unforgiving profession. They were inspired by Stanislavsky's chief precept, which was "to live in the truth." Now its students are exploited as props to the weekly, televised vanity of an institution—the New School—that apparently values fruit, but no labor, and that elevates personality over all the contexts that turn a resourceful, persevering personality into an artist.

JUNE 21, 2004

62 Oprah Winfrey

Now celebrating her twentieth year as the host of the world's most influential talk show, Oprah Winfrey is to television what Bach is to music, Giotto to painting, Joyce to literature. *Time* magazine hit the nail on the head when it recently voted her one of the world's handful of "leaders and revolutionaries." (Condoleezza Rice wrote Oprah's citation: "She has struggled with many of the challenges that we all face, and she has transformed her life. Her message is empowering: I did it, and so can you.") Like all seminal creative figures, her essential gift lies in her synthesizing power. She has taken the most consequential strands in modern life and woven them together into an hour-long show that is a work of art.

The boilerplate criticisms of Oprah—she exploits a culture of victimization that she did so much to create; she glamorizes misery; she amplifies already widespread narcissism and solipsism; she fills people's heads with hackneyed nostrums about life—are correct, up to a point. But that's not the whole story. Oprah's critics write as if her goal of extending to her audience empathy, consolation, and hope were intrinsically cheap and cynical. On the contrary: The question is whether that is really what she is offering.

Oprah's aspiration to inspire her audience with hope—elaborated on her TV show, in her magazine, and on her website—

is hardly ignoble. Her "victimized" viewers—not all her viewers, to be sure—are simply people who have been hurt and have nothing to guide them and nowhere to turn. So they make a virtue of necessity and convert their injuries into proactive forces in the world—just as some people turn their old school ties into proactive forces in the world.

Narcissism and solipsism? Sure. But why not call it withdrawal into a protective inner space instead? When Oprah, in the course of seven days, talks to thirteen-year-old boys who have been seduced by their teachers, features "flattering clothes for all figures," presents "five things that can make you younger," and follows that with the story of a woman whose husband set her on fire, she is hitting the different planes of the self like hitting the walls of a solitary fortress. In a world where it's hard for some people to know how to think about themselves, the assurance that fashion smiles on you however you are shaped (be content with who you are) and that some people have it a lot worse than you do (count your blessings) is worth gold.

In 1986, human nature in America started to change. That year, *The Oprah Winfrey Show,* based in Chicago, became nationally syndicated, and the country entered the beginning stages of a quiet cultural revolution. It took awhile for the transformation to take hold, but, four years later, the effects were unmistakable. Do you really think George H. W. Bush, who presided over the spectacularly successful Gulf War, lost to Bill Clinton in 1992 because of a sagging economy? It was Oprah, stupid. It was Oprah behind Clinton in 1992 and also in 1996; and it was Oprah behind George W. Bush in 2000 and 2004, electoral shenanigans notwithstanding.

It's safe to say that, with her parade of afflicted guests, Oprah helped along the perception of Clinton's childhood wounds as evidence of authentic character. With her emphasis on imperfect self-presentation as proof of genuine intention—she has appeared on the air in her bathrobe, without makeup—she also helped create an atmosphere that turned Al Gore, and then John Kerry, into fabricated con men who were too handsome (Kerry had his lanky Jimmy Stewart allure), articulate, and privileged to be trusted or true. Bush, on the other hand, was so inarticulate, awkward, and funny-looking that, when you thought of his own super-privileged background, you felt that at least he had *something* going for him. And all that unconcealed imperfection made him real—or at least electable.

It's ironic that *O*, Oprah's glossy monthly magazine, relies on the same formulas as do potent arbiters of perfect appearance like *Glamour, Cosmopolitan,* and *Self.* Like its founder and editorial director, *O* is on the front line in the American struggle between tyrannical appearances and the ordinary, imperfect, mortal person. Not just the suffering, injured person, but the unbeautiful person. In our society, not measuring up to resplendent appearances can cause a deep psychic wound. Every sphere of life has its heroic moments, and, in the War of Ordinary People against Ideal Images, this exchange between Oprah and Julia Roberts is the equivalent of that solitary figure confronting the tank in Tiananmen Square:

> **Oprah:** Does the pretty thing ever get to ya? . . . I'm wondering, I was having this discussion with my girlfriend the other day. I said, "It's a really great thing we were never, like, pretty women, because now we don't have to worry about losing that."
>
> **Julia:** You can't really complain about being in a movie called *Pretty Woman* when you're the woman.

It's hardly a coincidence that Roberts has been one of Oprah's select circle of favorite guests. Her full mouth and large, lustrous eyes contrast with and echo Oprah's own features. Just thirty-three years ago, when a nineteen-year-old Oprah got her start in television anchoring the news for a local Nashville station, society would not have been ready to acknowledge such a comparison. You can only talk about it now because Oprah has become so rich and famous—she attracts tens of millions of viewers around the world, and her net worth is said to be about $1.4 billion. But the way she orchestrates and manipulates appearances on her show is one of the sources of her success.

It is not hard to imagine that, for many middle-class black women in her audience, Oprah's dig at Roberts—"the pretty thing" fades, which is a tragedy when all you have is the pretty thing—is an affirmation of sorts. At that moment, the white movie star (the yuppies' very goddess) is diminished by the black host's humor, irresistible self-deprecation, and earthy wisdom—qualities that black women in her audience might identity with and that, in Oprah's inspiring case, helped her bypass the white standard of beauty on her sure-footed path toward power and riches. After all, Roberts is Oprah's guest, not the other way around. Oprah is the one asking the questions, and with all the self-assurance and astuteness of someone who knows the answers. With Roberts, Oprah's sharp tongue not only spoke a humble truth to powerful appearance; it repossessed, as it were, the black sensuality that collagen stole and gave to the white world.

For the middle-class white women who tune into Oprah every weekday afternoon, and who don't look like Roberts, the liberation from Hollywood standards—and from beauty magazine standards and fashion-world standards—is absolute. The star is being torn down with the movie that must have driven tens of thousands of white suburban girls into eating disorders. Roberts actually has to fall back on the unreality of a character she played in a film to defend herself against the real, the very real, woman sitting before her! Even as she treats ordinary wounded people like celebrities and eases celebrities into talking about their ordinary setbacks, disappointments, and wounds, Oprah has created and appeals to a kind of fourth race—the Oprah-people—which is not white, black, or celebrity. The Oprah-people stay glued to her show, because Oprah speaks to their true existence, the life they live away from the glamorous images purveyed by television and the movies.

The secret of Oprah's success on television is precisely that her show has been, until the recent "reality" craze, the antidote to the images of ideal happiness and physique that appear on television. From her first talk-show gig in Baltimore hosting *People Are Talking,* in which an overweight, awkward Oprah brought equally ordinary people in front of the cameras to speak with her, she has always thrust life in the face of imperial television. Think of it like this: The media is Caesar. Having mastered and then revolutionized its idiom, Oprah is Christ. Like changing water into wine, she has managed—through her elevation of hidden, obscure, or neglected experience into spectacle—to make the television set watch *you.*

As the culture focused more and more narrowly on personality—on *you*—Oprah brilliantly expanded her format to put personality at the center of radically diverse experiences. One day, she had physical makeovers (she was almost two decades ahead of shows like *Extreme Makeover*). The next, you "met" a woman who returned home to find her four children shot dead by her ex-husband. After that, a deep commiseration with thin, pale Renée Zellweger over her ordeals with the paparazzi. Then a convening of Oprah's Angel Network, a charitable club that saved enough spare change to send fifty poor kids to college for four years. Or cooking with Paul Newman, or weeping with Sidney Poitier, or hugging Diana Ross. Then a disfigured young victim of a drunk driver meeting with the driver's mother. Followed by *Your Wildest Dreams*. And then a psychologist—Dr. Phil for a while, until he started his own show—or a spiritual guru. And then a new book on Oprah's Book Club, almost always about a woman: a neglectful mother, a neglected daughter, an abused wife. Oprah has distilled the total American environment into a unified experience that is accessible to every individual ego.

There's something more, too. Something remarkable. A single week of Oprah takes you from bondage to all the violent terrors of life, to escape through vicarious encounters with celebrity, to visions of charity and hope, to hard resolve, to redemption and moral renovation. And running through these thoughts and sensations is the constant motif—reinforced by self-help gurus—of growth and strength through suffering. In other words, not even fifty years after segregation, America's first black billionaire is offering to her mostly white—if the composition of her studio audience is any indication—female, middle-class audience something fairly extraordinary. She is presenting to them the essential structure of the slave narrative of the antebellum South, right down to her Book Club's quest for literacy.

For all the show's seesawing between horror and inanity, and precisely because of its cunningly orchestrated subtext of racial catharses—à la the exchange with Roberts—*The Oprah Winfrey Show* is a racial utopia based on the exchangeability of colorless human pain. There is something beautiful and profound about that. As democracy seems more and more to be defined by the number of people who become rich—not many—Oprah's show has gotten more and more popular. In Oprah's universe, democracy is defined by the number of people who are "empowered" by knowing that their sadness and frustration is shared by other people—a lot of other people. It is a kind of egalitarianism from within.

Oprah has said, "If there's a thread running through each show we do, it is the message that 'you are not alone.'" No wonder either Oprah or her guest is almost always weeping. The fluidity of tears—the oceanic melting of the ego in high feeling—represents the essence of Winfrey-democracy. We are not alone because we can blur into another person or become another person at any moment. We can make over our appearance, achieve our "wildest dreams," or be heartened by the evidence of charity or by the revelation that the rich and famous are creatures of feeling, too, which makes their lives possibly habitable phases in the spectrum of exchangeability. And, if the very worst happened, and we came home to four murdered children, we would know what to expect, having been there, in a way, before. We would not be alone then, either. "Tears, tears, tears! / In the night, in solitude, tears," wrote Walt Whitman, the poet of American democracy. "Moist tears from the eyes of a muffled head; / O who is that ghost? that form in the dark, with tears?" Well, it could be anybody. Almost anybody at all. Oprah has accomplished an amazing trick, or even a miracle: She has turned living vicariously into living authentically.

Every *Oprah Winfrey Show* has about it the aura of Oprah's own life, just as the rituals and sacraments of a religion are suffused with the life of the religion's founder. Above the testimony of Oprah's guests hovers what viewers know about Oprah's experience. This is not unlike watching an actress like Nicole Kidman, over whose film characters hover the facts that we think we know about the real Kidman. Yet, in Oprah's case (as in Kidman's) we know only what we have officially been told. One of the ironies of Oprah's success is that this woman, who has made a gospel of publicizing private life, scrupulously keeps fans in the dark about her own.

What we do know, from scores of hagiographies, certainly sounds like an inspiring American story. Born in 1954 to an impoverished, teenage single mother in Kosciusko, Mississippi, Oprah was raised by her grandmother there and then by her mother in Milwaukee. She also lived part of the time in Nashville with her soldier father and her stepmother, both of whom gave her a love of reading. She received excellent grades in an Upward Bound program at an all-white elementary school in Milwaukee, then achieved academic success in high school in Nashville, where she was elected vice president of the student council. Around that time, Oprah was chosen, along with another student, to represent Tennessee at the White House Conference on Youth. A few months later, she entered and won a beauty contest, which led to a part-time job doing newscasts at a local radio station. At Tennessee State University, she majored in speech and drama. She won two more beauty contests, and major ones: Miss Black Nashville and Miss Black Tennessee. Before graduating from college, she landed her first TV job as a newscaster for a news show on a CBS affiliate in Nashville. From there, she went on to Baltimore, Chicago, and fame.

All the while, she was testing different styles of presenting herself. It was in Chicago, a year before her show went national, that Oprah's intimate style broke new ground. In 1985, she announced on the air that she had been raped by her cousin when she was nine. She later revealed that, the following year, a friend of her cousin started molesting her, abuse that she says continued into her teens. Pregnant at fourteen—she won't say by whom—she had the baby, who she says died. Around that time, in 1968, Oprah also claims that an uncle sexually abused her.

Oprah's public narrative of private victimization shadows every moment of the narratives that get spun on her show. It floats above her choice of books and authors for her Book Club: One of her idols, Maya Angelou, was also raped as a child; one of her first Book Club choices, *She's Come Undone,* by Wally Lamb, is about an obese young girl who is raped. Oprah's public story flickers in her choice of victims of sexual abuse among her guests. And it's present—a shadow that accentuates the light—in her works of charity, like the $10 million she recently donated to house victims of Hurricane Katrina: Out of great pain, goodness.

The Oprah tale is, as they used to say, a paradigm shift. In place of Horatio Alger's Protestant ethic-driven rags-to-riches story, Oprah's is a Christian fundamentalist-driven tale of the power of faith and grace. It's not that Oprah hasn't worked hard to get where she is. One of the most appealing things about her has got to be that she always looks exhausted. Oprah has always worked superhumanly hard, it seems, but the object of her work is different from the traditional Alger-type jobs: rag-picking, selling newspapers, and the like. Oprah's work has been her own life. That is her ministry.

Like any great artist mastering a genre in order to recast it, Oprah has revolutionized the presentation of self on television through the total deployment of every dimension of her life.

Her artfulness reached the peak of perfection the very same year that she went public with her tale of sexual abuse. In 1985, she landed the role of Sofia in Steven Spielberg's film of Alice Walker's *The Color Purple*. Like Oprah herself, Sofia was the victim of brutal male abuse. In one stroke, Oprah used her life to capitalize on her role and her role to capitalize on her life. And, by successfully transmuting herself into the fictional character, Oprah could prove to her fans the essential premise of her show: the fungibility of American experience. Exchangeable lives were possible through the democratic vessels of emotion and pain.

In TV terms, Oprah's multiplication of herself into simultaneous actual, fictional, and didactic selves was on the order of Picasso inventing cubism. But Oprah didn't stop there. Another story shadowed her public one, just as her public tale shadows every episode of her professional existence. Though she claims to have been romantically involved for years with a man named Stedman Graham, a businessman and former professional basketball player, the two have never married. Naturally, gossip has circulated for years that the relationship is a sham and that Oprah is actually gay. Provocatively enough, Oprah rarely refers to Graham on her show. Instead, her most frequent references are to Gayle King, an intimate friend of Oprah's since Baltimore. So, rather than refute rumors that she is homosexual, she seems to subtly encourage them—in fact, her official story is that she and King first formed an attachment when a snowstorm forced them to spend the night together.

Her detractors cry hypocrite. But there is nothing hypocritical about having a private life. If Oprah is in a fake romance, and if she is gay, neither reality would contradict her public advocacy of courage, fortitude, and growth through suffering.

Rather, her seemingly calculated intimations of a hidden second life only strengthen her hopeful message of ceaseless personal possibilities.

Oprah's response to skeptics has simply been: "I don't make things up." The success of her life affirms the veracity of her life. Oprah: "My initial dream for myself was to be able to stretch out of myself and create work that would touch people's lives." To stretch out of herself and to create work—once you stretch your life into your work, you are no longer responsible for what you do. Only for what you are. And you can *be* something different—anybody different—from minute to minute. Nobody questions the genuineness of someone who has just changed jobs. Being means survival, and survival is incontestably good. You measure what you *do* by its effectiveness at helping you achieve what you are and what you want to be. "Thank you for saying that," Oprah often declares to a suffering guest who admits her weakness or culpability, thus indicating a desire to change. The power of proclaimed purpose matters more than the density of a done deed.

The James Frey scandal, beaten to death by the press, horrified Oprah. If you live on planet Earth, you probably know the story. *A Million Little Pieces*—Frey's memoir detailing his drug addiction, descent into crime, time in jail, redemption, and reform—was selected by Oprah for her Book Club. As a result, *A Million Little Pieces* became a sensational best-seller, earning the thirty-six-year-old author a small fortune. It turned out, though, that Frey had made up substantial sections of his autobiography.

Oprah at first defended him, and then, when she became convinced that he had indeed fabricated his story—or when she saw the tide of opinion turning against her—she had Frey back on her show, where she scolded, shamed, and publicly rebuked him. Almost immediately after that imbroglio, she turned to her old friend, Elie Wiesel, whom she first had on her show in 1993. She made *Night,* Wiesel's 1956 semi-autobiographical account of his captivity as a boy in Auschwitz, her next Book Club pick. Some people saw this as a cynical attempt to use the subject of the Holocaust as a shield to make herself impervious to any further criticism about Frey. You might also suspect Oprah of using Wiesel to make a self-exculpatory point: *Night* is no less semi-autobiographical than *A Million Little Pieces,* yet no one ever questioned Wiesel's honesty.

A few commentators ventured that Oprah had gotten what she deserved. Frey, they said, had modeled his book on Oprah's successful formula of sin and/or suffering, leading to expiation and/or redemption. Such a phony "template," to use the trite term, had finally boomeranged into her comeuppance. But, of course, there is nothing phony about Oprah's inspiring, exemplary life: "I did it, and so can you." There is nothing false or artificial about the consolation she brings people; or especially about the way she has transposed the experience of the black ordeal onto white suffering, putting both races in the same hourly daytime boat. She may have done more for black-white relations in this country than anyone since Martin Luther King Jr.

Oprah didn't get what she deserved. What she got—and what horrified her—was a reminder of who she was, or wasn't. Frey had not followed some daytime TV formula; he had absorbed Oprah's most essential lessons. Like everyone, Frey had a life that unfolded in a singular, definite way. But in *A Million Little Pieces,* he stretched out of himself and created work that touched other people's lives. He turned his life into his job.

Just as Oprah created a talk-show host named "Oprah," making that character her work, improvising on it and experimenting with it, so Frey created a character named "James Frey," and improvised on it and experimented with it. He didn't need to act on the Winfreyist principle of exchangeability by feeling someone else's pain. He imagined a new persona for himself, constructed out of pain he had actually felt, and then proceeded to play his new role. After all, a person is free to do whatever he wants with his own pain. In this sense, Frey was not lying about his life. He was making his life his work, and, since work is a process of development and life is always open-ended and fragile and provisional, it can take any form you want it to take as you proceed toward your goal. Frey was doing what he had to do in order to be who he knew he really was, and who he wanted to become.

Every person and every ideology has its countertendency. With Frey, Oprah's countertendency surged into public view. The reverse side of making your life your work is a life in which your actions become mere propulsions along the rails of self-advancement. You are not responsible for what you do because your truth as a person lies in the future as your "goal." You don't tell lies, because what might seem like a fabrication to other people is the expression of your genuine feeling, which is authorized by who you know you really are and can be in the future. We are taught that "the end justifies the means" is a ruthless, amoral approach to life. But Oprah has taken that sword-like precept and beaten it into a benign ploughshare of planting, cultivation, and growth. She has made the sincerity of a statement more important than the content of it. Which is to say, she has made it virtuous to be amoral. *After all you have been through, you deserve this.* Oprah did it, and so can you.

Like Oprah herself, Winfreyism has an equally fraught countermotion. The reverse side of a democracy based on exchangeable feelings is the creation of a kingdom of mere sensations, in which no experience has a higher—or different—value than any other experience. We weep and empathize with the self-destructive mother, we weep and empathize with Sidney Poitier, we weep and empathize with the young woman dying of anorexia, we weep and empathize with Teri Hatcher, we weep and empathize with the girl with the disfigured face, we weep and empathize with the grateful recipients of Oprah's gift of a new car to every member of one lucky audience, we weep and empathize with the woman burned beyond recognition by her vicious husband. In the end, like the melting vision of tearing eyes, the situations blur into each other without distinction. They are all relative to your own experience of watching them. The fungibility of feeling is really a reduction of all experience to the effect it has on your own quality of feeling.

In fact, Oprah's universal empathy has an infinite flexibility. When critics complained that she focused too much on stories of physical and emotional horror, Oprah quickly responded, in the early 1990s, by mocking that very format. Publicly vowing to start diversifying her show, she immediately incorporated lighter fare more frequently. Several months after Jonathan Franzen dissed her Book Club, an incident that gave rise to a heated debate over its true function and value, Oprah disbanded it. (It has returned, but in a more peripheral and occasional way.) The Frey incident sent her spinning in appeasement yet again.

One of Oprah's most powerful visual metaphors is how she utterly transforms her appearance—her hairstyle, mode of dress, type of jewelry, even her manner of speaking—from day to day. It is her clever, dramatic embodiment of the possibility of personal change and growth. But ability to change is also a capacity for accommodation. It hints at a personality that will "stretch" itself in any rewarding direction, unconstrained by truthfulness or consistency. Unconstrained by the constraint of character, you might say.

The name Oprah gave to her production company—her business—is Harpo Productions, which is "Oprah" spelled backward. That is exactly right. Winfreyism is the expression of an immensely reassuring and inspiring message that has, without doubt, helped millions of people carry on with their lives. And it is also an empty, cynical, icily selfish outlook on life that undercuts its own positive energy at every turn. On her way to Auschwitz, sitting in her hotel room in Krakow, thinking about the masses of people who were murdered in the death camp, Oprah wrote in *O*, "I have never felt more human." Her empathy and moral growth seem to require human sacrifice. Yet watching Oprah does fill you with hope. It also plunges you into despair. She has become something like America itself.

MAY 26, 2006

Acknowledgments

I wish to thank the late Elizabeth Maguire, who created this book; my agent Gloria Loomis, who made so many good things happen; and Edwin Frank, who enlivened my mind.

Leon Wieseltier made these essays possible, and made the author possible while he was writing them, and then heroically kept him possible in an impossible situation.

Janet Malcolm's work has nourished me as a writer, and her decency and generosity have sustained me as a person. I am lucky to have her as a friend.

As always, my profoundest gratitude is to my beloved family, Christina and Julian.